DAVID NEMEC

THE RULES OF BASEBALL

An Anecdotal Look at the Rules of Baseball

and

How They Came to Be

L&B

LYONS & BURFORD, PUBLISHERS

Printed in the United States of America

Design by Howard P. Johnson

10 9 8 7 6 5 4 3 2 1

Nemec, David.
       The rules of baseball / David Nemec.
          p. cm.
       "Illustrated and annotated."
       Includes index.
       ISBN 1-55821-279-5.   ISBN 1-55821-280-9 (pbk.)
       1. Baseball—Rules. 2. Baseball—Rules—History.
       I. Title
       GV877.N47   1994
       796.357'02'022—dc20   93-48361
                                                         CIP

THE
RULES
OF
BASEBALL

CONTENTS

FOREWORD

I**T SEEMS** not too long ago that I wandered onto a sandlot diamond as an ambitious young catcher—a position no one else seemed to want. From that very first encounter, forty years past, I sensed that baseball would be an important part of my life.

I remember seeing pictures of the President in our local newspaper, throwing out the first pitch of the season. For some reason that seemed to legitimize the game for me—and clearly establish it as America's favorite pastime. After all, I had never seen our Chief Executive run a "down and out" to get the football season kicked off—or dribble down the court to start the basketball season.

I was happy playing "hardball" on the vacant lot in our neighborhood where we made up the rules as we went. We shared gloves, salvaged ragged balls with black tape, and kept our favorite bats together with nails from my dad's tool box. Uniforms . . . that was the least of our concerns. The Game! That's what it was all about. We could dream back then. Only darkness and the dinner bell could diminish our enthusiasm.

Baseball has been my professional life for the past twenty-five years. I still experience that same enthusiasm everytime I walk onto a baseball diamond. Whether it's the seventh game of a World Series, Opening Day in Fenway Park, or a ragged high school practice field in the dead of winter where I might be conducting a clinic, a genuine feeling of respect and love of the game swells within me once I step onto that field.

In *The Rules of Baseball*, David Nemec has magically inspired those same feelings. With this unique format, this talented author has created an anecdotal history that will stand the test of time. His exhaustive research and journalistic integrity are obvious to me. In my relentless efforts to ferret out meaningful information for my students at the Academy of Professional Umpiring, I have encountered many of the same sources. Nemec's attention to detail and accuracy in reporting is commendable.

Not only did I discover fascinating new information in *The Rules of Baseball*, but I also confirmed many of the interpretations and precedents I had long suspected.

As an umpire, player, coach, or fan, you are going to learn a lot from this book. More importantly, you are going to have fun along the way.

—JIM EVANS,
American League Umpire,
Owner/operator Academy
of Professional Umpiring

INTRODUCTION

FRENCH HISTORIAN
Jacques Barzun is best known to followers of our national pastime for having written: "Whoever wants to know the heart and soul of America had better learn baseball." Barzun's implication, of course, is that baseball epitomizes our nation and that its rules and rites spring from American roots. Yet that is not altogether true.

Europeans played many different types of bat-and-ball games for centuries before the earliest American Colonial settlements. These informal divertissements gradually evolved into the orderly games of cricket and rounders that had circumscribed rules and games like one ol'cat whose rules were often made up on the spot depending on the size of the playing field and the number of players. What all these early games had in common was that they were ancestors of baseball. For our national pastime did not have the "immaculate conception" Barzun's epigram would lead us to imagine but rather developed by trial and error.

The Rules of Baseball endeavors, among other things, to track the evolution of some of baseball's more interesting rules and rituals by reporting on key episodes that inspired the game's thinkers to redesign a piece of the rulebook. Many of its illustrative anecdotes come from the 19th century when the rules were in an almost constant state of flux, but the rulebook is still far from a perfect instrument. George Will has commented: "The real powers behind the rule book are the people who balance baseball's financial books." His observation is well taken and to a degree has always been true. All during the last century whenever the unequal balance between hitting and pitching threatened to affect attendance, to say nothing of TV contracts, major changes were made in the game's playing code. The most significant one in 1893 lengthened the stretch of ground between a pitcher and a batter by moving the pitching slab to its present sixty-foot six-inch distance from home plate.

But the rules are also continually being rewritten for other than financial reasons. Each new season brings at least one occurrence that cannot be resolved by the rulebook. The 1983 "Pine Tar Game" between the New York Yankees and the Kansas City Royals is a prominent example and is discussed in this book. But there are literally hundreds of remarkable moments in the game's history when a player or an umpire found himself in a situation that did not have a rule to govern it.

One of the earliest came in an American Association clash in 1887 between Louisville and Brooklyn when a Louisville baserunner, after scoring from third base on an infield error, began wrestling with the Brooklyn catcher so that a teammate could also score. At the time, rather amazingly, an umpire was left entirely to his own devices in such a predicament because there was as yet no rule addressing a situation in which a player who had scored, and was therefore by definition no longer a baserunner, interfered with a fielder. Nevertheless the arbiter that day, one Wesley Curry, worked out what seemed to him a logical solution, and in the process set a precedent that eventually triggered a new rule.

Curry's handling of the situation will be found in the section on the rules pertaining to umpires, but unfortunately not all of the fascinating incidents that led to rule changes can be tackled in a single book. In the years ahead, as interest in the game's evolution continues to spread rapidly from scholars to baseball buffs, there will doubtless be many more efforts to help us draw a better bead on the whys and wherefores of baseball's rules. Meanwhile I hope you have as much fun with this book as I did putting it together.

—David Nemec,
February, 1994

OBJECTIVES OF THE GAME

1.03

The winner of the game shall be that team which shall have scored, in accordance with these rules, the greater number of runs at the conclusion of a regulation game.

SEEMINGLY it would be safe to assume that the winner of à baseball game has always been the team that scored the most runs at the end of nine innings; but actually the 1857 season was the first in which a game was required to go nine innings, with five innings constituting an official contest if play were stopped for some reason. Prior to 1857 the objective was to score 21 runs or aces. A game thus could conceivably end after a single inning or finish without a winner if neither team was able to push across 21 aces before darkness set in.

The first game played by the Cartwright rules—devised by Alexander Cartwright and now recognized as having blended the best properties of several bat and ball games of his time to create the game we know as baseball—took place at the Elysian Fields in Hoboken, New Jersey, on June 19, 1846, between the New York Nine and Cartwright's club, the New York Knickerbockers. The contest lasted only four innings as the Nine tallied their 21st run in the top of the fourth, added two more scores for safe measure, and then blanked the Knicks in their last turn at bat to prevail 23–1.

ALL THE rules pertaining to the shape and size of the playing field have changed significantly since Alexander Cartwright's day, except one: The bases are still 90 feet apart. Nothing was actually said about the distance between bases in the first formal code of playing rules that Cartwright drafted in 1845; the only stipulation was that the stretch of ground from home to second base and from first to third base should be the same 42 paces. Since a pace for an athletic man walking briskly to lay out a diamond is roughly a yard, that worked out to about 126 feet, or only a foot and a third short of the present distance between home and second base.

Baseball historian Frederick Ivor-Campbell has speculated that Cartwright chose to measure in paces for the sake of ease and simplicity. An empty stretch of ground can be converted into a ball diamond in a matter of seconds if the distances between home and second and between first and third are stepped off, whereas using a yardstick or a tape measure takes considerable time. Ivor-Campbell has also theorized that Cartwright might have preferred 42 paces to 42 yards because it gave players bases at a distance fit for their legs. As an example, children or women pacing out a diamond will naturally come up with shorter base paths than adult men, resulting in a game more closely suited to their physical dimensions.

No one really knows what was behind the thinking of the game's early designers—the bases could as easily have been 80 or 100 feet apart and still would have allowed the playing field to retain its diamond shape—but it was as if Cartwright and those who helped him figure out how the game should be played instinctively knew that the 90-foot distance would give runners and fielders parity. Every other significant feature of the geometry of the playing field has changed since Cartwright's day.

FOR A LONG time after the first enclosed baseball fields were constructed in the late 1850s there was no minimum distance an outside-the-park home run had to travel. The Chicago White Stockings, for instance, played in Lake Front Park in the early 1880s, which had a leftfield fence only 180 feet from the plate and a rightfield barrier just 196 feet down the line. In 1884 the bandbox park helped the White Stockings to hit 142 home runs and the club's third sacker Ned Williamson to collect 27 dingers. These marks stood as team and individual major league records until the arrival of Babe Ruth.

By the 1890s fences in major league parks were required to be at least 235 feet from the plate. In 1892 the National League rated any ball hit over a barrier less than 235 feet distant a ground-ruled double. The minimum distance for an automatic circuit clout was lengthened in 1926 to 250 feet and remained at that figure until 1958, but clubs were urged, where possible, to set their fences at least 300 feet away.

Several parks extant in 1926 barely met the 250-

foot minimum. The Polo Grounds, home of the New York Giants and later the New York Mets' first domicile, was a mere 257½ feet down the right field line and just 279 feet to the leftfield foul pole. Baker Bowl, the Philadelphia Phillies' home until 1938, had a rightfield fence only 280½ feet away. In contrast, Boston Braves hitters in 1926 were confounded by a leftfield wall in Braves Field that was 403 feet from the plate at its shortest point. As could be expected, the Braves rapped just 16 circuit clouts that year, the fewest in the majors and 31 less than Babe Ruth hit all by himself.

ONE MIGHT wonder why home base is more commonly called home plate. The natural assumption is that it must originally have been shaped like a dish, and this is borne out by history. In all the early forms of baseball home base was round, and in casual games might be fashioned out of whatever circular device was handy, including at times a dish or even a player's cap. In 1869 the circular shape was abandoned and home base became a 12-inch square, usually made of white marble or stone. The square was set in the ground so that one corner pointed toward the pitcher's box and its opposite corner toward the catcher. The pitcher's and catcher's positions were therefore called "the points."

In 1885 the American Association stipulated that home base could no longer be stone but had to be made of white rubber, and two years later the National League added the same proviso to its rule manual. The purpose of the change was to cut down on abrasive injuries to runners sliding across the plate. But home base remained a square until 1900. Converting the plate to a pentagonal shape as the new century began was done to make it easier for both pitchers and umpires to pinpoint the strike zone, but it gave hurlers a huge additional boost. The larger 17-inch five-sided

---

1.05

Home base shall be marked by a five-sided slab of whitened rubber. It shall be a 17-inch square with two of the corners removed so that one edge is 17 inches long, two adjacent sides are 8-1/2 inches and the remaining two sides are 12 inches and set at an angle to make a point. . . .

W.P. Snyder captures a square home plate in this drawing of a 19th century game in a "domed stadium." The indoor site is the 13th Regiment Armory in New York. Note, too, that the players are wearing canvas shoes since the contest is being played on a wood floor. **Transcendental Graphics**

plate, plus the adoption of the foul-strike rule in 1901, contributed as much as anything to the sharp decline in offense that gripped the game from the early part of the century to the end of World War I and caused it to be dubbed "The Deadball Era."

THE FEATURE of the playing field that has changed the most dramatically since the first game was played by the Cartwright rules is the pitching station. As late as 1880 pitchers hurled from a rectangular box, the forward line of which was only 45 feet from home plate. A pitcher was required to release the ball either on or be-

1.07

The pitcher's plate shall be a rectangular slab of whitened rubber, 24 inches by 6 inches. It shall be set in the

(continued)

(continued)

ground so that the distance between the pitcher's plate and home base (the rear point of home plate) shall be 60 feet, 6 inches.

hind the forward line and was not allowed to advance beyond it after the ball left his hand. After the National League loop batting average dipped that season to .245 and the Chicago White Stockings ran away with the pennant, winning by a 15-game margin on a schedule that called for just 84 contests, the pitcher's box was moved back five feet to generate more offense. In 1881 the White Stockings still romped to an easy repeat pennant, but the league average jumped 15 points.

By 1892, however, a more drastic change was needed to restore a balance between hitters and pitchers as the NL batting average that season once again plummeted to .245, and stars like Cap Anson (.272), King Kelly (.189), and Jake Beckley (.236) all hit well below .300. With scoring on the wane, it was decided once again to move the pitcher's slab farther from the plate. One popular tale is that the present distance is the result of an error made by a surveyor who misread the 60' 0" written on the blueprint as 60' 6", and laid out the new pitcher's plates accordingly before the 1893 season. Whatever the case, the actual increase in distance was not as great as it might seem. Although required to release the ball at a point 60 feet 6 inches from the plate, the typical hurler finished his delivery with his front foot about 55 feet from home base or only five feet farther away from the batter than the forward line had been in 1892.

IN SHARP contrast to the following diagram showing the current layout of the pitching mound are drawings of the playing field prior to 1893. The pitcher's boxes are flat in all of them.

To give hurlers something in compensation when the pitching distance was lengthened in 1893, the pitcher's plate was raised. Nothing was said, however, about how high it could be elevated. Teams like the

New York Giants, with speedballers of the caliber of Amos Rusie and Cy Seymour, consequently worked to situate them high above the batter, whereas clubs that were about to face a Rusie or a Seymour would shave their mounds the night before beginning a series with the Giants.

This sort of shenanigans went on for a full decade since there was nothing in the rules to prevent it. Then in 1903 all organized professional leagues adopted a rule that the pitcher's mound must be limited to 15 inches

This diagram, taken from the Official Baseball Rules, shows the dimensions and circular layout of a modern pitching mound. Until 1893, diagrams of the pitching position featured a rectangular box.

Suggested Layout of Pitching Mound

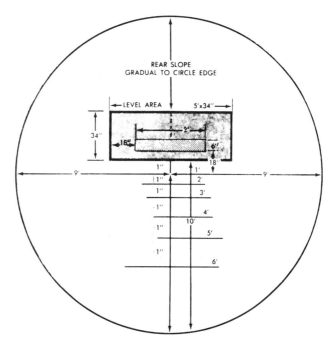

The degree of slope from a point 6″ in front of the pitcher's plate to a point 6′ toward home plate shall be 1″ to 1′, and such degree of slope shall be uniform.

above the baselines and home plate, and the slope must be gradual. The new rule was the first even to mention the term "mound." In 1904 the term "pitcher's box" was eliminated from the rulebook in favor of "pitcher's plate."

In the late 1960s the game's moguls faced a similar crisis that had forced their brethren to lengthen the pitching distance in 1893. After Carl Yastrzemski set an all-time nadir for a major league batting leader when he won the American League hitting crown in 1968 with a .301 average, Bob Gibson topped the majors with a microscopic 1.12 ERA, and the Cincinnati Reds were the only major league team to average as many as four and a half runs a game, one of the changes implemented in an effort to restore the balance between hitters and pitchers was to pare five inches off the mound and reduce its maximum height to ten inches.

Batting averages jumped in 1969 but not nearly as much as they had in 1893 after the pitching distance was increased. Continued experimentation with the rules was necessary in order to procure more offense. Among the changes that eventually impacted on the balance between hitters and pitchers were reducing the strike zone and, in the American League at least, allowing a designated hitter for the pitcher.

1.09

The ball shall be a sphere formed by yarn wound around a small core of cork, rubber or similar material, covered with two stripes of white horsehide or cowhide, tightly stitched together. It shall weigh not less than five nor more than 5-1/4 ounces avoirdupois and measure not less than nine nor more than 9-1/4 inches in circumference.

THIS IS ONE of the few rules in the manual that has changed little since the first rulebooks were written. In the 1840s balls differed substantially in both size and weight, depending on which team provided the game ball and where its strength lay. A hard-hitting club was likely to furnish a tightly wound ball on the small side, whereas a nine that prided itself on its defensive work was more apt to select a heavier and softer ball.

In 1854 all organized clubs adopted the rule that balls must weigh between five and five and a half ounces and be between two and three-quarters and

three and a half inches in diameter. Six years later the ball was reduced in size to its present dimensions as stipulated in Rule 1.09.

Since the 1879 season, the Spalding ball has been the National League's official ball. The American League adopted the Spalding-made Reach baseball when it first organized under its present name in 1900 and has used the same ball ever since. Other aspirant major leagues used brands of balls that in most cases have long since disappeared from the sporting goods market.

The National Association, the National League's forerunner, used many different balls during its five-year run from 1871 to 1875. When the American Association first opened its doors in 1882 as a challenger to the National League, it chose as its official ball one made by the Mahn Sporting Goods Company of Boston. After using the Mahn ball for just one season the AA abandoned it in favor of the Reach ball, which remained the official AA ball until the loop ceased operation following the 1891 campaign.

In 1884, its sole year as a major league, the Union Association employed the Wright & Ditson ball, designed and manufactured by George Wright, the game's first great shortstop and part owner of the Boston Unions franchise. The Reach and Spalding balls in 1884 were much alike, but the Wright & Ditson ball was purportedly a "hitter's" ball, chosen in the expectation that fans would be drawn more to high-scoring games than to pitchers' duels.

The official ball of the Players League during the 1890 season, its lone campaign, was the Keefe ball, devised by Tim Keefe, the Hall of Fame pitcher who hurled that year for the New York PL entry and operated a sporting goods store in lower Manhattan in partnership with Buck Becannon, a former teammate.

In 1914–1915, the Federal League, the last serious threat to the two established major league circuits, employed a ball made by the Victor Sporting Goods Company, at the time one of the leaders in the business.

Before we leave the rule on balls, we should dwell for a moment on the phrase "white horsehide." Many readers will remember that in 1973 Oakland A's owner Charlie Finley had his defending World Champions experiment with orange balls in a few spring training exhibition games, but, unlike many of Finley's innovations, this one died a quick death.

The last time a team played with balls that were a color other than white in a regulation major league contest was in 1939 when Brooklyn Dodgers general manager Larry MacPhail tried dandelion yellow balls in three games, two against the St. Louis Cardinals and one against the Chicago Cubs. The Dodgers also used MacPhail's yellow balls in a 1938 contest with the Cardinals on August 2 at Ebbets Field, but met resistance from the other National League teams, especially after they won 6–2.

UNTIL 1893 hitters were permitted to use bats that had one flat side, making it easier for them to execute "baby hits" (bunts) and also to slap pitches not to their liking deliberately foul. Even after being deprived

1.10 (A)

The bat shall be a smooth, round stick not more than 2-3/4 inches in diameter at the thickest part and not more than 42 inches in length. The bat shall be one piece of solid wood.

Bats with one side deliberately flattened were legal prior to 1893. This aid to hitters was removed in the same season that the pitching distance was increased by ten and a half feet. **Transcendental Graphics**

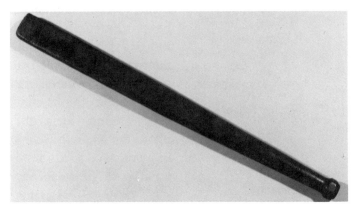

of this advantage, many hitters, including Willie Keeler, a leading exponent of the flat-sided bat, thrived in 1893 when the pitching distance was lengthened. As was true for hurlers who now had to tailor their deliveries to the increased distance, several batsmen proved unable to adapt to bats that were entirely round; they were soon out of the majors.

The major leagues have from time to time authorized bats that were not all of a piece. During the 1954 season, for instance, laminated bats were allowed on an experimental basis. Bats made of metal, in whole or in part, have never been permitted, however, and purists can only hope they never will be.

BEYOND ANY doubt the most famous violation in major league history of Rule 1.10 (c) was the "Pine Tar Incident" in 1983, which began on July 24 at Yankee Stadium in a game between the New York Yankees and the Kansas City Royals, but echoed deep into the off season, and did not culminate until late that December when Commissioner Bowie Kuhn fined the Yankees $250,000 for "certain public statements" made by Yankees owner George Steinbrenner about the way American League president Lee MacPhail had handled the incident.

The controversy was set off by Kansas City third baseman George Brett's two-run homer off Yankees reliever Goose Gossage with two out in the ninth inning of the game to put the Royals ahead, 5–4. As Brett started for the dugout after circling the bases, Yankees manager Billy Martin asked the umpires to check Brett's bat for excessive pine tar. Like many players, Brett used pine tar on his bat handle to improve his grip and prevent blisters, but Martin contended the application extended beyond the allowed 18 inches from the end of the handle. Plate umpire Tim McClelland looked at the bat,

---

1.10 (c)

The bat handle, for not more than 18 inches from its end, may be covered or treated with any material or substance to improve the grip. Any such material or substance, which extends past the 18 inch limitation, shall cause the bat to be removed from the game. NOTE: If the umpire discovers that the bat does not conform to (c) above until a time during or after which the bat has been used in play, it shall not be grounds for declaring the batter out, or ejected from the game.

George Brett registers a "mild" protest after being told his two-run homer has been disallowed because his bat contains too much pine tar. Moments later the guilty bat, seen at bottom right, was quietly purloined by Yankees pitcher Gaylord Perry, who tried to dispose of it while the argument still raged. UPI/Bettmann News-photos

then consulted with his three associates, and the onus fell on crew chief Joe Brinkman.

When Brinkman measured the pine tar on Brett's bat handle against the 17-inch width of home plate, he discovered the substance exceeded the 18-inch limit by an inch or so. Thereupon the umpires ruled Brett out for using an illegal bat to nullify his home run and end the game with the score reverting to 4–3, New York. Livid

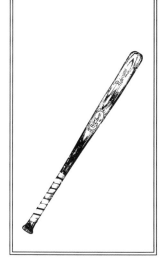

with rage, Brett raced back onto the field and had to be physically restrained from taking on the entire umpiring crew. While the argument roared around home plate, Yankees pitcher Gaylord Perry furtively snatched Brett's bat. Before he could make off with it, however, he was intercepted by a uniformed guard, who saw to it that the bat was taken to the umpires' dressing room.

The Royals lodged an official protest with Mac-Phail. Four days later MacPhail announced he was upholding the protest, marking the first time in his 10 years as American League president that he had overturned an umpire's decision. MacPhail contended the fault lay not with his umpires, however, but with the rule, which needed to be rewritten to make it clear that a bat coated with excessive pine tar was not the same as a doctored bat—one that had been altered to improve the distance factor or to cause an unusual reaction on a batted ball.

With the protest upheld, the score once again became 5–4, Royals, with two out in the top of the ninth. When MacPhail ruled the game had to be finished at Yankee Stadium on August 18, an open date for both the Yankees and the Royals, Steinbrenner at first said he'd rather forfeit. The completion of the game eventually took place as ordered by MacPhail, but not before there was an attempt by Yankees fans to get a court injunction barring the game and a last-ditch effort by Billy Martin to have Brett declared out.

As soon as the two clubs took the field on August 18, Martin had his infielders try appeals at first and second bases. When the umpires—not the same crew who had worked the original game—gave the safe sign, Martin filed a protest with crew chief Dave Phillips, contending that the four umpires could not know that Brett had touched all the bases on his home-run tour since none of them was in Yankee Stadium on July 24. But Martin's argument had been anticipated. Phillips whipped out a notarized letter signed by Brinkman's crew stating that

Brett and U. L. Washington, the runner who had scored ahead of him, had both touched all the bases.

The game took only 12 minutes to complete, as the Yankees meekly went down in order in the bottom of the ninth to seal the 5–4 Royals victory. However, the various court actions that the Yankees launched to have the result quashed were only just beginning. In the end none of them came to much, but over the winter the Official Playing Rules Committee clarified the so-called "pine tar rule" to stipulate, as per the note in Rule 1.10(c), that a violation of the 18-inch limit shall call for the bat's ejection but not for nullification of any play that results from its use.

Ironically, the Yankees were themselves once victimized by Rule 1.10(c) before it was rewritten. In a 1975 game against the Minnesota Twins, Yankees catcher Thurman Munson singled in the first inning to drive home a run but was called out by umpire Art Frantz when an inspection of his bat, instigated by Twins manager Frank Quilici, disclosed that the pine tar on it overstepped the 18-inch limit. Billy Martin still remembered Frantz's ruling eight years later when he requested that Brett's bat be checked.

1.11 (A)

(1) All players on a team shall wear uniforms identical in color, trim and style, and all players uniforms shall include minimal six-inch numbers on their backs. . . . (3) No player whose uniform does not conform to that of his teammates shall be permitted to participate in a game.

IT HAS ALWAYS been customary for all the players on a professional team to wear identical uniforms, but not until 1899 was the rule first imposed that every player on a team's bench had to wear a uniform that exactly matched those of his teammates in color and style. Prior to then it had been an unwritten rule that many clubs violated, particularly when on the road and forced to pick up a substitute at the last moment. To keep down expenses, teams sometimes took to the road with as few as ten players, the minimum a club could dress at the time, and then hired local amateurs in the city they were visiting when disabling injuries oc-

The 1882 American Association champion—the Cincinnati Red Stockings— showcase their multicolored uniforms. National League teams, in self-defense, copied the AA's bold innovation, but it died a quick death when fans, seeing two enemy players on the field wearing the same uniform pattern, often couldn't tell who was who. Transcendental Graphics

curred. Often these major league "temps" were outfitted with makeshift uniforms that were comprised of extra uniform parts donated by other team members. In some instances a temp was even allowed to wear the uniform of his amateur club, supplemented by the cap of his major league team for the day, and on at least one occasion a substitute played in street clothes. In an American Association game on May 10, 1885, John Coleman, who had not suited up that day, left the bench to replace Bobby Mathews in right field for the Philadelphia Athletics. Mathews had begun the game in the box but then switched to right when he hurt his hand. Coleman replaced him in the sixth inning after the rival manager acceded to the A's request for an injury substitution.

In 1882, its first season as a major league, the American Association violated the uniform dress code custom for a very different reason. AA teams were encouraged to be as gaudy in their attire as possible. In the inaugural AA season, clubs wore silk uniforms in as many different colors as there were positions on the diamond. The champion Cincinnati Red Stockings infield dressed as follows: First baseman Dan Stearns wore a candy-striped blouse, Hick Carpenter at third chose all white, and the two keystoners, lefty second sacker Jimmy Macullar and shortstop Chick Fulmer, showcased blue and red blouses, respectively.

The rule that all players must be wearing uniforms of exactly the same color harmed the Cleveland Indians in a 1949 game against the Boston Red Sox. Tribe ace Bob Lemon had a no-hitter going midway through the contest. It was a hot day, and before each pitch Lemon fell into the pattern of tweaking the red bill of his cap to rub the perspiration off his fingers. Noticing that Lemon's wiping was causing the bill's color to fade as the game progressed, Red Sox manager Joe McCarthy claimed that it was no longer the same color as the cap bills worn by the rest of the Indians and therefore was not regulation. To avoid a rhubarb that would only further break his rhythm, as was McCarthy's intention, Lemon obligingly changed caps, but the damage was already done. The Red Sox proceeded to hammer him and knock him out of the box. The following day Lemon, ever able to find humor in the game, appeared on the field in pregame practice wearing a fedora.

1.11 (B)

A league may provide that (1) each team shall wear a distinctive uniform at all times, or (2) that each team shall have two sets of uniforms, white for home games and a different color for road games.

ANOTHER LONGSTANDING custom that for many years was not formalized into a rule was for a team to possess two different uniforms, one to wear at home and the other to showcase while on the road. This practice first became an actual rule in 1904. Prior to then it had been customary since the early 1880s for the home team to dress in white and the visitors in gray or some other darker hue. Not until 1911 did it become

Bob Lemon is slightly out of uniform as he strolls toward the Cleveland dugout prior to a game with the Boston Red Sox on September 21, 1949. The Indians pitching great sported a fedora all during pre-game practice, after he was made to change his sweat-faded cap the previous afternoon by umpire Cal Hubbard. At far left in the dugout is Mickey Vernon. Waiting to greet Lemon are coaches Steve O'Neill (applauding) and Bill McKechnie. AP/Wide World Photos

mandatory, however, for the home team to wear white uniforms and the visitors dark uniforms as a way for fans, players, and umpires alike to distinguish the players on one club from the other more easily.

THIS RULE is comparatively new to the manual. When the entire rulebook was rewritten prior to the 1950 season, it was spelled out for the first time that a pitcher could not wear a garment with ragged, frayed,

1.11 (c)

(1) Sleeve lengths may vary for individual players, but the
(continued)

(continued)

sleeves of each individual player shall be approximately the same length. (2) No player shall wear ragged, frayed or slit sleeves.

Johnny Allen (R) lets Cleveland manager Ozzie Vitt examine the tattered sleeve that resulted in his ouster from a game in 1938. The previous year, the hot-blooded Allen nearly flattened a Tribe teammate whose error saddled him with his only loss of the season. American Photographic Archives

or slit sleeves, but long before then umpires had begun making pitchers shed offending garments, albeit on an arbitrary basis. One who escaped punishment for many years was Dazzy Vance, whose blazing fastball was rendered all the more effective by the tattered right undershirt sleeve he flourished over the vehement protests of rival batsmen.

Cleveland hurler Johnny Allen was not so fortunate, however. Long known for his monumental temper tantrums, Allen faced the Boston Red Sox in Fenway Park on June 7, 1938, with umpire Bill McGowan behind the plate. Allen and McGowan had crossed swords before in Fenway, so the stage was set for sparks to fly as soon as Allen began to complain about McGowan's decisions on pitches.

In the second inning McGowan stopped play, strolled out to the mound, and told Allen he would have to cut off a part of his sweatshirt sleeve that waved whenever he delivered a pitch, distracting the batter. Allen refused either to remove the shirt or slice off the offending sleeve, and instead stalked off the mound and went to sit in the Cleveland dugout. Indians manager Ozzie Vitt promptly took him out of the game and fined him $250.

The offending shirt became a *cause célèbre*. When Cleveland owner Alva Bradley learned of the incident, he bought the shirt from Allen for $250—in effect paying the fine for his pitcher—and had it mounted in a glass showcase of the Higbee Company, a large department store in downtown Cleveland. Bradley contended that the Higbee Company, and not he, had purchased the shirt, which may technically have been true. Bradley's brother, Chuck, was the president of the Higbee Company in 1938. By then the entire country knew the tale of Allen's frayed temper and tattered sleeve. His shirt was eventually placed in the Hall of Fame as a reminder of one of the game's wooliest episodes.

IN THE EARLY days it was recommended but not mandatory that a player wear spikes attached to his shoes. Interestingly, most players then wore shoes of the same high-top design that is now the rage in baseball gear. Later all clubs made spikes mandatory. The last player on record to be fined for not wearing spikes on his shoes was Pete Browning when he was with Pittsburgh in 1891.

Players have never been permitted to wear golf or track spikes for an obvious reason. No second baseman or shortstop would ever have stood in to take a throw at the keystone sack on a steal attempt if a Ty Cobb or a Rickey Henderson had come into the bag with track spikes flying.

During the 1976 season several players, including Dan Ford of the Minnesota Twins and Matt Alexander of the Oakland As, briefly wore spikes similar to those on golf shoes before a rival manager spotted the violation and protested to umpires, forcing the offending players to change to shoes with regulation spikes.

A QUESTION often asked by fans who are unfamiliar with the history of uniforms is: Why have the New York Yankees retired the numbers of all their great players like Ruth, Gehrig, and DiMaggio, whereas the Detroit Tigers have somehow never deigned to retire Ty Cobb's number? The answer has nothing to do with Cobb's thorny personality or lack of popularity. Rather, it is that Cobb never wore a number during his playing days. Nor for that matter did Walter Johnson, Pete Alexander, Eddie Collins, Honus Wagner, or many other great stars of Cobb's era.

Although major league teams as far back as the 1880s wore numbered uniforms on occasion, the experiment always failed, in part because many players did not like the notion of bearing a number like a convict. Not until 1929, when the Indians and the Yankees both adopted wearing numbers on the backs of their uniforms, did a team put numbers on its uniforms and keep them there. On May 13, 1929, at Cleveland's League Park, for the first time fans were treated to the spectacle of every player on the field wearing a numbered uniform, and were further delighted when Willis Hudlin of the Indians beat the Yankees, 4–3. Two years later the American League made numbered uniforms mandatory. Ty Cobb meanwhile retired in 1928 before players began having to wear numbers on their uniforms.

I N A SENSE it was Hoyt Wilhelm and other knuckleballers of his ilk who caused a rule to be adopted limiting the size of a catcher's mitt. To help Gus Triandos and his other catchers handle Wilhelm while he was with the Orioles from 1958 to 1962, Baltimore manager Paul Richards had an elephantine mitt constructed

Ty Cobb laces one in batting practice. This photo, taken late in Cobb's career, shows why the Detroit Tigers have never retired the uniform number of their greatest player. National Baseball Library & Archive, Cooperstown, N.Y.

that resembled the gigantic mockery of a catcher's mitt that Al Schacht, the Clown Prince of baseball during the 1920s and 1930s, sometimes incorporated into his comedy act. Even with the oversized mitt, Triandos still set all sorts of modern records for passed balls. On May 4, 1960, he became the first backstopper in American League history to let three pitches get by him in a single inning. Less than a week later Triandos's backup receiver with the Orioles, Joe Ginsberg, tied his record.

In 1962 another Baltimore receiver, Charlie Lau, fell victim three times in a single inning to the butterfly pitch.

After the 1964 season the rules committee voted to limit the size of a catcher's mitt, not that the lack of a restriction had ever seemed to offer much help to Triandos and the other receivers who had to cope with Wilhelm. In 1965, the first year the new rule was in effect, Wilhelm, by then with the White Sox, contributed heavily to the 33 passed balls Sox catcher J. C. Martin committed to set a post-1900 major league record.

A S LATE as 1938 a first baseman could still use a glove of any size or shape he wished. Detroit first sacker Hank Greenberg brought this practice to an abrupt halt when he concocted a glove with a web so elaborate that he looked as if he were flaunting a fishing net. Prior to the 1939 season a rule was inserted that a first baseman's glove could no longer be more than 12 inches from top to bottom and no more than eight inches across the palm and connected by leather lacing of no more than four inches from thumb to palm. The "Trapper" model, which first appeared in 1941 and quickly became the standard glove for the first-base position, was circumspectly designed to conform to the new rule.

I N THE early days the rules said nothing about the size and shape of fielders' gloves for the simple reason that for many years no self-respecting player would stoop to wearing a glove in the field. By the mid-1870s many catchers had begun using protective mittens while behind the bat and a few players, such as Al Spalding, also sported gloves that were employed more to protect their hands than to act as an aid in catching the ball, but gloves were not a standard item of equipment until the 1880s. Even then a number of players disdained field-

---

1.13

The first baseman may wear a leather glove or mitt not more than twelve inches long from top to bottom and not more than eight inches wide across the palm. . . . The webb of the mitt shall measure not more than five inches from its top to the base of the thumb crotch. The web may be either a lacing, lacing through leather tunnels, or a center piece of leather which may be an extension of the palm connected to the mitt with lacing and constructed so that it will not exceed the above mentioned measurements. . . .

1.14

Each fielder, other than the first baseman or catcher, may use or wear a leather glove. . . . The glove shall not measure more than 12" from the tip of any one of the 4 fingers, through the ball pocket to the bottom edge or heel of glove. The glove shall not measure more than

(continued)

(continued)

7-3/4" wide, measured from the inside seam at base of first finger, along base of other fingers, to the outside edge of little finger edge of glove. . . . The webbing may be constructed of two plies of standard leather to close the crotch area entirely, or it may be constructed of a series of tunnels made of leather, or a series of panels of leather, or of lacing leather thongs . . . .

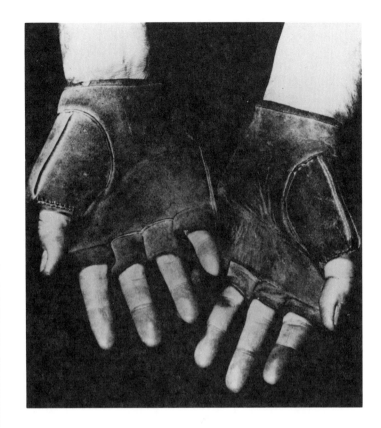

Typical catching gear, circa 1870s. These leather gloves, with the fingers cut off to facilitate throwing with either hand, were virtually all the protection a catcher wore at that time. **National Baseball Library & Archive, Cooperstown, N.Y.**

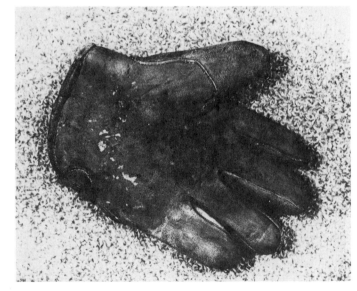

A glove used by a West Point player in 1893. The pancake style without webbing made every fielding play an adventure. Players were often fined in that era if they did not use two hands to make a catch. **National Baseball Library & Archive, Cooperstown, N.Y.**

ing a ball with anything but their bare flesh. The last two bare-handed players of note were second baseman Bid McPhee and third sacker Jerry Denny. Both balked at the notion of using a glove until deep into the 1890s.

Meanwhile, other players had long since recognized the advantages a glove could give them. When some began designing contraptions that resembled butterfly nets, in 1895 a rule was devised limiting fielders to gloves that were not over 10 ounces in weight or more than 14 inches in circumference around the palm of the hand. Catchers and first basemen were exempted from any restrictions on the size or weight of their gloves but were made to switch to a fielder's glove if they played another position. In the early 1890s it was still common practice for a catcher to use his mitt when filling in at shortstop or third base and for a first baseman to take his innings in the outfield with his first sacker's glove.

THE **1971** season was the first when it became mandatory for all players to wear protective helmets when batting, but most had adopted them long before then. In 1941 the Brooklyn Dodgers became the first team to wear plastic headguards after Pete Reiser, Ducky Medwick, and several of the team's other stars were beaned. By 1957 the American League had recognized the need for protective headgear and made it obligatory. Batters had the option, though, of using plastic inserts in their caps, which offered less protection than a helmet, particularly one with ear flaps, but were more comfortable and also allowed a player to hide his fear of being beaned, however healthy that fear might be.

1.16

A professional League shall adopt the following rule pertaining to the use of helmets: (a) All players shall use some type of protective helmet while at bat. (b) All players in National Association Leagues shall wear a double ear-flap helmet while at bat. (c) All players entering the Major Leagues commencing with the 1983 championship season and every succeeding season thereafter must wear a single ear-flap helmet (or at the player's option, a double ear-flap helmet), except those players who were in the Major League during the 1982 season, and who, as recorded in that season, objected to wearing a single ear-flap helmet.

2

DEFINITIONS OF TERMS

The term "balk" has always been part of the game's vocabulary. Section 19 of Alexander Cartwright's playing rules in 1845 stated: "A runner cannot be put out in making one base, when a balk is made by the pitcher." At the time, though, a balk was an illegally delivered pitch or one that was not served up underhand in the manner of a cricket bowler.

Forty years later, the first season that overhand pitching was legal throughout the game, the term had already begun to acquire its present meaning. A balk in 1885 occurred in any of the following instances according to Rule 29:

(1) If the Pitcher, when about to deliver the ball to the bat, while standing within the lines of his position, makes any one of the series of motions he habitually

makes in so delivering the ball to the bat, without delivering it. (2) If the ball is held by the pitcher so long as to delay the game unnecessarily; or, (3) If delivered to the bat by the Pitcher when any part of his person is upon the ground outside the lines of his position.

The second type of violation was a matter of the umpire's judgment, whereas the third referred to the boundaries of the pitcher's box, which in 1885 was a 4 × 6-foot rectangle.

BASE COACHES have been around ever since it was recognized that a player could not both track the ball and make time while running the bases. To assist base runners, teams in the early days customarily stationed two players not due up to bat for a while outside the first-base and third-base foul lines. These players were called "coachers." Once the realization set in that a coacher could do more than just stand and wait for a runner to come his way, a new breed of base coach evolved.

By the mid-1880s teams like the St. Louis Browns were employing their most vociferous players as coachers and licensing them to taunt opponents and umpires along with encouraging their teammates. The Browns' leading coacher was third baseman Arlie Latham, a torrential heckler and an ace sign stealer. So vaunted did Latham become at the job that he carved a new niche in the game after his playing days were over. In 1907 manager John McGraw of the New York Giants hired Latham to do nothing more than coach runners, making him the first contracted base coach.

ALEXANDER Cartwright made no reference in his playing rules to a base on balls. The reason for the omission is that until 1863 there was no such thing in baseball as a free trip to first base. To reach base, a player had to hit the ball, even if it took 50 pitches before he got one to his liking.

A BASE COACH is a team member in uniform who is stationed in the coach's box at first or third base to direct the batter and the runners.

A BASE ON BALLS is an award of first base granted to a batter who, during his time at bat, receives four pitches outside the strike zone.

In the 1863 season both balls and strikes were called for the first time, with a batter being granted his base on balls after he received three pitches that were deemed balls. However, before an umpire was permitted to call a pitch a ball, he was first obliged to warn a pitcher an unspecified number of times for not delivering "fair" pitches or for delaying the game. In essence, then, far more than three pitches had to be delivered outside the strike zone before a batter received a walk.

In 1874 umpires were mandated to call a ball on every third unfair pitch delivered, meaning that nine balls in all were needed to draw a walk, though technically it came after three called balls. Five years later the rule was again amended, allowing umpires to call every unfair pitch a ball until nine were reached. In 1880 a walk was pared to eight called balls, then to seven the following year.

The 1884 season saw the National League shrink the number of balls needed for a walk to six, but the American Association still required seven balls. In 1886 the AA dropped to six balls, only to have the NL again demand seven. The two leagues adopted a uniform code of rules in 1887, including a reduction to five balls. Finally, in 1889, the figure was set at four, where it has remained ever since.

In 1879, the last year that nine balls were required to walk, Charley Jones, at the time the game's leading slugger, topped the National League, with just 29 free passes, and there were only 508 walks issued throughout the loop. The league total more than doubled in 1881 when a walk came after six balls, and the figure continued to climb all during the 1880s, peaking in 1889, the first year that a batter could stroll to first base after only four called balls. That season National League pitchers handed out 3612 free tickets, 1519 more than in 1888.

The BATTER'S BOX is the area within which the batter shall stand during his time at bat.

CARTWRIGHT also made no reference to batter's boxes in his playing rules. In all forms of baseball prior to 1874 a batter had to stand with either his forward foot or his back foot on a line drawn across the center of the home plate area. If a batter struck a pitch without having a foot on the line, the umpire simply called the resulting blow "no hit" and called the batter back to the plate. There was no other penalty.

The 1874 season introduced a 6 × 3-foot rectangular box for the hitter to occupy, thereafter known as the "batter's box." The dimensions were increased to the present 6 × 4 in 1886.

BENCH OR DUGOUT is the seating facilities reserved for players, substitutes and other team members in uniform when they are not actively engaged on the playing field.

RATHER remarkably, the term "dugout" did not first appear in the manuals until 1950 when the entire rulebook was recodified and many features of the game that had slipped into existence without being given due recognition finally received formal acknowledgement. Dugouts had existed since 1909, when the first all concrete and steel stadiums were constructed in Pittsburgh and Philadelphia; previously players sat at field level on benches that were enclosed to sequester them from spectators. The new stadiums also contained the first dressing rooms for visiting teams. Before 1909 visiting clubs had changed at their hotels and then traveled by carriages to the ballpark in full uniform.

A BUNT is a batted ball not swung at, but intentionally met with the bat and tapped slowly within the infield.

HITS THAT we now call bunts were originally known as baby hits. No one has a clue who coined the term "bunt." It is even impossible to say for certain who laid down the first deliberate bunt. Some historians credit the ploy to Dickey Pearce, a stocky little shortstop active from the mid-1850s until 1877. A weak hitter even against underhand pitching, Pearce learned to bunt out of necessity, but whether he was the first to master the art will always be arguable.

ON SEPTEMBER 9, 1876, the Hartford Blues and the Cincinnati Red Stockings played two games against each other in the same day, the first such occurrence in National League history. But the pair of games was not a doubleheader by the strict definition of the term because the first contest took place in the morning and then, after a lengthy dinner break, a second game was played in the afternoon.

The first true major league doubleheader, whereby two games were played in immediate succession, came on September 25, 1882, when the Providence Grays split a pair with the Worcester Ruby Legs.

For many years major league clubs also occasionally played tripleheaders when postponements made it necessary. Only once did all three games of a tripleheader go the full nine innings, on September 1, 1890, when the Brooklyn Bridegrooms swept a trio from the Pittsburgh Innocents. Pittsburgh also took part in the last major league triplebill. The club, by then the Pirates, went three rounds with the Cincinnati Reds at Forbes Field on October 2, 1920. Peter Harrison umpired behind home plate in all three contests, although the finale lasted only six innings before darkness gave Harrison an excuse to bring a merciful halt to the long day, with the Pirates comfortably ahead 6–0.

THE TERM "infield fly" did not first appear in the rulebook until 1895, a full half century after Alexander Cartwright devised the first formal set of playing rules. Prior to 1895 with the bases occupied infielders, including pitchers and catchers, were free to drop infield pops or line drives on the gamble that they could then force out runners who had been frozen to their bases on the assumption the ball would be caught. Part of the reason it took so long for an infield fly rule to be adopted was that until the 1890s, when

Yankees second baseman Bobby Richardson calls for a pop fly in a 1958 game at Cleveland as Mickey Mantle pulls up to watch. Today a batter is automatically out if he hits an infield fly with less than two out and when first and second base, or all three bases, are occupied. Prior to an 1895 rule change, infielders would let pop-ups drop safely so they could then turn an easy double play. American Photographic Archives

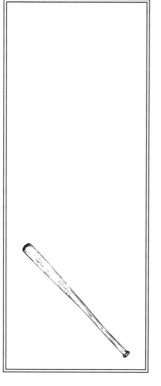

gloves became a fielding tool as well as a protective device, there was little assurance that a pop fly would be caught, and it seemed absurd for an umpire to rule a batter automatically out and then sheepishly watch as the ball fell safely.

A typical example of the way a quick-thinking fielder could take advantage of the absence of an infield fly rule was displayed in an American Association game at Cincinnati on June 22, 1882, between the Cincinnati Red Stockings and the Pittsburgh Alleghenys. In the bottom of the 14th inning with Cincinnati ahead 5–2, Pittsburgh had Mike Mansell on second base and Ed Swartwood on first with none out when Johnny Peters lifted an easy pop toward Cincinnati shortstop Chick Fulmer. After setting himself for a catch, Fulmer let the ball drop and then scooped it up and in swift order retired both Mansell and Swartwood. Heeding a shout from his first baseman, Fulmer saw that Peters in disgust had not bothered to run out the hit and fired to first to end the game with a triple play.

ANOTHER wonderful question that no one can answer is who first brought the term "inning" to baseball. In his original playing rules Alexander Cartwright made no mention of innings, calling a team's stint at bat a "hand" and stipulating that even after one club achieved 21 runs or aces, a game could not end until an equal number of hands had been played. In Cartwright's day, however, it was already common parlance to say a nine must be given its innings. An inning is a period of prosperity or luck and every team, from the dawn of baseball history, has looked to prosper when it took its turn at bat.

THE FIRST baseball teams to band together to play under the rules of the game then in existence for a so-called "league championship" were a group of New York clubs who gathered in 1857 to form the National Association of Base Ball Clubs. The fledgling loop played its games at the Fashion Race Course in Jamaica, New York, assessed spectators a 50-cent admission fee, and adopted the nine-inning format to replace the old first-team-to-score-21-runs-wins rule. All the players in the NABC were simon-pure amateurs, however, or at least that was the circuit's claim; the notion of openly paying players to perform was still more than a decade away from being popularly accepted.

The first professional league did not organize until 1871. Calling itself the National Association, it fielded nine teams and played its first game on May 4,

1871, with Cleveland (Forest City) facing Fort Wayne (Kekionga). The Fort Wayne club played just 19 championship contests before it folded, and no team played more than 33. By 1875, its last year of existence, the NA had swelled to 14 teams, but only the top three—Boston, Hartford, and the Philadelphia Athletics—played anywhere near a complete schedule. Rife with weak clubs, corrupt players, and lackadaisical team officials, the loop gave way the following season to a new circuit that christened itself the National League and has remained alive under that name ever since.

I N THE early professional game the individual on a team who performed the same functions as a manager does today was generally called a field captain and was drawn from the ranks of the team's active players. A prime example was Adrian Anson, who was dubbed "Cap" when he assumed the captaincy of the Chicago White Stockings in 1879. Working in conjunction with the field captain on most teams was a manager, responsible for making travel arrangements, paying players, enforcing fines, etc. On some teams both roles were handled by one man, who sometimes also owned all or part of the club. Charlie Byrne was the prototypical manager who consulted with and answered to only himself when he ran the Brooklyn Bridegrooms in the mid-1880s.

By Byrne's time few owners were still so egocentric or so penurious as to sit at the field helms of their clubs, and most teams now called the individual who did the manager. Playing managers remained common, but the two best teams during the 1890s, the Boston Beaneaters and the Baltimore Orioles, were skippered by Frank Selee and Ned Hanlon, men who were exclusively bench pilots. The duties that the manager had formerly executed were in most cases now the province of another club official, often the secretary.

THE MANAGER is a person appointed by the club to be responsible for the team's actions on the field, and to represent the team in communications with the umpire and the opposing team. A player may be appointed manager.

A STRIKE is a legal pitch when so called by the umpire, which—(a) Is struck at by the batter and is missed; (b) Is not struck at, if any part of the ball passes through any part of the strike zone; (c) Is fouled by the batter when he has less than two strikes; (d) Is bunted foul; (e) Touches the batter as he strikes at it; (f) Touches the batter in flight in the strike zone; or (g) Becomes a foul tip.

A **T ONE** time a ball hit foul by a batter with less than two strikes was not considered a strike. As a result, the American League record for the highest batting average was established in a season when the junior loop did not yet recognize the foul strike rule. In 1901, while Nap Lajoie was hitting .426 to set an AL mark that looks safe now forever, the National League for the first time was counting any pitch fouled off by a batter with fewer than two strikes as a strike. The AL did not follow suit until two years later. Hence Lajoie's record, already suspect because the AL in 1901 was operating for the first time as a major league and many of its teams were

stocked with minor leaguers, was further tainted by the fact that he was not charged, as were NL players that year, with a strike for hitting a foul ball.

In 1901 the AL outhit the NL by 10 points and upped the margin of difference to 16 points in 1902. The following year, the first in which both leagues counted foul balls as strikes, the NL outhit the AL by 14 points, seeming to support the argument that the hitters hadn't been better in the AL during the previous two campaigns, only given the equivalent of an extra strike or two in many of their at bats.

Incredible as it now seems, a player was not even assessed a strike on a fouled off bunt attempt until the 1894 campaign. Heretofore bat magicians like Willie Keeler and Jack Crooks, as long as they were not too obvious about it, could poke pitches foul all day without penalty in wait for one to their liking. Beginning in the mid-1880s, umpires were licensed to charge a batsman with a strike if they felt he was delaying the game by purposely fouling off pitches, but this rule was seldom invoked and often resulted in turmoil when an umpire did attempt to sanction an offender. An American Association game between St. Louis and Brooklyn on September 5, 1888, crumbled into mass confusion when umpire Fred Goldsmith, a star pitcher earlier in the decade with the Chicago White Stockings, instantly called a strike on Browns catcher Jack Boyle when he bunted a foul pop, claiming it was a deliberate effort to hit foul, and then found himself obliged to void Brooklyn receiver Bob Clark's catch of the popup owing to his previous call of strike.

In 1895, the year after the foul bunt rule came on the books, the National League for the first time decreed that a foul tip was a strike but only if it was caught by the catcher within the 10-foot lines of the catcher's box. Between the increased mound distance in 1893 and the impunity with which batters could foul off pitches, it was small wonder that strikeout totals tumbled to an all-time low during the mid-1890s. In 1893, as an extreme example, the entire Louisville Colonels' hill staff notched only 190 strikeouts in 114 games, and the New York Giants topped the National League with a mere 395 Ks, an average of about three and a half a game.

The STRIKE ZONE is that area over home plate the upper limit of which is a horizontal line at the midpoint between the top of the shoulders and the top of the uniform pants, and the lower level is a line at the top of the knees. . . .

IN THEORY, the present definition of the strike zone was established in 1969 when the strike zone was reduced at its upper limit from the top of a batter's shoulders to his armpits and at the lower limit from the bottom of a batter's knees to the top of his knees. The upper limit, though now defined as the midpoint between the top of the shoulders and the top of the uniform pants, is still for all practical purposes the armpits.

The actual truth, however, is that umpires subsequent to 1969 gradually shrunk the upper limit of the strike zone until it became the beltline. To end this practice, the Official Playing Rules Committee rewrote the definition of the strike zone prior to the 1988 season. But some older arbiters have allegedly ignored it and still go by the pre-1988 strike-zone configuration, whereas others find it easier to picture the armpits as the upper limit than an imaginary midpoint between the beltline and the top of the shoulders.

Until the National Association came into being in 1871, the strike zone was rather nebulous. Beginning in 1858, when the concept of calling strikes was first introduced, umpires were authorized to assess a strike on any pitch that was "within fair reach of the batter." In 1871 the National Association adopted a rule allowing a batter to request either "high" or "low" pitches. The strike zone for a high ball was between a batter's waist and forward shoulder, whereas the low strike zone ranged from the waist to the forward knee. A batter was required to declare verbally his choice of pitches when he stepped up to the plate and was not permitted to change his mind during his turn at bat. If a batter did not declare himself, the strike zone then became the entire area between the shoulder and the knee.

Quaint as the notion of a high and a low strike must now seem, it endured for the first 16 seasons of professional play, from 1871 through the 1886 season. In 1887, when the number of balls needed for a walk was pared to five and the number of strikes hiked to four, the high-low rule was eliminated. Confronting hitters with a strike zone nearly double in size seemingly ought to have resulted in markedly lower batting averages, but quite the opposite occurred. In 1887 the National League hitting average jumped 18 points over the previous year and the American Association mark gained a whopping 30 points. Giving batters an extra strike and granting a walk after only five balls instead of six apparently more than compensated for the larger strike zone, at least initially.

AGAIN, we cannot be sure when the word "tag" became part of baseball lingo. In the infant forms of baseball a fielder did not retire a runner by tagging him with the ball or tagging a base before he reached it but by hitting or "soaking" him with a thrown ball. This barbaric method had vanished by the time the Cartwright rules were adopted, but the idea of requiring a fielder to tag a runner was not embraced until 1848. Prior to that season it had been possible to nail a runner at any base, including home, simply by tagging it before he got there. Runners in the pre-1848 era were tagged only when they clashed between bases with a fielder who happened to have the ball. As of the 1848 campaign, however, it became necessary to tag a runner coming into a base on any play except a force out.

A TAG is the action of a fielder in touching a base with his body while holding the ball securely and firmly in his hand or glove; or touching a runner with the ball, or with his hand or glove holding the ball, while holding the ball securely and firmly in his hand or glove.

GAME PRELIMINARIES

3.01 (c)

Before the game begins the umpire shall—
(c) Receive from the home club a supply of regulation baseballs, the number and make to be certified to the home club by the league president. Each ball shall be enclosed in a sealed package bearing the signature of the league president, and the seal shall not be broken until just prior to game time when the umpire shall open each

(continued)

Originally it was the challenging team's duty to provide the game ball. If, say, the Pittsburgh Pirates were to challenge the Philadelphia Phillies for bragging rights in the State of Pennsylvania, the rules in 1858 would have bade the Pirates to spring for the sphere regardless of where the game was played.

When teams began to meet for more than a single contest, the policy was for the visiting nine to furnish the balls if a series of games was played and the home side if the match called for only one game. In either case, at the close of each game the ball became the property of the victorious club. Even after the job of

(continued)

package to inspect the ball and remove its gloss. The umpire shall be the sole judge of the fitness of the balls to be used in the game.

3.01 (D)

The umpire shall be assured by the home club that at least one dozen regulation reserve balls are immediately available for use if required.

supplying the balls fell always to the home team, this custom was retained. In 1887, when the National League and American Association first agreed to be governed by the same rules, both circuits stipulated in their rule manuals that the last ball in play belonged to the winning team.

I N 1887 the home team in both major leagues had to furnish the umpire with two balls. Both had to be handed to him prior to a game enclosed in a paper box that was sealed with a seal of the secretary of either the National League or the American Association. Upon receiving the sealed boxes, the umpire would call "Play" and then break open both of them in the presence of the two rival team captains. If either of the two game balls was lost or damaged to an extent that it could no longer be used, the home team was required to replace it with another new ball so that an umpire would always have on his person an extra ball.

In the very early years of professional play the home team had to furnish the umpire with just one new ball and there was no rule that it had to be given him in a sealed box. What some frugal teams would do was remove a new ball from play after it had been served up to the required leadoff batter of the game and substitute a used ball. If the leadoff batter was luckless enough to make out on the first pitch, the new ball would only be in play for that one delivery. This practice encouraged pitchers on the clubs that utilized it to lay the first pitch in there hoping to retire the leadoff batter as speedily as possible and so preserve the team's new ball. Oftentimes the so-called "new" ball would be used in this manner for several games before an opponent or an umpire refused to accept it as new any longer.

A Cleveland fan's head thwarts Orioles first baseman Eddie Murray from catching a pop foul hit by the Tribe's Junior Naboa. Fans have not always had the privilege of fighting players for foul balls in quest of a souvenir.
American Photographic Archives

UNTIL FAIRLY deep into this century spectators were expected to return any ball hit into the stands, whether fair or foul, and it often remained in play. For many years any fan who attempted to keep a ball he caught invited a struggle with the ballpark security force for possession of it.

Cubs owner Charles Weeghman in 1916 brought an end to the warfare in Wrigley Field (then called Weeghman Park) between park policemen and fans looking to obtain souvenir balls when he decided to cede all balls hit into the stands to his customers. But other teams were loath to be so generous. In 1923 a

Philadelphia lad was arrested and housed overnight in the slammer for refusing to relinquish a ball hit into the Baker Bowl bleachers during a Phillies game. Fourteen years later a New York fan was violently set upon by ushers when he tried to retrieve a foul ball that had become lodged in the home plate screen at Yankee Stadium. His suit against the Yankees in 1937, which the club ultimately settled for $7500, resulted in an unofficial truce between fans and major league teams on the issue.

As for balls hit out of the park, they too were customarily returned to the playing field—at least until the tag end of the last century. Most teams stationed guards and sometimes even substitute players outside the park to retrieve balls that were fouled out of its confines or home runs that cleared the outfield barriers.

Prior to 1886 an umpire was required to wait five minutes before declaring a ball hit out of the playing field lost and putting a new ball in play. Even after 1886 teams continued to chase down balls hit out of the park and return them to play, depending on their condition. Whether a ball was still playable was often the subject of a furious debate. In a Union Association game at St. Louis on October 11, 1884, between the Washington Nationals and the St. Louis Maroons, St. Louis won by forfeit when Washington refused to continue after arguing in vain that a ball fouled out of the park in the fourth inning by Maroons pitcher Pudge Boyle was too lopsided to be kept in play.

Some four years later American Association umpire Herman Doscher levied over $300 in fines stemming from a dispute midway through a game on July 6, 1888, between Cincinnati and Philadelphia. Doscher contended that a ball knocked over the outfield fence was useless when it came back covered with mud, and threw it out of play, overriding the protests of the A's pitcher. After Doscher broke out a new ball, A's centerfielder Curt Welch grabbed it and heaved it out of the Cincinnati park, prompting Doscher to tender his resignation after the game and aver that "he would not again pass through such a scene."

RARELY was a ball taken out of play in the last century or, for that matter, in the early part of this century because it was too heavily stained by grass or mud or tobacco juice or any combination thereof. No one worried whether the ball remained white, only that it remained reasonably round.

By the early 1920s, however, umpires were strongly urged to remove balls that were discolored or difficult for players to see, and the one incident more than any other that caused both major leagues to stop economizing on the price of balls occurred at the Polo Grounds on August 16, 1920. That afternoon the New York Yankees entertained the first-place Cleveland Indians on the home site they shared at the time with the New York Giants. Pitching for the Yankees, who trailed Cleveland by just a game and a half, was Carl Mays. The club's ace, Mays, threw the ball with an underhand sweep that was hard for batters to follow even when visibility was good, and conditions that afternoon were execrable. By the top of the fifth inning, when shortstop Ray Chapman led off for the Indians, a light drizzle was falling. The ball Mays held was damp and mudstained. Down he dipped and swung his arm. His submarine delivery shot out of bleachers in the deep background of the Polo Grounds.

The following day the *Cleveland Press* reported, "Mays tossed an inshoot that seemed to hypnotize Chapman, or else he miscalculated it and believed the ball would sail by. Anyhow, it struck him on the temple, fracturing his skull, and paralyzing the nerve chords, making it impossible for him to talk."

Ray Chapman is considered by many students of the game to have been the best shortstop of his time. He was just reaching his prime when he was killed by a mud-spattered pitch on a dark, drizzly day in 1920. **American Photographic Archives**

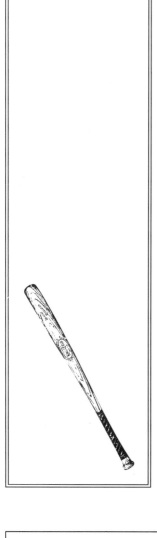

After the beaning Chapman underwent a delicate brain operation that evening and then hung on for several hours unconscious before expiring during the night. Mays was at first accused of deliberately throwing at Chapman, and there was a push, particularly in Cleveland, to charge him with manslaughter before he was exonerated of any wrongdoing. But in any event, Chapman's death, the only fatality resulting directly from an injury suffered in a major league game, hastened long-overdue legislation to remove balls from play as soon as they become scuffed or discolored.

Balls were taken out of play long before the Chapman incident, however, if they were severely damaged. In 1882 the National League introduced a rule to allow an umpire, at the request of either team captain, to call for a new ball at the end of any even inning if the old ball was badly ripped to expose its yarn or otherwise cut or misshapen. The American Association adopted the same rule but authorized an umpire to replace a ball even if neither captain appealed to him. A year later the NL permitted an umpire to replace a ball "at once" if in his judgment it was no longer fit for play, but the AA continued to direct its umpires to wait for the close of an inning until the two circuits adopted the same rulebook in 1887. Seldom, though, was a ball declared unfit for play unless it was palpably damaged. Typical of the time was a National League game between the Philadelphia Phillies and the Cleveland Blues on September 13, 1883. Played at Cleveland's Recreation Park after a heavy rain, the contest pitted Philadelphia's John Coleman against One Arm Hugh Daily of the Blues. Coleman, loser in 1883 of a major league record of 48 games, was virtually unhittable that afternoon, but Daily was literally unhittable. Despite a boyhood accident that deprived him of his left forearm and made him play with a pad attached to the stump of his amputated limb as an aid to fielding his position, Daily set the Phils down without a safety in a 1–0 win. His hitless gem was met with disdain, though, by Phillies' followers. One account of the game said the rain had rendered the field in a "wretchedly soggy condition and this soon made the ball so mushy it was impossible to hit it effectively."

No umpire in 1883 would have considered replacing the ball Daily hurled in his no-hitter merely because it was waterlogged. In fact, if a ball was not lost or obviously damaged, it could remain in play for the entire game. On August 4, 1908, the St. Louis Cardinals and the Brooklyn Superbas played a full nine innings at Brooklyn's Washington Park using just one ball. That doesn't say it was the last time this occurred, only that there was a documented instance of it as late as 1908.

SOME historians have mistakenly attributed Ray Chapman's fatal beaning partly to the fact that pitchers in the 1920 season could still legally throw spitballs and other deliveries that involved applying a foreign substance to the balls in addition to hurling scuffed and discolored balls. Actually, however, the rule abolishing the spitball, the shine ball, the emery ball, the licorice ball, and all the other deliveries that licensed a hurler to soil, deface, or in any way mar the texture of a ball was instituted on February 9, 1920, some six months before Chapman was beaned. A special provision allowed each team to designate two spitball pitchers for the 1920 season at least ten days prior to April 14, 1920, or the opening day of the campaign, and stated that thereafter none would be allowed.

Though the spitball had ostensibly been banned by the time of the Chapman incident, there were several spitball pitchers still legally plying their trade. For the most part they were hurlers who relied so heavily on the spitball that depriving them of it would have severely impaired their chances of continuing to earn a living on the major league level.

Following the 1920 season, eight National League and nine American League pitchers were given special dispensation to continue to throw spitballs for the rest of their careers. The NL hurlers were: Bill Doak, Phil Douglas, Dana Fillingim, Burleigh Grimes, Ray Fisher, Marv Goodwin, Clarence Mitchell, and Dick Rudolph. The junior circuit exemptees were: Yancy Ayers, Ray Caldwell, Stan Coveleski, Red Faber, Dutch Leonard, Jack Quinn, Allan Russell, Urban Shocker, and Allan Sothoron. Coveleski, Faber, and Grimes went on to fashion careers that have since been deemed worthy of the Hall of Fame. Had the spitball been removed from their arsenal, all of them might have suffered instead the fate of the many skilled practitioners of the spitball in the late teens who had not yet advanced to the major league level. Since they were not on the exempted list, these pitchers were forbidden from throwing a spitter in the event that they reached the majors, though they were permitted to continue using the spitball in the minor leagues. A few, like Hal Carlson, nevertheless worked their way up to the majors after developing other pitches to replace the spitball, which had been central to their repertoire, but most languished in the minor leagues for the remainder of their careers. Among them were Frank Shellenback and Paul Wachtel, both of whom had pitched in the majors prior to the spitball abolition but not enough to be included on the exempted list. Subsequent to 1920, Shellenback won a record 295 games in the Pacific Coast League and Wachtel dominated the Texas League, collecting a record 233 wins in that circuit.

FOR MANY years a manager was allowed to substitute for a player in his lineup only when a disabling injury occurred. Even then the opposing manager could refuse to allow the substitution if he felt the injury was not severe enough. Oftentimes an argument ensued, with the umpire forced by the rules to side against the team with the injured player. Unable to substitute, the loser of the argument would then either have to struggle along as best it could with the player who had been injured or else would have to play a man short.

There can be no doubt that players in the 19th century were a hardy breed. In 1878 the Boston Red Caps went through the entire National League season with only ten players, winning the pennant in the process. At that, the team's lone sub, Harry Schafer, got into just two games.

But most clubs were not as free of injury or mishap as the 1878 Red Caps. One of the most famous instances when a team was compelled to finish a contest

---

3.03

A player, or players, may be substituted during a game at any time the ball is dead. A substitute player shall bat in the replaced player's position in the team's batting order. A player once removed from a game shall not re-enter that game. . . .

with only eight men came on July 22, 1884, in a match between the Providence Grays and Philadelphia Phillies at Providence. In the box for the Grays was Charlie Sweeney, who only the week before had been made the club's ace after Hoss Radbourn was suspended for drunkenness and insubordination. Holding a 6–2 lead after seven innings, Providence manager Frank Bancroft decided to save Sweeney's arm and ordered him to right field, bringing right fielder Cyclone Miller in to pitch.

As though offended by the idea, Sweeney walked off the diamond and headed for the dressing room. Finding him there changing into his street clothes, Bancroft demanded he return to the field, but Sweeney refused to comply. One theory was that he engineered the showdown with Bancroft so that he could gain his release from Providence and sign with the St. Louis Maroons of the rebel Union Association. At any rate, the Grays had to play the rest of the game a man short, the rules of the time giving Bancroft no other recourse when a player who was not injured refused to remain in action. Providence somehow survived the eighth inning unscathed, but then the roof fell in. According to one account: "In the ninth Miller was hit freely, the ball going just where the (two remaining) outfielders could have handled it had they been in their regular places. Errors crept in fast, and the Philadelphias scored eight unearned runs."

After the disheartening 10–6 loss, Providence released Sweeney, reinstated Radbourn, and went on to bag the National League flag that year. But teams continued to play shorthanded on occasion until 1889, when a limited substitution rule was drafted, allowing one player for each team whose name was printed on the scorecard as an extra player to be put into the game for any player on the field at the end of any complete inning, with the replaced player not permitted to return to the game.

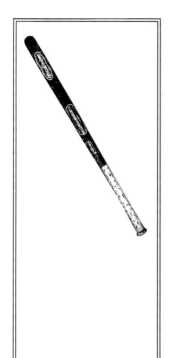

The ill-fated Charlie Sweeney. After he walked off the field in 1884, leaving his Providence team to play a man short, his life plunged sharply downward until 1902 when he died at age 38, shortly after being released from San Quentin. **Transcedental Graphics**

The following year the rule was revised to let a second substitute for each team also enter a game at the end of a complete inning. In 1891 the rule was further liberalized so that it now resembled the current rule. Beginning with the 1891 campaign, any player on the field could be substituted for at any time during a game. Among other things, the revamped rule ushered in a new type of specialist: the pinch hitter. Previously a

Rules were regarded as only mild inconveniences by Mike "King" Kelly. Tales abound of the ways in which he circumvented them, but not all the stories have much basis in fact. **National Baseball Library & Archive, Cooperstown, N.Y.**

player had sometimes been sent up to bat for a teammate but only when an injury made the opposition willing to accept the substitution. Like so many innovations, however, the concept of a pinch hitter was slow to take hold. In the early 1890s pinch hitters were used so infrequently that until 1896 the record for the most pinch hits in a season stood at a mere two, first done in 1893 by Jack Sharrott, a reserve outfielder with the Philadelphia Phillies.

According to baseball legend, the one player who more than any other forced the game's lawmakers to tighten the 1891 substitution rule was Mike "King" Kelly. There is an often-told tale that one afternoon in the early 1890s shortly after the rule was liberalized to allow substitutes to enter a game at any time, Kelly, then with the Boston Beaneaters, was on the bench nursing a hangover when a pop foul headed his way. Seeing that Charlie Ganzel, the Beaneaters catcher, had no chance to reach it, Kelly hopped to his feet, announced himself in the game for Ganzel, and snared the pop. The problem with that story is that if Kelly really pulled off this stunt, one would imagine that so obvious a loophole in the rules would have been immediately sealed. However, there was no further important legislation regarding substitutions until 1910, when it was mandated that the captain of a team making a substitute must immediately notify the umpire, who in turn must announce the change to the spectators. By 1910 Kelly was not only out of the game but had been dead for some 16 seasons. Hence the probability is strong that the Kelly tale, if not altogether apocryphal, has been embellished over the years.

3.03

...A pitcher may change to another position only once during the same inning; e.g. the pitcher will not be allowed to assume a position other than a pitcher more than once in the same inning...

THE PROVISO prohibiting pitchers from assuming a position other than pitcher more than once in the same inning was added to Rule 3.03 largely to thwart managers like Paul Richards, who created delays with his maneuvers in the 1950s that would have made four-hour games the norm nowadays. In a 1953 game with a right-handed hitter up in a tight situation, Richards, then at the helm of the Chicago White Sox, removed southpaw Billy Pierce and brought in Harry

Paul Richards (R) demands a full explanation. During his long tenure as a manager, Richards was the bane of umpires—constantly testing the rules in ways they could not anticipate. **National Baseball Library & Archive, Cooperstown, N.Y.**

Dorish, a righty reliever. Rather than take Pierce out of the game, though, Richards stationed him at first base while Dorish faced the right-handed batter. Then, with a lefty up next, Pierce returned to the mound. Richards had first pulled this maneuver two years earlier with Dorish, sending him to third base while Pierce took the mound in relief to face Ted Williams. After Pierce retired Williams, Dorish again assumed the pitching chores and a new third baseman came into the lineup.

Richards also employed the maneuver twice more in 1954, once with righthander Sandy Consuegra and finally with southpaw Jack Harshman. Without a rule to prevent it, a manager with Richards's kind of mind could orchestrate a lefty-righty switch again and again during an inning, or for that matter during every inning if he happened to have a couple of pitchers like

Harshman, who was originally a first baseman. The machination obviously has the potential to make a game seem interminable.

UNTIL 1950 courtesy runners were permitted with the consent of the opposing team. If Babe Ruth, for example, were struck in the ankle by a Lefty Grove pitch and temporarily incapacitated, a teammate could run for him if A's manager Connie Mack agreed to it. Ruth would still be eligible to return to the game as long as he was able to take his place in the field at the start of the next inning.

A **FORM** of this addendum first appeared in rulebooks prior to the 1910 season. Managers like New York Giants leader John McGraw made it necessary to stipulate that any player who assumes the position of pitcher must pitch to at least one hitter before he can be replaced on the mound. Prior to 1910 whenever one of McGraw's starting pitchers ran into trouble and he had no one ready, he would replace the beleaguered hurler with a substitute player, sometimes even himself, who would then stall around on the mound until the relief pitcher the Giants really wanted was warmed up. Since the first sub, whether McGraw or one of his utility infielders, would exit without having thrown a single pitch while time was in, his name would never even appear in the box score.

Despite the presence of Rule 3.05 (b), a pitcher

3.04

A player whose name is on his team's batting order may not become a substitute runner for another member of his team. This rule is intended to eliminate the practice of using so-called courtesy runners. No player in the game shall be permitted to act as a courtesy runner for a teammate. No player who has been in the game and has been taken out for a substitute shall return as a courtesy runner. Any player not in the lineup, if used as a runner, shall be considered as a substitute player.

3.05 (B)

If the pitcher is replaced, the substitute pitcher shall pitch to the batter then at bat, or any substitute batter, until such batter is put out or reaches first base, or until the offensive team is put out, unless the substitute pitcher sustains injury or illness which, in the umpire-in-chief's judgment, incapacitates him for further play as a pitcher.

can still receive credit for a mound appearance without throwing a single pitch while time is in. Many pitchers have come on in relief and promptly picked off a runner to end an inning or even a game before they delivered a pitch. In such an instance a pitcher still is credited for having worked a third of an inning.

Once announced into the game, a hurler can gain a mound appearance even without toeing the rubber while the ball is in play. On June 21, 1957, Jim Brosnan, later the author of several fine baseball books, including *The Long Season*, came out of the Cubs bullpen to face the New York Giants at the top of the tenth inning. While taking his warmup tosses, Brosnan slipped off the rubber and pulled the Achilles tendon in his left ankle. The umpire-in-chief properly waived the rule requiring Brosnan to face at least one batter and allowed Cubs manager Bob Scheffing to bring Dave Hillman into the game. Hillman was swiftly tagged for solo home runs by Danny O'Connell and Bobby Thomson to give the Giants a 12–10 victory.

Brosnan recovered from his Achilles injury to enjoy a long and productive major league career, but Robin Yount's older brother Larry was not as fortunate. The elder Yount's entire taste of life in the bigs consisted of a single warmup toss for the Houston Astros. After being called up from the Astros' Oklahoma City farm club in 1971, Yount was summoned in relief to face the Atlanta Braves in the ninth inning of a game on September 15. In his exuberance he aggravated an old elbow injury on the first preliminary pitch he delivered and had to be removed. But even though Larry Yount never faced a single batter in earnest, his name is in the record books as having pitched in a major league game.

The compelling question now is can there be a situation in which an umpire will allow a pitcher who is not injured to exit from a game before he pitches to the required one batter? Indeed there can, and Western International League fans saw one of the strangest examples of it on June 17, 1952.

While outfielder John Kovenz of the Tri-City Braves was at bat in the ninth inning, pitcher Bill Wisneski of Victoria was removed when his first serving to Kovenz was a ball. Eric Gard came in on relief. As Gard wound up to make his first pitch, Kovenz stepped out of the box. When Gard paused in his windup, plate umpire Herman Ziruolo assessed him with a balk and waved the tying run in from third base.

Storming in from the mound to protest that he thought time had been called when Kovenz stepped out, Gard brushed against Ziruolo and was promptly tossed out of the game. Another Victoria reliever, Ben Lorino, then took the hill, finished pitching to Kovenz, and went on to blank Tri-City and earn credit for a ten-inning 10–9 win. Gard is only one of several hurlers to be thumbed from a game before they could pitch to the required one batter, but Kovenz may be the lone hitter ever to face three pitchers in a single turn at bat.

FOR A LONG time it was left up to each individual team to monitor its own players when it came to fraternizing with opponents, but the early rulebooks clearly stated that players in uniform were not permitted to sit among spectators. They also forbade umpires, managers, captains, or players from addressing the crowd during a game but added the stipulation "except in case of necessary explanation." It was not unusual in the 1870s and 1880s for an umpire to stop play for a few moments while he explained a ruling to the audience or for a team captain to appeal to spectators for help when an umpire's decision did not go his way.

The fraternization rule, in no matter whose hands its enforcement is placed, has always been abused pret-

3.09

Players in uniform shall not address or mingle with spectators, nor sit in the stands before, during, or after a game. No manager, coach or player shall address any spectator before or during a game. Players of opposing teams shall not fraternize at any time while in uniform.

ty much without penalty. Everyone who has gone early to a major league game has seen players on both teams mingling casually around the batting cage during pregame practice. Rules against players and managers talking during a game to spectators have been likewise ignored. Prior to the 1883 season the management of the Philadelphia Athletics team in the American Association handed down a list of club rules that included the following: "No member of the team while dressed in his uniform shall be permitted to flirt with or 'mash' any female or lady." This edict had about as much chance of being obeyed as did another club rule that said: "While away from home every player must report at the hotel to the Manager before 11:30 P.M. and retire to his room for the night. No player shall lie abed after eight o'clock in the morning while on a trip unless he is sick or disabled."

PRIOR TO 1896 it was left to the judgment of the home team captain whether the field was fit to continue after play had been stopped. Naturally this had a high potential for abuse. A home side trailing 10–0 before a game had gone the required five innings to become an official contest was unlikely to want to continue to play if there was a single drop of water on the field that could be cited as a possible hazard. Conversely, the home captain was apt to wait until dark before calling a game if his team happened to be down a run in the late innings when the heavens parted.

Members of the Florida Marlins ground crew struggle with the tarp during a cloudburst on June 29, 1993. In a 1941 game at Washington, an inept ground crew took so long to cover the field in Griffith Stadium that the contest was later forfeited to Boston. **Allen Eyestone**

OFFICIALLY control of groundskeeping crews was first given to the umpire-in-chief in 1906 for the purpose of making a playing field fit to resume action after a rain delay, but groundskeeping crews at that time were small and often swiftly overwhelmed if a sudden rainstorm hit. The umpire consequently was unlikely to make an issue out of it if the crew was slow in protecting the field. By the middle of the 20th century, however, most teams had a sizable staff of grounds-keepers, and expectations had risen accordingly. On August 15, 1941, with the Washington Senators leading the Boston Red Sox 6–3 in the eighth inning at Washington's Griffith Stadium, a thunderstorm caused a 40-minute delay. By the time the squall abated, the field was too wet to resume play, so the umpires called the game and declared Washington the victor, 6–3. Boston manager Joe Cronin immediately lodged a protest, contending that the game could have continued if the Washington crew had not been laggard in covering the field. American League president Will Harridge agreed with Cronin and awarded the game to the Red Sox by forfeit.

Midway through the 1993 season the New York Mets nearly became only the second team in history to collect a forfeit win because of a rain-delay snafu. On June 29, the day after Mets hurler Anthony Young sustained his record-breaking 24th consecutive loss, the 40-member Florida Marlins' grounds crew fumbled with a tarp for 15 minutes in Miami's Joe Robbie Stadium before getting the infield covered after a storm stopped play. The crew's ineptness eventually had players on both teams laughing hysterically in their dugouts while the public-address system played the theme to "Mission Impossible."

A **GOOD** example of a special ground rule of the type discussed in this rule occurred in the very first modern World Series in 1903 between the Pittsburgh Pirates and the Boston Pilgrims. The two clubs played to overflow crowds in several games at both Boston's Huntington Park and Pittsburgh's Exposition Park. Both managers—Fred Clarke of the Pirates and Jimmy Collins of the Pilgrims—agreed to call any ball hit into an overflow crowd in fair territory a groundruled triple. As a result, Boston slugged a team World Series record 16 triples and Tommy Leach of the Pirates set an individual Series mark with four three-baggers. Boston ultimately won the fray 5 games to 3.

Twelve years later the Boston club, known by then as the Red Sox, was the beneficiary of another overflow-crowd ground rule in a World Series. Facing the Philadelphia Phillies in 1915, the Sox played to a sellout crowd in Philadelphia's Baker Bowl on October 13, 1925, in what turned out to be the final game when Boston outfielder Harry Hooper homered in the top of

3.13

The manager of the home team shall present to the umpire-in-chief and the opposing manager any ground rules he thinks necessary covering the overflow of spectators upon the playing field, batted or thrown balls into such overflow, or any other contingencies. If these rules are acceptable to the opposing manager they shall be legal. If these rules are unacceptable to the opposing manager, the umpire-in-chief shall make and enforce any special ground rules he thinks are made necessary by ground conditions, which shall not conflict with the official playing rules.

The scene following a World Series game in 1903 at Huntington Avenue Grounds, home of the Boston Pilgrims. Most of the overflow spectators had been packed into the outfield, forming a ring inside the wall that caused a special ground rule to be adopted that covered any ball hit into the crowd. **Transcendental Graphics**

the ninth to give his club a 5–4 win over Hall of Famer Eppa Rixey. It was Hooper's second home run of the contest and both were fly balls that bounced into temporary seats in right field that had been installed to accommodate the overflow crowds and declared, by mutual agreement, territory for a groundruled four-base hit. At the time batted balls that ended up in the stands in fair territory, whether it be on the bounce or on the fly, were home runs.

Rule 3.13 is now virtually an anomaly on the major league level, since big league teams no longer allow overflow crowds that infringe on the regular playing field.

3.14

Members of the offensive team shall carry all gloves and other equipment off the field and to the dugout while their team is at bat. No equipment shall be left lying on the field, either in fair or foul territory.

ONLY someone under the age of 50 could ask if there is any truth to the tale that players in the old days were permitted to leave their gloves on the playing field while their team was at bat. But then many who have not yet turned 50 might consider 1953 the old days. That was the last season that players on all levels, including the major leagues, could leave their gloves in the field when they came in to bat. The popular custom was for outfielders to deposit their gloves near their positions, infielders to spread theirs around the edge of the outfield grass, and pitchers and catchers to haul their fielding tools into the dugout. Many players also left their sunglasses in the field, folded inside their gloves.

A thrown or batted ball that struck a glove left on the field was in play, and if a fielder tripped on the glove while chasing a hit, it was considered an occupational hazard. Everyone wondered how an umpire would rule if a fielder, while diving for a line drive, caught it with an opponent's glove after somehow getting his bare hand entangled in it. But this unlikely event never happened. What often did happen was that teammates or opponents of squeamish players would tuck rubber snakes and such in their gloves while they were left unattended and then wait for their owners to shriek when the repellent discovery was made.

Rule 3.14 became necessary because by the mid-1950s improvements in design had made gloves so large as to be much more of a potential menace to fielders. After the new rule was adopted, some players, out of force of habit, for years continued to try to leave their gloves in the field until they were called on it by an umpire. Once in a while before a glove was ordered removed it would be allowed to remain on the field for a time, perhaps as a lorn reminder of a vestigial custom of the game whose passing most did not even know to mourn until long after the fact.

SPECTATOR interference, especially on a fly ball, was another hazard that was addressed for the first time in the rulebook for the 1954 season. That was the first year in which an umpire was licensed to declare a batter out on a foul or fair fly even when the ball was not caught, if in his judgment a fielder would have made the catch had a spectator not reached out of the stands to hinder him. On balls hit into the stands, however, unless an act of interference was particularly blatant fielders continued to be on their own if they reached in among a throng of spectators to make a catch.

3.16

When there is spectator interference with any thrown or batted ball, the ball shall be dead at the moment of interference and the umpire shall impose such penalties as in his opinion will nullify the act of interference. . . .

THE 1994 season marks the twentieth anniversary of the last occasion when a visiting team collected a win by forfeit after spectators invaded the field while a game was in progress and the home team was unable to stem the havoc. To bolster attendance, the Cleveland Indians designated their June 4, 1974, contest with the Texas Rangers a special "10-cent Beer Night" and lived to regret it. With the score tied 5–5 in the bottom of the ninth and the winning Cleveland run perched on third base with two out, Tribe fans in various stages of inebriation poured out of the rightfield stands and began tussling with Texas outfielder Jeff Burroughs. When Burroughs fought back both benches emptied to protect him. Order was eventually restored, but the peace was short-lived. After umpire Nestor Chylak was struck on the head in a fresh melee, the game was forfeited to Texas.

The Indians brass bewailed the needless defeat because Cleveland during the early summer of 1974 mounted what promised to be a serious pennant bid. By the end of September, however, theTribe was in its usual spot, well off the pace.

Interestingly, the Rangers had also been involved in the last previous forfeit that was triggered by a crowd-related incident while a game was in progress. On September 30, 1971, the Rangers' franchise was still based in the nation's capital and about to conclude its last game as the Washington Senators, a night contest against the New York Yankees at RFK Stadium. The game meant nothing in the standings to Washington, which was buried deep in fifth place in the American League East Division, but New York stood at 81–80, needing a win to finish above .500.

Behind 7–5 with two out in the top of the ninth, the Yankees were suddenly given an unexpected gift as Horace Clarke strolled to the plate to face Washington reliever Joe Grzenda. Outraged at owner Bob Short's

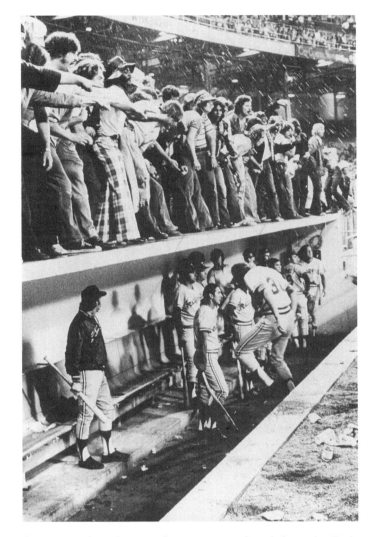

Members of the Texas Rangers hunker under their dugout roof at Cleveland Stadium for protection on "10-cent Beer Night." At center is manager Billy Martin, holding the bat he has just broken while pounding on the dugout roof in a vain effort to stop the Cleveland fans standing on the roof from dumping beer over his players. American Photographic Archives

decision a few days earlier to move the club to the Dallas area, thus bringing an end to major league baseball in a city that had had a team for the past 71 years, the bulk of the Washington crowd of 20,000 swarmed onto the field and began ripping up home plate, the bases, and the pitching rubber. Realizing the chances of completing the game were nil, the umpires had no choice but to award the Yankees a 9–0 forfeit victory, thereby assuring them of a winning season.

4

STARTING AND ENDING A GAME

4.02

The players of the home team shall take their defensive positions, the first batter of the visiting team shall take his position in the batter's box, the umpire shall call "Play" and the game shall start.

R ule 4.02 says in effect that the home team must bat last, but such has not always been the case. In fact, the opposite was true in 1877 when a new rule required the home club to take the bat first. The following season the National League reverted to the pre-1877 custom, which called for the two captains to determine which club first took the bat. The usual method was to flip a coin, with the visitors accorded the honor of making the call and the winner of the flip then given the option of batting first or last.

In 1885 the American Association allowed the home captain to choose which club batted first, and the National League adopted the same policy in 1887, when the two circuits agreed to be governed by one rulebook. It remained more an ingrained tradition than a rule that the home team would bat last until 1950, when Rule 4.02 was added to the manual. By the early part of the present century having your last at bats was viewed as an advantage. Previously, though, teams had often preferred to bat first, largely because it gave them first crack at the game ball, which was likely to be the only new ball put in play that day.

In the very first World Series played to completion between two rival major leagues, the 1884 matchup between the National League champion Providence Grays and the American Association champion New York Metropolitans, the Mets batted first in the opening game despite being the home club. Six years later, in the last World Series between the two loops, the home side batted last in all seven contests, but there were still occasions in 1890 when the home boys elected to bat first. One came in a Players League contest on June 21 between the Chicago Pirates and the Brooklyn Wonders, played at Chicago's South Side Park. Chicago manager Charlie Comiskey opted to put his Pirates up first and his decision deprived his pitcher that day, Silver King, of an opportunity to achieve the only no-hitter in Players League competition. The lone run of the game was tallied by Brooklyn's George Van Haltren in the seventh inning after he reached second base on a double error by Dell Darling, a catcher filling in that afternoon at shortstop. Because Brooklyn did not have to bat in the ninth after Chicago sealed the 1–0 verdict by going scoreless in the top of the frame, although King hurled a complete game, he did not work the necessary nine innings that a pitcher must to gain credit for a no-hitter.

4.03

When the ball is put in play at the start of, or during a game, all fielders other than the catcher shall be on fair territory.

SINCE NO team in its right mind would station its players anywhere but in fair territory nowadays, Rule 4.03 on the surface might seem superfluous. The rule was put in partly to keep any team or player from making a travesty of the game. Rube Waddell reputed-

ly would call all his infielders and outfielders to the sidelines sometimes in exhibition games and then strike out the side while working with just his catcher. No one cared to see a pitcher have the license to try this in a regular game.

There was a time, however, when players not only could legally be stationed in foul territory but it behooved them to play there. In 1876, the National League's first season of operation, it was still a rule that any batted ball that struck earth initially in fair territory was fair regardless of where it ended up. Many players mastered the fair-foul hit, which involved chopping down on the ball with their bats in such a way that it hit in front of the plate and then immediately spun off crazily into foul territory. To protect against these batsmen, teams were forced to position their first and third basemen outside the foul-line boundaries.

In 1876 Ross Barnes of the Chicago White Stockings collected 138 hits and scored 126 runs in just 66 games while posting a .429 average to win the inaugural National League batting crown by a whopping 63-point margin over runner-up George Hall of Philadelphia. Barnes's totals were swelled by his expertise at manufacturing fair-foul hits. When this skill was taken away from him by the rule change prior to the 1877 season, his average sagged to .272. Barnes never again hit even that high in the remainder of his major league career.

REQUIRING a catcher to remain within the lines of the catcher's box until the ball leaves the pitcher's hand makes issuing an intentional walk more of a challenge. If it were meant to be less, both major leagues, bent now on speeding up the game, would adopt the high school rule that requires a defensive team only to signal the desire to issue an intentional walk for it to occur.

There was a time when some batters could make any attempt to issue an intentional walk to them an adventure. Cleveland Indians player-manager Lou Boudreau once foiled an effort to purposely pass him by throwing his bat at a wide pitch and sailing the ball into right field for a single. Don Mueller, known as "Mandrake the Magician" because of his dexterity with a bat, also is well-remembered by New York Giants fans during the 1950s for thwarting efforts to walk him. Boudreau's and Mueller's legerdemain was a rarity only in that it was successful. Batters in the preexpansion era commonly fought against accepting intentional walks and were ever ready to lash out if a pitcher slipped a hair and delivered a ball close enough to the plate that it could be tagged.

In recent years either pitchers have become more skilled or batters less audacious. Wild pitches and passed balls still occur with a fair degree of frequency during an attempt to walk a batter intentionally, but ploys like Boudreau's and Mueller's are almost extinct.

IN AMATEUR and sandlot games teams often use people as base coaches who are not in uniform. This first became illegal on the major league level in 1957. Until then a Connie Mack or a Burt Shotton—to name two of the managers who have piloted their teams while wearing street clothes—was free to coach third or first any time the mood struck him.

4.06 (A)

No manager, player, substitute, coach, trainer or batboy shall at any time, whether from the bench, the coach's box or on the playing field, or elsewhere—. . . (2) Use language which will in any manner refer to or reflect upon opposing players, an umpire, or any spectator.

THE PROBLEM of base coaches who unduly taunt umpires or badger opposing players was first addressed by the rulebook way back in 1887, though umpires usually tried to ignore the offender unless he became inordinately loud or foul-mouthed. All the rules prohibiting it notwithstanding, heckling a thin-skinned opponent or arbiter has always been part of a base coach's job. Pitchers in particular are considered fair game.

In almost every case it is now against the rules for a base coach to distract a pitcher while he is in the midst of his delivery. It is not illegal, however, for a base coach to try to disrupt a pitcher's rhythm or to outright bamboozle him. One nugget, now forbidden by Rule 7.09 (j), that was worked on many unwary pitchers, particularly in the early 1920s right after the spitball was banned, involved a base coach, ideally with a runner on third, calling to a pitcher that he was morally certain the pitcher was doctoring the ball and then to demand to be shown it when the pitcher glanced his way. If the unsuspecting pitcher was so foolish as to toss the coach the ball for a look, the coach then stepped aside and let the throw go by him while the runner waltzed home. In 1915 the St. Louis Cardinals pilfered a game from the Brooklyn Dodgers when St. Louis player-manager Miller Huggins, coaching at third, pulled this trick on rookie hurler Ed Appleton.

4.08

When the occupants of a player's bench show violent disapproval of an umpire's decision, the umpire shall first give warning that such disapproval shall cease. If such action continues—

(continued)

MANY TIMES an umpire has invoked the ultimate power bestowed on him in Rule 4.08 and expelled every player on a team's bench from a game. One of the most volatile incidents occurred on September 27, 1951, in a game between the Brooklyn Dodgers and the Boston Braves at Braves Field and resulted in the only ejection of a player who never participated in a major league game. Trying to hold a slim first-place

(continued)

PENALTY: The umpire shall order the offenders from the bench to the club house. If he is unable to detect the offender, or offenders, he may clear the bench of all substitute players. . . .

4.09 (B)

HOW A TEAM SCORES. When the winning run is scored in the last half-inning of a regulation game, or in the last half of an extra inning, as the result of a base on balls, hit batter or any other play with the bases full which forces the runner on third to advance, the umpire shall not declare the game ended until the runner forced to advance from third has

(continued)

lead over the onrushing New York Giants, the Dodgers were tied 3–3 with Boston in the bottom of the eighth when Jackie Robinson speared a ground ball and fired it home to catcher Roy Campanella seemingly in time to nail Bob Addis trying to score from third. But plate umpire Frank Dascoli called Addis safe. Campanella was swiftly dispatched for arguing, then coach Cookie Lavagetto followed when the debate continued to rage, and finally Dascoli cleared the entire Dodgers bench.

Among the record 15 players who were banished was outfielder Bill Sharman, just up from the Dodgers' Fort Worth farm club in the Texas League. Sharman failed to get into a game with Brooklyn in 1951, however, and then quit baseball after one more season in the minors to pursue an NBA career with the Boston Celtics. After joining with Bob Cousy, Bill Russell, and Sam Jones to play on several championship Celtic teams, Sharman eventually made the pro basketball Hall of Fame, but he never had the thrill of seeing his name in a major league box score, even though it once appeared in an umpire's report on players who were booted from the game.

PROBABLY THE most famous instance of an umpire awarding a runner home plate because of fan obstruction was the wild ending to the 1976 American League Championship Series that saw George Brett of the Kansas City Royals rifle a three-run homer into the seats at Yankee Stadium in the top of the ninth to tie the game 6–6, only to have Yankees first sacker Chris Chambliss lead off the bottom half of the inning by belting a solo dinger off Kansas City reliever Mark Littell to clinch the pennant for the Yankees. In describing the pandemonium that ensued when Yankees fans, unable to control their exhilaration, began streaming

(continued)

touched home base and the batter-runner has touched first base. An exception will be if fans rush onto the field and physically prevent the runner from touching home plate or the batter from touching first base. In such cases, the umpires shall award the runner the base because of the obstruction by the fans....

onto the field almost the moment Chambliss's shot cleared the rightfield barrier, Thurman Munson later said, "By the time Chambliss got to third base all hope of reaching the plate was gone. He never did make it."

Though Kansas City made no protest and the umpires seemed inclined to let Chambliss's interrupted journey around the bases pass without comment, hours later the Yankees first baseman took time away from the team's pennant celebration to creep out of the clubhouse, accompanied by two policemen, and touch home plate to make his flag-winning run official.

Joyous New York fans mob Chris Chambliss as he tries to circle the bases after homering to give the Yankees the 1976 American League pennant. The umpires were authorized by Rule 4.09 (b) to award Chambliss home plate even though he never touched it in their presence. AP/Wide World Photos

AS IS STILL true in most minor leagues, the second game of a doubleheader was often scheduled for only seven innings in both major leagues prior to World War I. Much of the reason for the abbreviated second contest was because games in those days often did not start until midafternoon, making it a constant challenge to end before darkness. None of the parks as yet had lights, nor had Daylight Savings Time been adopted in the summer months.

Between 1903 and 1910 no fewer than nine doubleheader nightcaps that went less than nine innings resulted in no-hitters and one was a perfecto. On August 11, 1907, Ed Karger of the St. Louis Cardinals retired 21 straight Boston Braves in a seven-frame contest as he cruised to a 4–0 win.

THE EXCEPTION to the present rule enabling a team to win by more than one run when a game is ended by a "Sudden Death" home run was first added in 1920. Before then the rule was hard and fast that a team batting last could not win by more than one run when it won the game in the ninth or an extra inning. If with the score tied and the bases loaded a player hit a "Sudden Death" outside-the-park home run, rather than a grandslam he was given credit only for one RBI (the number of runs needed to win the game) and a single (the number of bases the runner scoring the winning tally needed to make). Among the 38 players who lost home runs to the old rule was Babe Ruth. When Ruth homered for Boston on July 8, 1918, with Red Sox teammate Amos Strunk on first base to end a ten-inning 0–0 game with Cleveland, he was credited at the time with only a triple.

In 1968 the Special Baseball Records Committee, which was formed to resolve historical disparities or errors, voted to credit all the players who had hit

Babe Ruth was still a pitcher in 1918 when he lost a home run to a rule that has since been rescinded. Fifty years later, in 1968, the four-bagger was added to his career total, only to be removed again a few months later.
National Baseball Library & Archive, Cooperstown, N.Y.

"Sudden Death" home runs before 1920 with an additional career four-bagger. Ruth's home run total was hiked from 714 to 715, where it remained for all of about a year before the committee reversed its decision on May 5, 1969, and again assigned Ruth only a triple for his 1918 blow.

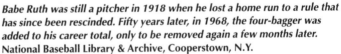

A GAME nowadays is suspended when darkness halts it because the stadium lights fail or a local ordinance prevents them from being turned on. At one time, however, a team was not allowed to turn on the lights in its home park during the course of a game unless it was a scheduled night or twi-night encounter. When darkness intervened the game was stopped at that juncture. If it had gone the necessary five innings, it was considered an official game. When darkness forced a halt short of the five-inning mark, that was the breaks.

One of the more unfortunate examples of the old tradition occurred on June 1, 1947. That afternoon, after a crowd of 47,132 in Cleveland Stadium sat through a 33-minute rain delay prior to the first game of a scheduled doubleheader between the Indians and the New York Yankees, the weather broke long enough to play two innings before another storm front moved in, forcing a second stoppage that lasted an hour and 18 minutes. When the game resumed in the mud and fog, New York and Cleveland waged a slugfest that took four and a half hours to finish, including the two rain delays. Finally, with the clock approaching 6:00 P.M. and New York ahead 11–9, Yankees relief ace Joe Page stifled a Tribe rally in the bottom of the ninth to preserve Al Lyons's lone win with the Bronx Bombers.

After the two teams retired to their dressing rooms, the crowd had to endure another wait before the second game began. By the time the clubs took the field again it was nearly 6:30 P.M. and the fog made the hour seem even later. Cleveland owner Bill Veeck would happily have turned on the lights, but the rules in 1947 prevented it. Yankees leadoff hitter Snuffy Stirnweiss stepped reluctantly to the plate to face Indians righthander Al Gettel. After each pitch Stirnweiss turned to home plate umpire Red Jones and complained that he was having trouble seeing the ball. Finally Stirnweiss took a called third strike and even before he could turn to complain again, Jones threw up his hands and announced that the game was being called on account of darkness. Although the crowd loudly voiced its dissatisfaction with Jones's decision, the *New York Times* reporter at the game said: "But it seemed the sensible thing to do." No one thought to grumble then about Veeck not being allowed to use the stadium lights so that the twinbill could be completed.

4.12 (A)

. . . . (4)Darkness, when a law prevents the lights from being turned on. (5) Weather, if the game is called while an inning is in progress and before it is completed, and one of the following situations prevails: (i) The visiting team has scored one or more runs to tie the score, and the home team has not scored. (ii) The visiting team has scored one or more runs to take the lead, and the home team has not tied the score or retaken the lead.

THE MARATHON 26-inning 1–1 tie game between the Brooklyn Dodgers and the Boston Braves on May 1, 1920, came 49 years too soon. Now the game would have been suspended when darkness made it impossible to continue and then resumed at the top of the 27th inning the next time the teams met. Before 1969, however, a game called at the end of a completed inning with the score tied after nine innings was declared a draw and then replayed from scratch later in the season.

The 1969 rule change made it possible for the Chicago White Sox and Milwaukee Brewers to break the record in 1984 for the longest game in American League history. On May 8 the two clubs battled for 17 innings to a stalemate at Chicago's Comiskey Park and then resumed the struggle the following day. Eventually Harold Baines slammed a homer off Chuck Porter with one down in the bottom of the 25th inning to give the White Sox a 7–6 triumph. Tom Seaver, who worked the final inning of the suspended game in relief on May 9 and then started the regularly scheduled game and went 8.1 innings, won both contests for Chicago.

Previously, the record for the longest game in American League history had been 24 innings, last done on July 21, 1945, at Philadelphia when the A's and the Detroit Tigers were forced to settle for a 1–1 tie.

Had the current rule been in effect then, the game would have been completed at a later date, as would have the Dodgers and Braves 26-inning classic.

4.12 (c)

A suspended game shall be resumed and completed as follows: (1) Immediately preceding the next scheduled single game between the two clubs on the same grounds; or (2) Immediately preceding the next scheduled double-header between the two clubs on the same grounds, if no single game remains on the schedule; or (3) If suspended on the last scheduled date between the two clubs in that city, transferred and played on the grounds of the opposing club, if possible; (i) Immediately preceding the next scheduled single game, or (ii) Immediately preceding the next scheduled double-header, if no single game remains on the schedule. (4) If a suspended game has not been resumed and completed on the last date scheduled for the two clubs, it shall be a called game.

ALTHOUGH major league teams nowadays not only make every effort to complete suspended games and make up postponed games but are in fact required to do so, especially when the game in question could have a bearing on a pennant race, this has not always been the case. The issue was first seriously addressed after the 1908 season. That year Detroit copped the American League pennant by a half-game over Cleveland. The margin of victory was a postponed game the Tigers had not been required to play, leaving Detroit at 90–63, whereas Cleveland, playing a full 154-game slate, finished at 90–64.

Cleveland fans were understandably up in arms, but Chicago White Sox followers also had a strong grievance. The White Sox finished a game and a half behind Detroit at 88–64 after failing to make up two postponed games. Had the Tigers played their postponed game and lost it and the White Sox won both of their unplayed games, the 1908 American League race would have ended in a three-way tie with Detroit, Cleveland, and Chicago all at 90–64.

Few historians have noted that the 1908 season was the fifth in a row in which postponed games were a significant factor in the American League pennant race. In 1904, the first year that both major leagues adopted a 154-game schedule, Boston and New York tied in victories with 92, but Boston had three fewer losses. Philadelphia and Chicago both garnered 92 wins in 1905, but postponements reduced the A's slate to 148 games, whereas the White Sox played 152. The following year the Sox benefitted by postponements, finishing three games ahead of New York as both teams were

held to 151 contests; had the clubs been required to play out the schedule, New York could have tied the Sox at 93–61.

The 1907 season was the only time in major league history that a pennant winner lost more games than an also-ran. An extraordinarily rainy summer in the East shaved nine games off the Philadelphia A's schedule while Detroit lost only four contests to the weather. Philadelphia finished at 88–57, a game and a half behind Detroit's 92–58 mark. Had the full slate been played, the A's could have come in at 97–57 and the Tigers five games back at 92–62.

Despite a pledge following the 1908 campaign to make up postponed games that had a potential bearing on a pennant race, there have been several occasions in the years since when this was not done. The most glaring was in 1915 when three teams were bunched within half a game of each other at the close of the Federal League season. Owing to postponements, the flag-winning Chicago Whales played just 152 games and finished at 86–66; the Pittsburgh Rebels with the same number of wins but one more loss ended in third place half a game back at 86–67. Finishing second were the St. Louis Terriers at 87–67. The Terriers were just one percentage point off the pace and are the only team in major league history to lead its circuit in victories yet fail to win the pennant.

Some critics tend to excuse the Federal League, contending it was not a true major league, but no satisfactory explanation has ever been presented for the American League's failure to order meaningful postponed games to be made up in 1935 or an even more serious gaffe by the National League three years later. Detroit copped the 1935 American League flag by a three-game margin over the New York Yankees that could have turned into a one-game deficit if both clubs had fulfilled their 154-game commitments. In 1938 the

Chicago Cubs triumphed by two games over Pittsburgh, but could likewise have wound up one game in arrears had the Pirates played and won four postponed games while the Bruins were losing their two unplayed contests.

The 1918 and 1972 seasons also saw teams benefit from the full schedule not being completed but for reasons that were unavoidable. Owing to America's involvement in World War I, the 1918 campaign was terminated on Labor Day with huge disparities between the number of home and road games the Boston Red Sox and Cleveland Indians played, contributing to a Red Sox triumph by two and a half games. In 1972, after a spring-training lockout delayed the start of the major league season, it was ruled that all games that were canceled as a result of the lockout would not be made up. Detroit then proceeded to win the American League East crown over Boston by a scant half-game. This memory prompted both major leagues to make up all canceled games during the course of the season when another labor lockout delayed the start of the 1990 campaign.

TECHNICALLY the last time a major league game was forfeited because a team failed to show up was in 1902, when the Baltimore Orioles were unable to field a team for an American League game on July 17 with the St. Louis Browns. The Orioles were in total disarray at the time after ex-National Leaguer John Mc-Graw jumped the club to join the New York Giants and spirited several key players back to the National League with him.

Before the Baltimore decimation, the last time a team was saddled with a no-show loss was on May 25, 1893, when the Chicago White Stockings left the Louisville Colonels holding the bag. By the 1890s for-

---

4.15

A game may be forfeited to the opposing team when a team— (a) Fails to appear upon the field, or being upon the field, refuses to start play within five minutes after the umpire has called "Play" at the appointed hour for beginning the game, unless such delayed appearance is, in the umpire's judgment, unavoidable.

---

feits for nonappearance were a rarity, but ten years earlier, owing to the vagaries of train travel, they had been fairly common. In September 1884 the Washington Unions bagged two victories in the space of 12 days when railway delays prevented, first, the Pittsburgh Stogies and then the Cincinnati Outlaw Reds from reaching the Washington ballyard by gametime.

IT HAS been 40 years since a major league team last received the ultimate penalty for stalling or deliberately trying to delay a game. On July 18, 1954, facing the Philadelphia Phillies at home in Sportsman's Park, the St. Louis Cardinals trailed 8–1 in the second game of a rain-delayed doubleheader with one out in the top of the fifth and darkness fast approaching. Since the game was not yet official and the rules then did not permit turning on the stadium lights to continue play, Cardinals manager Eddie Stanky thought he saw a way to escape defeat.

After changing pitchers twice in the fifth, though the Phils had made just one hit, Stanky went to his bullpen a third time. The umpires had already warned Stanky that his tactics bordered on stalling. When crew chief Babe Pinelli saw Stanky wave in Tom Poholsky, he picked up the field phone and announced that the game was forfeited to the Phils. Because the game went fewer than five innings the official scorer did not send in a box score. Many of the Phils lost hits and RBIs, and rookie Bob Greenwood was denied an almost certain victory in his first major league start.

A MAJOR league game has never been forfeited because a team was unable to put nine players on the field. Ever since the rules forbade a team playing shorthanded for any reason, clubs have always managed to scrape together a full crew. There have been

---

4.15 (B)

A game may be forfeited to the opposing team when a team employs tactics palpably designed to delay or shorten the game.

4.17

A game shall be forfeited to the opposing team when a team is unable or refuses to place nine players on the field.

---

many instances, however, when a team sustained a forfeit because it *refused* to put nine players on the field, or even any players.

One of the more interesting cases involved a season-closing series in 1886 between the Washington Senators and the Kansas City Cowboys. The two teams were locked in a struggle to avoid the National League cellar. When the Cowboys arrived in the nation's capital on the evening of October 6, they were angry to learn the Senators had scheduled three successive morning and afternoon doubleheaders in order to make up postponed games. The Cowboys had expected to play only a single contest on all three dates. Since they had what seemed a comfortable four and a half game lead on Washington, they slept in on the morning of October 7, allowing the Senators to claim a victory by forfeit.

The Cowboys pursued this same pattern for three straight mornings to present Washington with a trio of gift wins, the most any team has won by forfeit in a season, let alone in a three-day period. When the Senators also won the afternoon games on October 7 and 9, Kansas City manager Dave Rowe, suddenly finding his team in last place, begged that a 2–2 tie in the afternoon game on October 8 be replayed after the season's regular closing date. Washington manager John Gaffney grudgingly agreed, and the two clubs clashed for a final time on October 11. Despite the five successive defeats, three of them by forfeit, the Cowboys nevertheless managed to escape the National League basement when 18-year-old Silver King bested Washington's John Henry, 7–5, to post his first of 204 major league wins.

A **GOOD** question here is why are some protested games replayed in their entirety rather than resumed at the juncture when the point under contention occurred, as happened in the "Pine Tar" game in 1983. The explanation is that George Brett's "Pine Tar"

4.19

PROTESTING GAMES. Each league shall adopt rules governing procedure for protest-

(continued)

(continued)

ing a game, when a manager claims that an umpire's decision is in violation of these rules. No protest shall ever be permitted on judgment decisions by the umpire. In all protested games, the decision of the League President shall be final. Even if it is held that the protested decision violated the rules, no replay of the game will be ordered unless in the opinion of the League President the violation adversely affected the protesting team's chances of winning the game. . . .

home run to put his Kansas City Royals ahead, 5–4, occurred in the ninth inning. Often a contested play will develop so early in the going that it makes better sense to start from scratch, especially when an inability to duplicate the circumstances surrounding the protested game would put one team at a severe disadvantage. A good example took place in the 1932 contest between the Detroit Tigers and the New York Yankees. The fun began when second baseman Tony Lazzeri came to bat in the second inning under the assumption that he was the fifth hitter in the Yankees batting order. Plate umpire Dick Nallin informed him that he was listed in the sixth spot on the lineup card. When Yankees manager Joe McCarthy pleaded that he'd made a mistake in filling out the card and Lazzeri always hit fifth, Nallin relented and allowed Lazzeri to bat.

Detroit manager Bucky Harris remained mum on the issue until Lazzeri singled. Then he immediately appealed to Nallin, saying that Lazzeri had batted out of order. When Nallin pointed out that Lazzeri had batted in the fifth slot with his permission, Harris changed his appeal to a protest that Nallin had no right to change the batting order after the game had started.

After the Yankees won the game, 6–3, American League president Will Harridge upheld the protest and ordered the contest replayed in its entirety since Lazzeri's illegal hit had been made way back in the second inning. The two clubs met again a month later but ran into a further snag when the replay ended in a 7–7 tie that was called on account of darkness.

The following day the game was played for the third time. Detroit prevailed, 4–1, to put an end finally to the mammoth amount of work that was required to unravel the tangle Nallin's effort to be accommodating had created. At the close of the 1932 season Nallin's tenure as an American League umpire was terminated by Harridge after 18 seasons.

5

PUTTING THE BALL IN PLAY: LIVE BALL

5.02

After the umpire calls "Play" the ball is alive and in play and remains alive and in play until for legal cause, or at the umpire's call of "Time" suspending play, the ball becomes dead. While the ball is dead no player may be put out, no bases may be run and no runs may be scored, except that runners may advance one or more bases as the result of acts which occurred while the ball was

(continued)

Notice that although this rule covers when a ball is alive and in play, it skirts one of the umpire's greatest nightmares—a situation in which there is more than one ball in play. One of the most memorable occasions when this occurred came on June 30, 1959, in a game at Wrigley Field between the St. Louis Cardinals and the Chicago Cubs. With one out in the fourth inning, Stan Musial of the Cardinals walked on a pitch that hit Cubs catcher Sammy Taylor and home plate umpire Vic Delmore and then skipped to the backstop.

Taylor thought the pitch had ticked Musial's bat for strike two and began to argue with Delmore. When

(continued)

alive (such as, but not limited to a balk, an overthrow, interference, or a home run or other fair ball hit out of the playing field). . . .

Musial saw that Taylor was otherwise absorbed, he rounded first base and headed for second. Realizing what was afoot, Cubs third sacker Al Dark sped to the backstop to retrieve the ball. But before he could reach it a batboy picked it up and flipped it to field announcer Pat Pieper. Surprised by the toss, Pieper muffed it and the ball bounded toward Dark, who scooped it up and flung it to shortstop Ernie Banks covering second base.

Taylor meanwhile had absently been given a second ball by Delmore as the two continued to argue. Cubs pitcher Bob Anderson, by now also part of the debate, grabbed the ball from Taylor when he saw Musial streaking for second and threw it over Banks's head into center field. Musial, who had slid into the bag, picked himself up when he saw the wild heave thinking he had third base cold. But to Musial's dismay, with almost the first step he took off second, Dark's throw arrived at the bag, and before he could retreat Banks put the tag on him.

After a 10-minute delay while all four umpires—Delmore, Al Barlick, Bill Jackowski, and Shag Crawford—conferred, Musial was ruled out. The Cardinals lodged a protest, but it was withdrawn when they won the game anyway, 4–1.

Rule 5.02 makes it apparent, however, that "Time" can be called at any point by any umpire and that any action that results after the call is nullified.

Many games would doubtless have had a different outcome were it not for the strict enforcement of this rule. In a contest on August 28, 1960, at Baltimore's Memorial Stadium between the Orioles and the Chicago White Sox, pinch hitter Ted Kluszewski slammed a three-run homer in the eighth inning to vault the Sox from a 3–1 deficit to an apparent 4–3 lead. But the blow was erased because third base umpire Ed Hurley had called time a split second before Orioles pitcher Milt Pappas threw Kluszewski the gopher ball.

Hurley had observed Earl Torgeson and Floyd Robinson playing catch outside the Sox bullpen in foul territory and stopped play while he told them to get inside the restraining barrier. Made to bat over, Kluszewski lined out to center field to end the inning, and Chicago went on to lose the game, 3–1.

In 1976 Don Money of the Milwaukee Brewers lost an apparent game-winning grandslam homer in a similar manner. As he came to bat on April 10 at County Stadium against Dave Pagan of the New York Yankees, the bases were jammed in the bottom of the ninth and his team trailed, 9–6. Concentrating only on the task at hand, Money failed to notice that Yankees manager Billy Martin was waving to his outfielders to reposition themselves. New York first baseman Chris Chambliss saw Martin gesturing, however, and asked first base umpire Jim McKean for time.

McKean granted the request just before Pagan released the ball. When Money drove the pitch into the left-field stands, Milwaukee fans erupted in the belief that the blow was a grandslam, giving the Brewers a last-ditch 10–9 victory.

Money started circling the bases while many of his teammates headed jubilantly for the clubhouse. But throughout the celebration McKean continued to wave his arms until finally he got everyone's attention, whereupon he announced that he had to disallow the four-run homer because he had called time.

Returning to the batter's box, Money hit a sacrifice fly to bring the score to 9–7, New York, which is how it stood when the game ended moments later.

Before we leave this rule, it should be pointed out that more than one pitch or play can be nullified after an umpire's unrecognized call of "Time" is belatedly acknowledged. During a 1959 game at Briggs Stadium (now Tiger Stadium), Boston Red Sox third baseman Frank Malzone fouled off a pitch from Detroit's Paul

Noted ___ / ___ i ___
Damage _____

Foytack and then looked at a called strike. Down 0-and-2 in the count, Malzone suddenly breathed a new life upon hearing first base umpire Ed Hurley cry that he had called time before the first strike.

Unnoticed by the other three arbiters, Hurley had gone down to the Boston bullpen as Malzone stepped into the box to warn a player who was riding the umpires. When Hurley returned to his position and found that two strikes had been registered in his absence, he told plate umpire Joe Paparella to erase them because he had not been prepared to call a play at first base. Paparella tried to compromise and leave at least one strike on the board, but Hurley insisted time had been out for both pitches.

Standing in against Foytack with a fresh 0-and-0 count, Malzone smacked the Tigers righthander's next pitch for a home run.

ALTHOUGH allowed by this rule to do so, an umpire will seldom kill a play just because a player is injured. Many runners have been retired after being knocked unconscious by errant throws or in base-path collisions, sometimes right in front of a base coach who was powerless to come to their assistance.

But although a base coach cannot physically help a stricken runner, a teammate who is also a baserunner can offer assistance. Many years ago in a New Jersey sandlot game a player scored after collapsing at third base and dying of a heart attack when the runner coming along behind him picked him up and dragged him all the way home, making sure that his dead teammate's foot touched the plate before his own.

One of the most famous moments when a player's teammates failed to rally to his aid came in Game 4 of the 1939 World Series between the New York Yan-

---

5.10

The ball becomes dead when an umpire calls "Time." The umpire-in-chief shall call "Time"— (a) When in his judgment weather, darkness or similar conditions make immediate further play impossible; (b) When light failure makes it difficult or impossible for the umpires to follow the play;... (c) When an accident incapacitates a player or an umpire.

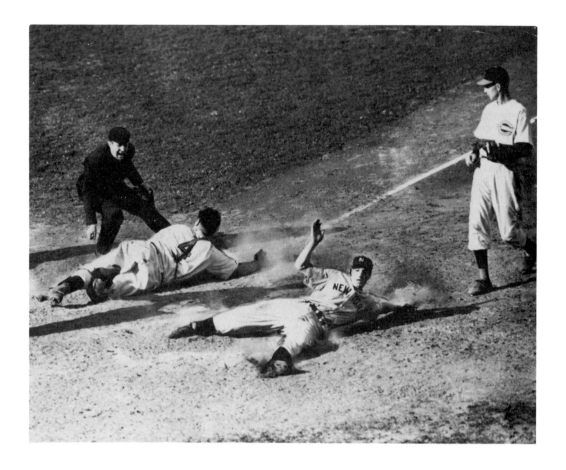

Cincinnati catcher Ernie Lombardi lies prostrate in front of Babe Pinelli as Joe DiMaggio slides home with the third Yankees run on his own single in Game 4 of the 1939 World Series. Reds pitcher Bucky Walters has just drifted into the picture at far right, too late to repair the damage done when Yankees outfielder Charlie Keller crashed into Lombardi moments earlier. AP/Wide World Photos

kees and the Cincinnati Reds. The two clubs were knotted at 4-all in the top of the 10th inning when Joe DiMaggio singled to chase home Frank Crosetti.

Charlie Keller also tried to tally on DiMaggio's hit but seemingly was beaten on the throw home to Reds catcher Ernie Lombardi. Instead of giving himself up, Keller crashed into Lombardi so violently that the ball was jarred loose. As Lombardi languished in the dust beside the plate, dazed and barely conscious with the ball inches away from him, his teammates, as if expecting time to be called, stood by in a trance of their own and allowed DiMaggio to circle the bases and score the

Yankees third run on the play. But the umpires were not bound to call time until Reds pitcher Bucky Walters stood on the rubber with the ball in his hand.

5.10 (F)

The ball becomes dead when a fielder, after catching a fly ball, falls into a bench or stand, or falls across ropes into a crowd when spectators are on the field. As pertains to runners, the provisions of 7.04 (c) shall prevail. If a fielder after making a catch steps into a bench, but does not fall, the ball is in play and runners may advance at their own peril.

IF AN outfielder sees that a batted ball is headed for home run territory, and catches it after jumping into the stands, it will still be a home run. If, however, he falls into the stands when jumping to make a catch, it will count as an out provided he catches and holds onto the ball. Any runners who are on at the time will be allowed to advance one base per Rule 7.04 (c).

The umpire can only make an educated guess sometimes whether an outfielder who disappears into the stands in pursuit of a ball actually caught it. Probably the most classic example of an arbiter who was put in this unenviable spot came in Game 3 of the 1925 World Series between the Washington Senators and the Pittsburgh Pirates, played at Washington's Griffith Stadium, where temporary bleachers had been installed in center field to provide added seating. In the eighth inning, with the Senators ahead, 4–3, Pittsburgh catcher Earl Smith drilled a long drive toward the temporary seats. Washington center fielder Sam Rice raced back for it, jumped to his limit, and toppled into the stands. For a good 15 seconds Rice was lost to view, but at last he emerged from the crowd, holding the ball triumphantly over his head. Umpire Cy Rigler ruled it a catch, and thus began a furious argument. Eventually even Pittsburgh owner Barney Dreyfuss bowled through the crowd of players on the field to make his voice heard in the protest. Commissioner Judge Landis, in attendance, was at last persuaded to confer with Rice, hoping for clear direction, but Rice would only say, "The umpire said I caught it."

In the end Rigler's ruling stood for the lack of any contradictory evidence, and the Pirates lost the game,

Even when a fielder tumbles into the stands after making a catch, as Philadelphia A's catcher Buddy Rosar is doing in this 1945 shot, the batter is almost always out—assuming an umpire can establish that the catch was made. Havoc can occur, however, when he is forced to make a guess. **American Photographic Archives**

5.10 (H)

Except in the cases stated in paragraphs (b) and (c) (1) of this rule, no umpire shall call "Time" while a play is in progress.

4–3. Rice lived nearly 50 more years without ever saying anything more definite about the play than he had offered on October 10, 1924. It seemed that his baseball epitaph would be: The umpire said he caught it. When Rice passed away, however, it emerged that he had left behind a letter to be opened upon his death. The letter averred that he had made the catch but provided no explanation for why he had refused to settle the issue while he was still alive.

ALTHOUGH an umpire-in-chief is the sole judge whether to terminate or interrupt a game for one of the reasons cited in this rule, players will nevertheless try to give a stubborn arbiter a nudge. There have been instances of fielders taking their positions wearing raincoats and batters coming to the plate carrying flashlights

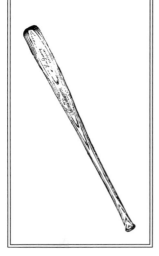

to clue an umpire that playing conditions warranted stopping the game. Usually these dramatic asides are ignored, but sometimes a man in blue will listen.

In a 1960 game between the Chicago Cubs and the Milwaukee Braves the umpires allowed play to continue into the fifth inning at Milwaukee's County Stadium, even though outfielders on both teams griped incessantly that a heavy fog that had blown in from Lake Michigan early in the proceedings was cutting their visibility to near zero.

Finally, in the bottom of the fifth, with the game still scoreless, the three Cubs outfielders got the four umpires to stroll out to center field to inspect conditions. What they saw induced them to ask Frank Thomas, a Cubs player not in the game, to stand at the plate and fungo a fly ball to the outfield. When none of the umps could see the ball coming their way, the game was halted.

It is worth noting here that Rule 5.10 (h) by inference corrects a common misconception. Many players, coaches, and managers have assumed that time was automatically out when they started to protest an umpire's decision only to discover the game was still very much in progress.

In the second inning of a game on September 8, 1923, between the Brooklyn Dodgers and the Boston Braves, Boston had Stuffy McInnis on third, Hod Ford on second, and Bob Smith at bat. After Smith singled to tally both McInnis and Ford, Brooklyn catcher Zack Taylor began jawing with home plate umpire Hank O'Day that Ford had run out of the baseline to elude Taylor's tag on the throw to the plate. During the argument Smith quietly took second base. Then, seeing that Taylor was still occupied with O'Day, Smith darted to third. When Taylor continue to pay the Braves runner no attention while he argued, Smith trotted home. Taylor then started a new argument that time had been out, but that too went nowhere.

Gregg Jeffries (R) tries unsuccessfully to call Mets teammate David Cone's attention to the fact that two Atlanta Braves runners are scoring as he jaws with umpire Charlie Williams. The incident occurred in a 1990 game and was instrumental in Atlanta's 7–4 win. AP/Wide World Photos

On April 30, 1990, New York Mets pitcher David Cone allowed the Atlanta Braves two free runs when he got caught up in a debate with first base umpire Charlie Williams.

With Dale Murphy on second and Ernie Whitt on first and two out, Cone raced to cover first on a grounder between first sacker Mike Marshall and second baseman Gregg Jeffries. Jeffries came up with the ball and tossed it to Cone, who crossed the bag with what he thought was the inning-ending out. But Williams said Cone's foot had missed the bag. Cone quickly blew a fuse.

Noticing Cone's back was to the infield as he argued with Williams, Murphy, who had taken third on the play, stole a few feet down the line and then broke

for home when Cone didn't turn around. Other Mets, including Jeffries, tried unavailingly to call Cone's attention to Murphy. Seeing that Cone was oblivious, Ernie Whitt took third and then sprinted for home too after Murphy scored. Jeffries finally grabbed Cone and tried to spin him around so that he could see what Whitt was doing. But Cone continued to sputter until two runs had been tallied after what he was morally certain should have been the third out. The pair of freebies helped the Braves to a 7–4 win. Cone later admitted sheepishly, "I just snapped."

Rule 5.10 (h) also helps correct another common misconception that time is automatically out when a bat flies out of a hitter's hands as he swings and sails into the playing field. Hall of Famer Pee Wee Reese had to learn the hard way that there was no such rule.

The Dodgers all-time greatest shortstop was on first in a 1947 game against the Chicago Cubs with Dixie Walker at the plate. A vicious swing and a miss by Walker brought the bat flying out toward first base. Reese stepped off the bag to retrieve it for his teammate, and Cubs catcher Clyde McCullough immediately snapped the ball to first sacker Eddie Waitkus. Even as Waitkus was slapping the tag on him, Reese began to proclaim that time must surely be out. But he was mistaken. Instead he was out.

6

THE BATTER

Alexander Cartwright's rules in 1845 said that "players must take their strike in regular turn," meaning that all nine players on a team had to come to the plate in regular rotation. However, it has not always been the case that an inning began with the player following the one who made or contributed to the making of the last batted out. Because the rules on the matter were still fuzzy, in the early days a batter could lose his turn if he was at bat when a teammate terminated an inning by being retired in a base-running mishap. Now, of course, the next inning must begin with the same hitter who had been at the plate when the previous inning ended since he had not as yet legally completed his time at bat.

The batter shall not leave his position in the batter's box after the pitcher comes to Set Position, or starts his windup.... The batter leaves the batter's box at the risk of having a strike delivered and called, unless he requests the umpire to call "Time." The batter is not at liberty to step in and out of the batter's box at will....

NOWADAYS when a batter steps out of the box causing a pitcher to pause in the middle of his delivery, the plate umpire will not call a balk. Instead the arbiter will just signal that time is out and then resume the game as if the incident had not occurred. If in the umpire's judgment the disruption was deliberate, he can take further action, including tossing the batter out of the game.

Before 1957, as a pitcher was about to deliver the ball, a batter was free to step out of the box and take his chances. The absence of an equivalent to Rule 6.02 (b) opened the door to incidents like the one in Chapter 3 that occurred in a 1952 Western International League game. It also allowed a batter to try a ruse that is now obsolete. With a runner on third base a batter could drop his bat as the pitcher went into his windup in an effort to induce a balk.

Incidentally, there is still nothing in the rulebook to say that a player must have a bat in his hands as he awaits a pitch. There is not even an edict that he has to bring a bat with him when he comes to the plate.

6.02 (C)

If the batter refuses to take his position in the batter's box during his time at bat, the umpire shall order the pitcher to pitch, and shall call "Strike" on each such pitch. The batter may take his proper position after any such pitch, and the regular ball and strike count shall continue, but if he does not take his proper position before three strikes are called, he shall be declared out.

EARLY RULEBOOKS had no equivalent to Rule 6.02 (c). It used to be that an umpire, for the lack of an alternative, would simply rule a player out for "refusing to bat" if he did not come up to the plate for whatever reason. In a National League game against the Philadelphia Phillies on August 22, 1891, New York Giants hurler Amos Rusie was declared out in this fashion by umpire Tim Hurst. The following notation appeared in the box score of the game to explain why the Phillies registered only 26 putouts: "Rusie declared out for refusing to bat."

Whatever reason Rusie had for declining to take his cuts, it was not that he was a poor hitter. In 10 seasons he had a .247 career batting average, well above the norm for a moundsman.

But if the rules in 1891 on batters who were loath to bat were open-ended, there is still considerable leeway in how they are enforced. For instance, the amount of time a batter has to return to the batter's box after being warned to do so depends heavily on the situation and the umpire. At the beginning of the 1993 season, with umpires under pressure to speed up games, there was an illustrative incident on April 16 in the Atlanta Braves' first visit of the campaign to San Francisco's Candlestick Park. In a game already studded with several heated disputes involving home plate umpire Mark Hirshbeck, the Braves trailed the host Giants 1–0 in the top of the ninth with two out, the potential tying run on second base, and Ron Gant at bat.

With a 1-ball count, Gant looked at a pitch from Giants reliever Rod Beck that he was certain was ball two. Hearing it called a strike, Gant stepped out of the box and swatted the air with his bat—the traditional way for a batter silently to voice his disagreement with a strike call. Hirshbeck ordered Gant back into the box, and when Gant dallied, Hirshbeck signaled Beck to throw and then called the pitch a strike. Braves manager Bobby Cox flew out of the dugout to protest and was speedily ejected. Behind now in the count 1–2, Gant flied to right on the next pitch to end the game.

Afterward, Gant said of Hirshbeck's decision, "It was worse than anything I've seen in Little League. What a joke." Crew chief Bruce Froemming contended that Hirshbeck was merely following Rule 6.02 (c) that had been on the books for a while, albeit seldom invoked until umpires were told to enforce it conscientiously to help speed up games. One San Francisco reporter chortled that the pitch to Gant while he was out of the box had looked low and outside but, given Hirshbeck's wrath toward the Braves by that point, he probably would have called the delivery a strike even if Beck had heaved it into the stands. The reporter was apparently unaware that once Hirshbeck set the machinery of Rule 6.02 (c) into motion, he was obliged to call Beck's pitch a strike regardless of where it was delivered.

SOME playground forms of baseball consider a batter out if his batted ball is caught either on the fly or the first bounce. Remarkably, the first-bounce rule was once in effect in all forms of baseball. Until 1864 any ball hit to the outfield that was caught on the first bounce was an out; exceptions were flies that were bobbled and then scooped up on one bounce after they hit the ground.

Champions of the one-bounce-out rule felt that it saved injuries to players' hands, whereas its detractors contended that it not only made the game unmanly but that there was nothing more frustrating to an admirer of good fielding than to see an outfielder nullify a hard hit simply by stationing himself near enough to it to take it on the bound. When the proponents of a more manly game finally carried their point in 1864, however, the new rule in 1864 applied only to fair-hit balls. A foul ball snared on the first bounce remained an out as late as 1882 in the National League and May of 1885 in the American Association. Upon the elimination of the first-bounce out on foul hits, *Spalding's Official Baseball Guide* for 1884 offered this accolade to National League moguls: "The continuance of the foul-bound catch would have been simply the retaining of a feature of the early period of base ball, in order to gratify the crowd and to help 'business,' and not the game."

A fascinating example of how the foul-bounce out rule could impact on the outcome of a game occurred in an American Association contest between the New York Metropolitans and the Louisville Eclipse in Louisville's park on June 21, 1884. The AA for reasons that are impossible to fathom now had refused to follow the National League's lead two years earlier when the senior loop eliminated the foul-bounce out, but the finale of the Mets-Louisville game fostered a belated reconsideration. Jack Lynch of the Mets battled Eclipse ace Guy Hecker to a 2-all draw at the end of regulation length. New York solved Hecker for two runs in the second extra frame, but Louisville roared back in the bottom of the 11th inning, filling the bases with two out. Louisville catcher Dan Sullivan then sent a foul drive down the rightfield line that Steve Brady of the Mets speared on the first bounce to stifle the threat and end the game. Had Sullivan's hit landed fair instead of foul without being caught on the fly, it would not have been the third out. Instead it would have resulted in at least a single, and in all likelihood would have sent home two runs and tied the game again. This sort of absurdity goaded AA officials to abolish the foul-bounce rule early in the 1885 season.

6.05 (B)

A batter is out when a third strike is legally caught by the catcher.

AS A BATTER could be retired if his fly ball was caught on the first bounce, so at one time he could be put out when a catcher caught his third strike on the first bounce. In 1858 a rule was first introduced to allow a batter to run on a missed third strike. Until 1880, though, a batter was considered out if the catcher snagged his third strike either on the fly or the first bounce. The rule was so liberal largely because catchers wore little protective apparel in the early days, necessitating that they play well back of the batter. Mitts and masks were rudimentary, chest protectors were skimpy, and shinguards did not really come into popular use until the early 1900s. Beginning in 1880, catchers had to move up right behind batters when the count reached two strikes. Before then it had been customary for a receiver to move up only with men on base and otherwise to play back and take balls on the

An action drawing of a game between the Brooklyn Atlantics and the Elizabeth Resolutes at Union Grounds, the first enclosed ball park. The catcher at this point in history stood so far in back of the batter that the umpire, unable to see from behind him, often stationed himself beside home plate. Transcendental Graphics

first bounce, including third strikes. In 1901 it became mandatory in the National League for a catcher to play within 10 feet of home plate at all times; the American League adopted the same rule the following year.

SINCE THE foul lines intersect the batter's box in such a way that the vast majority of it is in foul territory, the home plate umpire will almost always give the batter the benefit of the doubt if a ball hits his bat twice while he is still in the box. The same is generally true of balls that strike part of a batter's body after hitting his bat.

So rarely does an umpire rule a batter out in such a case that a protest is almost *de rigueur* when it happens. In a 1976 game between the Mets and the San Diego Padres, plate umpire John McSherry voided a sacrifice bunt attempt by New York rookie Leon Brown, claiming Brown's bat made contact with the ball twice. Mets manager Joe Frazier lodged the expected protest, but it was withdrawn when the Mets won the game, 5–4.

6.05 (H)

A batter is out when, after hitting or bunting a fair ball, his bat hits the ball a second time in fair territory. . . .

EVERY FAN has seen a batter try to pull away from or hold up on a pitch only to have it hit his bat and dribble into fair territory, making him an easy out. At one time balls that were hit unintentionally in this manner were not necessarily considered in play even if they went fair. Until 1892 whether a batter meant to hit a pitch that trickled off his bat was a matter for an umpire to judge. If it seemed the ball had been struck unintentionally, it was deemed dead and not counted as a pitch. Increasingly, however, during the 1880s umpires would rule the ball in play regardless of what they perceived the hitter's intent was, their logic being that no batter was about to let himself be deprived when a checked swing resulted in an accidental base hit.

But umpires in that era were particularly vulnerable to being talked out of their calls or influenced by the desire to avoid an argument with such contentious players as Cap Anson or King Kelly, so a rule was inserted prior to the 1892 season clarifying that any fairly delivered ball that hit a batter's bat was in play if it went fair regardless of whether or not the batter intended to hit the ball.

THE THREE-FOOT boundary outside the first base foul line was first contained in the playing rules for 1858. In 1882 the National League mandated that the three-foot line had to be marked on the field in all its parks, but the American Association did not require it to be marked until three years later.

Normally a batter is allowed to run either within the three-foot boundary or inside the first base line, but there are notable exceptions. One is on a bunt fielded by the catcher or pitcher when a runner can impede the throw to first if he runs inside the line. In Game 4 of the 1969 World Series, with the score tied 1–1 in the bottom of the tenth inning, New York Mets catcher J. C.

Martin dropped a sacrifice bunt with runners on first and second. Baltimore pitcher Pete Richert fielded the ball and fired it to first sacker Boog Powell. But Richert's toss struck Martin on the wrist and bounded off into foul territory as Jerry Grote raced home with the winning run. Orioles manager Earl Weaver screamed that Martin had run the last half of the distance to first illegally inside the foul line, but the umpires disagreed and the run stood. A videotape of the play made it appear that Weaver had a solid case and that the run should have been nullified with Martin ruled out.

THERE IS a commonly held belief that this rule is only present to deter a batter from jumping out of the box to hit a pitch when he is being intentionally walked, but the rule can be enforced any time a batter steps behind, in front of, or to either side of the chalk rectangle. In a 1965 game against the St. Louis Cardinals at Sportsman's Park, none other than Hank Aaron had a home run rescinded when he left the batter's box in his hunger to tackle a Curt Simmons change-up. The Milwaukee Braves slugger rocketed the ball onto the rightfield roof, but even before Aaron could start his tour of the bases, plate umpire Chris Pelekoudas signaled him out.

"Aaron was running up on the pitch," Pelekoudas said later in defense of his call. "His left foot was at least three feet out when he swung." The lost four-bagger deprived Aaron of a home run that would have hiked his career total to .756. However, almost every other great slugger, including Babe Ruth and Lou Gehrig, also lost at least one home run during his career to a rule technicality or violation.

IN SANDLOT games an argument often arises if a batter switches from batting right-handed to hitting lefty or vice versa when an opposing team has not

---

6.06

A batter is out for illegal action when—(a) He hits a ball with one or both feet on the ground entirely outside the batter's box....

6.06 (B)

A batter is out for illegal action when he steps from one
(continued)

96

THE   RULES   OF   BASEBALL

(continued)

batter's box to the other while the pitcher is in position ready to pitch.

changed pitchers while he is batting. As Rule 6.06 (b) reads, however, a batter is free to switch to the opposite side of the plate after every pitch. Before 1907 a batter could switch sides even while a pitcher was in the midst of his delivery. Since then the rule has been that if the batter is in the batter's box and the pitcher is in position to deliver the ball, the batter cannot switch unless time is called by the umpire, allowing him to step out of the box and make the change.

Rule 6.06 (b) makes an attempt by a batter to switch sides while time is in cause for an umpire to declare him out for an illegal action. One of the first victims of the new rule was Philadelphia Phillies outfielder Johnny Bates. In a game against the Cincinnati Reds on August 27, 1910, Bates, a left-handed hitter, was called out when he changed to the right side of the plate while the Reds pitcher was in motion.

The problem becomes more complex for an umpire, however, when a switch-hitter faces a switch-pitcher. In a Western Association game in 1928 Paul Richards of Muskogee (the same Paul Richards who would later vex umpires with his ingenious tests of the rules as a major league manager) baffled Topeka hitters by throwing left-handed to lefty hitters and right-handed to righty hitters until switch-hitter Swamp Baby Wilson came up in the ninth inning as a pinch hitter. Each time Richards changed his glove from one hand to the other Wilson matched him by moving to the opposite side of the plate. Said Richards in recalling the incident: "Finally I threw my glove down on the ground, faced him square with both feet on the rubber, put my hands behind my back and let him choose his own poison."

6.06 (C)

A batter is out for illegal action when he interferes with

(continued)

THIS RULE allows an umpire considerable latitude, as the Boston Red Sox learned in the bottom of the tenth inning in Game 3 of the 1975 World Series. With the score tied 5–5, Cincinnati center fielder Cesar

(continued)

the catcher's fielding or throwing by stepping out of the batter's box or making any other movement that hinders the catcher's play at home base. . . . If the batter interferes with the catcher, the plate umpire shall call "interference". . . .

6.06 (D)

A batter is out for illegal action when he uses or attempts to use a bat that, in the umpire's judgment, has been altered or tampered with in such a way to improve the distance factor or cause an unusual reaction on the baseball. This includes, bats that are filled, flat-surfaced, nailed, hollowed, grooved or covered with a substance such as paraffin, wax, etc. . . .

Geronimo led off with a single. Reds manager Sparky Anderson then sent up Ed Armbrister to pinch-hit for pitcher Rawley Eastwick. Upon laying down a sacrifice bunt, Armbrister became entangled with Red Sox catcher Carlton Fisk as Fisk sprang out from behind the plate to field the ball. The two seemed to lock together forever before Armbrister finally broke away to run to first, freeing Frisk to get the ball and throw it to second.

When Fisk's heave went into center field, the Reds ended up with runners on second and third, and plate umpire Larry Barnett wound up with Fisk and Red Sox manager Darrell Johnson in his face, howling that Armbrister should be out for interference and Geronimo made to return to first base. Barnett insisted the collision did not constitute interference because it had not been intentional, and first base umpire Dick Stello came to his support even though there was nothing in the rule to stipulate that a batter's interference must be intentional for it to be deemed an illegal action. A few minutes later the Reds won the game 6–5 on a single by Joe Morgan.

THIS RULE was first inserted in 1975. Before then if a batter was discovered to have struck a ball with a "loaded" or doctored bat, the hit counted and the offending bat was simply removed from the game, although the batter could be subject to further sanctions if it was a repeat violation or a particularly flagrant one. The procedure, if a bat was protested, was for the umpires to inspect it and then either allow it to continue in play or else confiscate it for a more thorough examination if it looked suspicious.

Loaded bats have been part of the game almost from its inception. Players in the last century would often pound nails into the meat ends of their bats and then coat the nail heads with varnish or some other substance that would conceal them from chary opponents. A much more recent incident occurred in 1954 when Cleveland third baseman Al Rosen was found to be using a bat studded with nails after slugging three home runs in a two-game set with the Boston Red Sox on May 18–19. At the time Rosen was hitting .382 with nine homers and 38 RBIs in just 30 games and coming off a season in which he had paced the American League in every important slugging department and almost won the Triple Crown. Soon after being deprived of his "magic" bat, Rosen suffered a broken finger. The dual setback caused a dramatic decline in his production. For the remaining 124 games of the 1954 campaign Rosen hit well below .300 and notched just 15 home runs and 64 RBIs. The sharp drop, even though some of it was definitely attributable to Rosen's injury, fostered speculation that he may have been using a loaded bat for some time before he was caught.

HERE WE discover that a player can be declared out and charged with a time at bat even though he never steps up to the plate. This deprivation has happened many times, and to some of the game's greatest stars. In a game against the Philadelphia Phillies on July 24, 1953, St. Louis Cardinals immortal Stan Musial was ruled out in the following manner for violating Rule 6.07.

Cards player-manager Eddie Stanky turned in a lineup card showing shortstop Sollie Hemus leading off, himself batting second, and Musial up third. Stanky then mistakenly led off the game by fanning. After Hemus followed Stanky and singled, Phils skipper Steve O'Neill bolted from the dugout to appeal. Hemus's hit was nullified and Musial was declared out because he, rather than Hemus, had been slated to follow Stanky according to the lineup card. The extra time

6.07

BATTING OUT OF TURN—
(a) A batter shall be called out, on appeal, when he fails to bat in his proper turn, and another batter completes a time at bat in his place.

at bat cost Musial a point on his batting average. He finished the season at .337 but would have had a .338 mark were it not for Stanky's oversight.

Ironically, less than a month after he saddled Musial with an unused time at bat, Stanky was involved in another batting order snafu that saw his team profit from having a player hit out of turn even though the mistake was caught. In a game against Cincinnati on August 21, 1953, first baseman Steve Bilko led off the Cardinals' half of the second inning by rolling out. As rookie third sacker Ray Jablonski strolled to the plate, Stanky, suddenly realizing that Jablonski, and not Bilko, had been scheduled to lead off the frame, sprinted up to home plate umpire Bill Stewart and notified him of the mixup. Stewart ruled Jablonski out for missing his turn, and Bilko was sent back to the plate since he was due up after Jablonski. Given a second opportunity, Bilko homered for the game's first run, and the Cardinals went on to win, 4–0.

The incident, though it stemmed from an honest mistake by Stanky, raised an interesting issue that Baltimore manager Paul Richards seized upon in a 1960 game against Detroit. Knowing full well that his pitcher, Gordon Jones, was due up, Richards instead sent leadoff hitter Jerry Adair to the plate. Richards later said he had purposely had Adair bat out of turn hoping he would work the count to 3-and-0 and Jones could then be rushed to the plate to finish the at bat and get a walk before the Tigers appealed Adair's batting out of order. But Adair foiled the plan by hitting a two-run single that was nullified when Tigers skipper Jimmy Dykes brought the violation to the umpire's attention.

As the rule presently stands, however, a manager, particularly in the National League where there is no DH for the pitcher, can still send up his leadoff batter with a weak-hitting pitcher due at the plate. Even if the leadoff batter reaches base and the opposing manager appeals, little is lost since the pitcher is an almost certain out anyway. Meanwhile the leadoff hitter has gotten an extra look at the pitcher that he may be able to turn to his advantage, as did Bilko.

ALTHOUGH the question is not specifically addressed in this rule, the absence of any proscription to the contrary licenses a vigilant fan to lean over the railing behind his favorite team's dugout and whisper to the manager that an opposition hitter is batting out of turn. Indeed, the only people in a ballpark who are forbidden by rule to call such a violation to a manager's attention are the official scorer and the umpiring crew. An umpire in particular is required to keep still, which is not to say that all arbiters know or abide by this rule. In her book *You've Got to Have B*lls to Make It in This League*, Pam Postema recalled the following moment in a minor league game she was officiating:

> "Once in a while I even showed up a manager or one of my own partners. For instance, one night I had the plate and noticed a batter step into the box who wasn't supposed to be there. He was batting out of order. Stupid rookie. Just as I was getting ready to call the batter out for hitting out of order, I heard the scorekeeper yell down to her husband, who happened to be one of the managers, 'Woody, that's the wrong batter, honey,' she said.
>
> Too late. I called the guy out and quickly figured out who was supposed to be up next. Meanwhile, my partner, who didn't have a clue what the rule said, whispered, 'Are you sure you're right?' Hey, it was no big deal to me. I knew the rule. I called it. End of discussion."

Postema's recollection makes it distressingly apparent that neither she nor her partner nor the official scorer nor the official scorer's manager-husband knew the rule on a player batting out of order.

6.08

The batter becomes a runner and is entitled to first base without liability to be put out (provided he advances to and touches first base) when— (a) Four "balls" have been called by the umpire;...
(b) He is touched by a pitched ball which he is not attempting to hit unless (1) The ball is in the strike zone when it touches the batter, or (2) The batter makes no attempt to avoid being touched by the ball....

A S ALEXANDER Cartwright made no mention in his playing rules of bases on balls, he also made no provisions for a batter who was hit by a pitch. The notion of awarding a batter his base for being hit by a pitch was not embraced by the rules until the game was nearly half a century old. As late as 1886, a full decade after the National League was founded, the senior loop still refused to penalize pitchers like Hoss Radbourn and John Clarkson for throwing at enemy hitters to intimidate them.

As a consequence of the National League's slowness to address the hit-batsman problem, situations like the following one often arose to confound umpires. In a game on July 29, 1884, between the Chicago White Stockings and Detroit Wolverines, with Stump Weidman of Detroit on first, rookie Wolves backstopper Chief Zimmer was struck in the arm by a pitch as he swung at it and missed. The ball then caromed off Zimmer and skipped past Silver Flint, the Chicago catcher, allowing Weidman to move to second base. Cap Anson, the White Stockings first baseman-manager, heatedly protested that the ball should be ruled dead and Weidman made to return to first.

The lone umpire working the game, Stewart Decker, then had to decide whether to call the pitch a strike or to rule it no pitch and a dead ball. Rule 30 in 1884 defined a ball "striking the batsman's person while standing in his position, and without it being struck at" as a dead ball. Decker, feeling that the rule supported Anson's argument, sent Weidman back to first and deemed the delivery to Zimmer no pitch.

Detroit manager Jack Chapman contended in vain that Zimmer's act of swinging at the pitch precluded it being called a dead ball and that Zimmer should have been assessed a strike and Weidman allowed to advance. League officials later realized, however, that both Anson and Chapman had an equally valid argu-

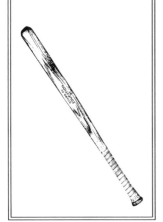

ment and also foresaw that if Decker had sided with Chapman, as he well could have, there was nothing in the rules to deter a batter from deliberately allowing a pitch to hit him as he swung at it in the hope of providing runners with an opportunity to move up a base.

But for all their recognition that a more comprehensive rule covering hit batsmen was long overdue, National League moguls still tarried for another two years before finally decreeing prior to the 1887 season that a batter hit by a pitched ball was entitled to first base provided he had not first swung at the ball, in which case it was automatically dead.

The American Association, meanwhile, adopted the hit batsman rule in 1884, largely to combat the tactics of two of its pitchers, Will White and John Schappert, both of whom were notorious for deliberately trying to plunk batters. Schappert was looked upon as so dangerous an intimidator that after the 1882 season other AA moguls persuaded St. Louis owner Chris Von der Ahe not to renew his contract with the Browns. Released by St. Louis, Schappert hooked on with Harrisburg of the Interstate League in 1883. The campaign was barely a month old before his welcome was nearly worn out in that circuit too. In the June 10, 1883, edition of *Sporting Life*, Schappert was accused of the "cowardly habit . . . in maliciously crippling men at the bat. . . . The manager of the Columbus club, defeated by the Harrisburg team last week, attributed the defeat to Schappert's action, the Ohio men being afraid to stand up at the plate."

Before the hit batsman rule was adopted, an umpire had only one tool at his disposal to stop a potential beanball war if a pitcher like Schappert was working the points. In 1879 the National League authorized its arbiters to fine hurlers for deliberately hitting batters with pitches, the levy ranging from $10 to $50. Even a $10 fine could be painful in that era, since many play-

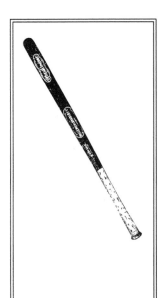

ers made less than $1000 for the season. But umpires were reluctant to make pitchers dig into their pockets unless the offense was too brazen to be allowed to pass unpunished. Part of the reason was because an umpire in the late 1870s could not afford to alienate a team if he wanted to keep his job. Umpires had to be approved by clubs in order to receive assignments to work games, and one of the surest ways to be denied approval was to anger a team's pitching ace by socking him in the pocketbook.

Even after National League umpires were first made salaried employees of the loop in 1883, fines for hitting batters were few and far between. What mostly deterred pitchers from throwing at rival batters was the fear that they themselves would become clay pigeons when they batted. Not only were pitchers required to hit in 1883, but the majority played other positions on days when they were not in the box. Though the schedule that season called for just 98 games, Hoss Radbourn collected 381 times at bat and another Hall of Fame twirler, Pud Galvin, took 322 official turns at the plate.

Since the National League batters who were hit by a pitch were not given their base until 1887, we can only wonder now if Lee Richmond's perfect game on June 12, 1880, the first of its kind in baseball history, was really a perfecto by today's rules. It is entirely possible, and even likely, that Richmond hit at least one Cleveland batter in the course of shutting down the Blues, 1–0. We do know that he surrendered what would have ordinarily been a single if his right fielder, Lon Knight, had not been playing shallow and thrown a Cleveland player out at first on a liner that landed in front of him.

We also know that without the hit-batsman rule Hooks Wiltse of the New York Giants would almost undoubtedly have had a perfect game on July 4, 1908. Facing the Philadelphia Phillies that day with two out in the ninth, Wiltse got two quick strikes on his mound opponent, George McQuillan. One strike away from a perfect game, Wiltse then blazed a pitch that McQuillan took for what Wiltse and his catcher Roger Bresnahan were both certain would be called a third strike. But umpire Cy Rigler granted the Phillies pitcher a reprieve when he ruled it a ball. Disconcerted, Wiltse then hit McQuillen with his next delivery to give the Phils their first baserunner.

What was the pitcher doing up at bat with two out in the ninth inning of a potential perfect game? The score at the time was 0–0. Wiltse subdued the mild threat by retiring Phillies leadoff hitter Eddie Grant, continued to hold the Phils hitless in the tenth, and then got a run in the bottom of the frame to win 1–0.

The next point to consider when contrasting today's hit-batsman rule with its ancestors is whether a batter has always been given his base as he is now if a pitch merely touches him. The American Association rule in 1884, the first season it was enforced, read that if a batsman be *solidly* hit by a ball from the pitcher when he evidently cannot avoid the same, he shall be given his base by the umpire. However, if a batter was struck on the hand or the forearm, the pitch was considered a dead ball unless it happened to be in the strike zone, in which case it was a strike.

What constituted a solid hit was left to an umpire's judgment, and not all AA arbiters were on the same page. In a July 1884 game between Louisville and Cincinnati at Cincinnati, umpire Robert Ross ruled that a pitch by Guy Hecker grazed Cincinnati hurler Billy Mountjoy's uniform blouse and awarded Mountjoy his base to force home the tying run in the ninth inning. After Cincinnati tallied four runs off Hecker in the eleventh to win the game, Mountjoy gleefully confessed to a local reporter that the pitch had never touched him at all, let alone hit him solidly.

Now let's turn to how an umpire determines that a batter is not entitled to be given his base because he did not make sufficient effort to get out of the way of a pitch. Not being a mind reader, an umpire obviously has no sure way of knowing whether a batter deliberately let a pitch hit him. Experienced arbiters know that even a Phil Niekro knuckler can freeze a batter expecting a fastball and prevent him from dodging it. Umpires therefore almost always give a hit batsman his base unquestioningly, and a fan can go to a game every day for several seasons without seeing a batter denied a free trip to first after being zapped by a pitch.

Those fans who were at Dodger Stadium, however, on May 31, 1968, witnessed perhaps the most famous enforcement of stipulation (2) to Rule 6.08 (b). That night, after pitching four successive complete-game shutouts, Dodgers right-hander Don Drysdale was on the threshold of breaking Walter Johnson's 55-year-old record for the most consecutive scoreless innings pitched (56) as he entered the ninth frame protecting a 3–0 lead over the San Francisco Giants. Drysdale then stumbled and loaded the bases with none out. After going to a 2–2 count on Giants catcher Dick Dietz, Drysdale hit Dietz with his next pitch, apparently forcing home a run and ending his bid to shatter Johnson's mark. But plate umpire Harry Wendelstadt ruled that Dietz hadn't made a sufficient effort to avoid the pitch and called it simply ball three.

With the count now full, Dietz skied out to left field, too shallow for the runner on third to tag up and score. Drysdale then retired the next two batters to tally his fifth straight shutout and preserve his scoreless skein, which ultimately reached 58 innings before it was halted.

After the game, the Dodgers claimed to a man that Wendelstadt's call was both correct and courageous. Giants vice president Chub Feeney said it would

The late Don Drysdale, seen here letting a fastball fly, in 1968 benefited from a special stipulation to Rule 6.08 (b), breaking Walter Johnson's record for the most consecutive scoreless innings. Transcendental Graphics

have been courageous if Wendelstadt had made it at San Francisco's Candlestick Park.

Dietz and Giants manager Herman Franks of course argued their cause at the time the incident occurred, but it was in vain. Another argument pertaining to Rule 6.08 (b) that is almost always a futile exercise for a batter, is contending that a pitch hit him when an umpire failed to see it. On rare occasions, however, the dispute can hinge on some scrap of evidence of his claim that a batter is able to show an umpire. In Game 4 of the 1957 World Series, Nippy Jones of the Milwaukee Braves won his case in the following manner.

With his team trailing the New York Yankees, 5–4, Jones led off the bottom of the tenth as a pinch hitter for Warren Spahn. Yankees southpaw Tommy

Byrne fed Jones a wicked low and inside pitch in the dirt that scooted all the way to the backstop in Milwaukee's County Stadium and then came almost back to the plate on the rebound. Already embroiled in an argument that the pitch had hit his foot, Jones retrieved the ball, located a black smudge on it, and showed the mark to plate umpire Augie Donatelli. Jones contended the smudge was shoe polish and the Yankees said it had been caused by the ball hitting the backstop.

Donatelli sided with Jones and awarded him his base. Felix Mantilla ran for Jones and was sacrificed to second by Red Schoendienst. Johnny Logan followed with a double to tie the game and then Eddie Mathews hit a two-run homer to win it for the Braves, 7–5. Whether Jones was right in his argument or simply lucky will forever be a topic of debate. But in any case his shoe was immortalized even if its owner was soon history. After the "Shoe Polish" incident, Jones never again reached base safely in a major league game.

I N THE LAST century, when most games were worked by only one umpire who stood behind the pitcher with men on base, catchers would often flagrantly tip an opponent's bat without being detected. Connie Mack reputedly was among the receivers who were masters at hindering a batter's stroke. The rulebook for the 1899 season was the first to stipulate that

Connie Mack shows Honus Wagner how he used to tip enemy bats in his heyday. The two Hall of Famers were united for this droll photo late in 1952, shortly before Mack's 90th birthday. David Nemec collection

a batter became a baserunner if a catcher impeded his swing. Not until 21 years later, however, did the manual specify that catcher's interference occurred even if a receiver merely tipped a batter's bat. In amateur games Rule 6.08 (c) is often invoked, but so few infractions are seen at the major league level that it earned Baltimore receiver Clint Courtney a spot in the record book when he was cited twice on June 19, 1960, in a game against the Detroit Tigers. In the fourth inning home plate umpire Ed Hurley nailed Courtney for tipping Tigers outfielder Sandy Amoros's bat, and two frames later Hurley caught Courtney repeating the offense against first sacker Steve Bilko.

6.09

The batter becomes a runner when— (a) He hits a fair ball.

THIS RULE seems so self-evident at first look as to be unnecessary. Surely a batter has always become a baserunner the moment he hits a fair ball. On the evidence, however, the rules were originally silent on the point. As a result, in 1874 a rule was introduced saying that when a batter has fairly struck a fair ball, he shall vacate his position and is considered a baserunner until he is put out or scores a run. This seemed clear enough, until some players began to test the rule in ways that its originators had not considered.

On June 30, 1883, in a National League game between the Providence Grays and the Boston Red Stockings, Boston scored the winning run in its 3–2 victory through an imaginative bit of baserunning—or more accurately, nonbaserunning—by Red Stockings left fielder Joe Hornung. With teammates Ezra Sutton on second base and Sam Wise on first, Hornung hit a routine ground ball to Providence second baseman Jack Farrell. Sensing an easy double play in the making, Hornung stood fast in the batter's box rather than run to first base. Since Hornung refused to try to make his base, he kept Sutton and Wise from being forced to vacate theirs, although both had started running as soon as the ball was hit. No longer subject to being forced out at second base, Wise had to be tagged in a rundown play between first and second involving Farrell and Providence first sacker Joe Start while Sutton whipped around third and scurried home safely.

Hornung's maneuver helped tighten the 1883 equivalent to Rule 6.09 (a) and apprise both umpires and the defensive team that even if a batter refused to leave the batter's box, it could no longer be a sanctuary once he put the ball in play.

THIS RULE makes it clear that a batter must make a complete tour of the bases after hitting an outside-the-park home run unless he is so severely disabled that he cannot, in which case a pinch runner has to finish the base tour. One of the more painfully amusing examples of the extremes to which umpires sometimes must go in order to enforce this rule was seen by Brooklyn fans on August 5, 1926. Hall of Famer Zach Wheat, in his 18th season with the Dodgers, pasted a home run over the wall at Ebbets Field in the tenth inning of a game against the St. Louis Cardinals. But by the time Wheat reached second base he had pulled muscles in both legs, forcing him to sit down on the bag while he tried to massage them into allowing him to continue. When five minutes had passed and Wheat was still in too much agony to cover the final 180 feet, Dodgers manager Wilbert Robinson requested permission to have a pinch runner complete the home run. Wheat begged for more time, however, and eventually was able to crawl to his feet and limp the rest of the way home. The trip was worth the effort, though Wheat could not have known that then. The home run was the last he ever hit at Ebbets Field, for he was released after the 1926 season.

The batter becomes a runner when a fair ball, after touching the ground, bounds into the stands, or passes through, over or under a fence, or through or under a scoreboard, or through or under shrubbery, or vines on the fence, in which case the batter and the runners shall be entitled to advance two bases.

UNTIL 1931 a batted ball that got under, through, or over an outfield fence in fair territory in any manner whatsoever was a home run. The first pinch-hit grandslam homer in American League history by Marty Kavanagh of Cleveland on September 24, 1916, reportedly squirted through a hole in the fence at Cleveland's League Park. That same season Brooklyn second baseman George Cutshaw beat the Philadelphia Phillies with a home run that mysteriously scaled the fence at Ebbets Field. With the score knotted in the bottom of the eleventh, Cutshaw smacked a liner to right field that skipped to the fence. As the Phillies right fielder prepared to take the ball on the carom, Cutshaw's hit struck an embankment in front of the fence that gave it a weird spin. Instead of ricocheting off the fence, the ball began to climb it. Reaching the top of the barrier, the ball teetered there for a precarious instant and then toppled into the stands. Apart from his fluke homer, Cutshaw hit only one other four-bagger in 1916.

Beginning in 1931 all batted balls that stuck in or bounced through or over an outfield fence were groundruled doubles unless the special ground rules of a park stated otherwise. In Brooklyn's Ebbets Field a batted ball that went through the wire on the rightfield fence was a home run as was a ball that stuck in the wire if a fielder could not dig it out in time to keep a batter from circling the bases. Pee Wee Reese hit a famous home run that lodged on a ledge in the right-field-screen sector at Ebbets Field in the final game of the 1950 season to tie the Dodgers with the Philadelphia Phillies at 1–1 and set up Dick Sisler's three-run homer in the tenth inning that brought the Phils their first flag since 1915.

6.09 (G)

The batter becomes a runner when any bounding fair ball is deflected by the fielder into the stands, or over or under a fence on fair or foul territory, in which case the batter and all runners shall be entitled to advance two bases.

WHEN JOSE Canseco's skull got an assist on the homer Carlos Martinez of the Cleveland Indians hit on May 26, 1993, the Texas Rangers outfielder became perhaps the most celebrated player to be beaned by a long fly that evolved into a four-bagger. But many gardeners have suffered the ignominy of seeing a ball they mishandled disappear over the fence for a circuit clout. There are several ways it can happen. The most straightforward development is something on the order of what Western Carolina League fans saw on June 7,

1961, in a night game between Belmont and Newton-Conover. Belmont right fielder Eddie Montellanico tracked a towering fly ball hit by Newton-Conover player-manager Joe Abernathy back to the fence when he suddenly lost it in the lights. The ball struck Montellanico on top of the head, knocking him unconscious, and caromed over the fence for Abernathy's only home run of the season.

More controversial is the type of four-bagger that helped Denver's Bill Pinckard win the Western League home run crown and the Bears the loop flag in 1952. Facing Omaha in a 0–0 pitcher's duel on August 9 at Denver, Pinckard socked a drive to deep left field. Omaha leftfielder Dick Cordell leaped high for the ball as he crashed into the fence, but Pinckard's blow ticked his glove and hit the fence, then came back to clip Cordell in the forehead and ricochet over the retaining barrier. After a long argument with the managers of both teams, the umpires awarded Pinckard a home run. Cordell's testimony must have been ignored, for if Omaha could have established that the ball struck the fence before it caromed off Cordell's head and then went over the fence, the hit properly should have been called a groundruled double because it became a bounding ball the instant it hit the fence rather than a ball in flight, as defined in Rule 2.00. In any case, Pinckard's circuit clout proved to be the game's only run and enabled the Bears' Barney Schultz to win a 1–0 verdict over Gary Blaylock of Omaha.

When the Western League season ended a few weeks later, it developed that Pinckard's disputed roundtripper had spelled the difference in the pennant race. Had Omaha rather than Denver won the game of August 9, Denver, Omaha, and Colorado Springs would have all tied for the flag with identical marks of 87–67.

NOTE THAT no mention is made in this rule about what happens when a batted ball that will clearly be a home run is short-circuited because it hits an object that is not a regular part of the playing field. In such an instance the number of bases awarded, if any, depends on the park ground rules.

No one has ever struck a low-flying plane in a major league game, but Mike Schmidt hit a blast on June 10, 1974, that smacked into the public-address system hanging from Houston's Astrodome roof 326 feet from home plate and 117 feet above the playing field. Left unimpeded, Schmidt's shot would probably have traveled around 450 feet. In any event, it would have been a home run in every other park in the country. But according to Astrodome ground rules, the ball remained in play, and Schmidt had to settle for a single.

In contrast, Larry Walker of the Expos hit a lazy fly ball on May 5, 1992, that struck one of the loudspeakers hanging 150 feet above the field at Montreal's Olympic Stadium. Even though the ball was descending when it hit the speaker and would likely have been an out, the existing ground rule in the Expos' park forced umpire Terry Tata to call it a home run. "It's the easiest out turned into a home run that I've ever had," Walker said after the game. "I like that ground rule."

ODDLY, the first major league official to champion the notion of a DH was National League president John Heydler, way back in 1928. Senior loop owners felt that action lagged when pitchers batted and were solidly behind Heydler's proposal, but it fell flat after American League moguls vetoed it, believing the game already had enough offensive punch. Forty-five years later, when the concept was next seriously entertained, the two circuits were still at opposite poles, only by then each had undergone a complete 180-degree reversal.

(continued)

exhibition games, the rule will be used or not used as is the practice of the home team. 2. In All-Star games, the rule will only be used if both teams and both Leagues so agree.

In 1972, the last season that pitchers batted for themselves in both leagues, NL teams outhit AL clubs by nine points and tallied 824 more runs.

DESIGNATED hitters first appeared in World Series action in 1976, when the Cincinnati Reds swept the New York Yankees. Dan Driessen served as the Reds DH in all four games, whereas the Yankees divided the assignment among Carlos May, Lou Piniella, and Elliott Maddox. For reasons that made little sense in 1976 and still seem quixotic at best, major league officials voted to allow DHs every other year in Series play. Series participants continued to use DHs only in even years until 1986 when the present rule was adopted, limiting their use to games hosted by American League teams.

In 1985, the last time that pitchers were required to bat for themselves in every World Series game, hurlers for the Kansas City Royals and the St. Louis Cardinals went a combined 0-for-30.

SINCE THE designated hitter rule now seems here to stay, it is time to consider the offshoot of it that seems destined to generate the most controversy in future years. Although some reactionaries will never stop lamenting that the perfectly symmetrical game Alexander Cartwright devised was irrevocably impaired the moment all nine men in the field were no longer required to take their fair turn at bat, Cartwright never intended for there to be pinch hitters or defensive substitutions either, and few now will quibble with their usage. Almost every baseball analyst and historian is disturbed, however, by the way the DH rule has enabled so many players to achieve career and single-season stats that seem bogus in comparison to the accomplishments of players who had to do full duty both in the field and at bat.

Included among the ersatz achievements are the hit, home run, and RBI career totals compiled by Dave Winfield, Paul Molitor, Brian Downing, Orlando Cepeda, Rico Carty, Tony Oliva, George Brett, Al Kaline, Rusty Staub, Reggie Jackson, and Jim Rice, to name just a few of the many players whose careers were extended when they were relieved of any necessity to play in the field. But less obvious is the impact of the DH rule on pitchers' career totals. In 1990 Frank Tanana became the first pitcher to post 200 wins, even though he had yet to score a run in a major league game. One must doubt too that Phil Niekro would still have been a starting pitcher at age 48 and amassed 318 wins if he had not been exempted from having to bat and run the bases during the last few years of his career.

7

THE RUNNER

7.03

Two runners may not occupy a base, but if, while the ball is alive, two runners are touching a base, the following runner shall be out when tagged. The preceding runner is entitled to the base.

There is no situation, however far-fetched, whereby two runners can legally occupy the same base, but for all the rules against it a far-fetched situation once occurred in which *three* runners tried to occupy the same base. The bizarre development came at Brooklyn's Ebbets Field on August 15, 1926, with the Dodgers facing the Boston Braves in the opening game of a doubleheader. Trailing 1–0 in the seventh inning against right-hander Johnny Wertz, Brooklyn tied the count when Johnny Butler led off with a single and came home on catcher Hank DeBerry's double into the left-field corner. After pitcher Dazzy Vance dribbled a single down the third base line and leadoff batter Chick Fewster was hit with a pitch to load the bases, Braves manager Dave Bancroft lifted Wertz in favor of George Mogridge.

Mogridge got Merwin Jacobson to hit a weak pop to the mound, and up came rookie first sacker Babe Herman with one out. Getting a pitch he liked, Herman belted a towering fly to deep right. DeBerry properly tagged at third base even though it seemed likely the ball would fall safely. Vance, at second, also held up, however, fearing it would be caught. Fewster meanwhile traveled nearly to second and waited on developments. Certain that the ball was out of right-

Yankees outfielder Mickey Rivers points to himself in disbelief as if to say, "You mean me?" when umpire Marty Springstead calls him out. Rivers thought he had beaten out a dribbler to Cleveland first baseman Andre Thornton (behind Springstead), but when Willie Randolph (middle), who was on first at the time, retreated to the bag, it remained his by right and Rivers became, literally, the odd man out. **American Photographic Archives**

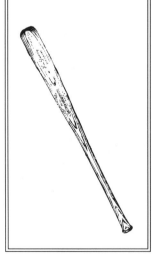

fielder Jimmy Welsh's reach, Herman put his head down as soon as he left the plate and ran at top speed.

The ball bounced off the fence, allowing DeBerry to score easily. But Vance, who had loitered near second until the ball dropped, was convinced after he rounded third that he would be a dead duck if he tried to score, and retreated to the bag. At the same time Fewster was reaching third. Seeing Vance returning, Fewster headed back to second. But before he could get more than a few yards from third, Herman, who had run the whole way with his head down, roared past him and slid into the bag. Dumbfounded, Fewster decided that he too might as well add to the logjam at third. For a few seconds, Brooklyn had three runners on the same base.

Only Vance rightfully belonged there, though, and he was not about to budge. After getting the relay throw from catcher Oscar Siemer, Boston third sacker Eddie Taylor had no idea who belonged where, but he knew he had someone dead to rights. First he tagged Vance and then he slapped the ball on Herman, upon whom it was just dawning that he might not have hit a base-cleaning triple. In fact, Taylor's tag was unnecessary; Herman was automatically out the moment he passed Fewster between second and third, though he would be credited with a double on the hit.

Fewster, the only one of the three Brooklyn runners who had done his job correctly thus far, set sail for second when he saw the clutter at third. Taylor rifled the ball to second baseman Doc Gautreau. Realizing he could not beat the throw, Fewster left the basepath and ran into the outfield with Gautreau chasing him. After the tag was made on Fewster, the three umpires working the game, Beans Reardon, Charlie Moran, and Ernie Quigley, huddled briefly and then came forth with the verdict that it was a twinkilling, ending the inning. Herman thus had doubled into a double play.

Almost lost in the turmoil was the fact that DeBerry had scored on the two-bagger, putting Brooklyn up, 2–1. When the Dodgers won, 4–1, Herman's blow became the game-winning hit, but that will never be how it is remembered.

An interesting footnote to the Herman *faux pas*: Not until 1907 did it become a rule that a baserunner was immediately out if he passed a teammate on the base paths. If the three-men-on-third incident had occurred before then, the Dodgers could have emerged unscathed assuming Fewster had somehow managed to scramble back safely to second base and Herman all the way to first.

Meanwhile the decision as to who gets the putout on a play like the one in which Herman passed Fewster will sometimes flummox even members of baseball's inner circle. As an example, in the fourth inning of Game 3 of the 1992 World Series the Atlanta Braves had Terry Pendleton on first, Deion Sanders on second, no outs, and David Justice at the plate. Justice walloped a pitch from Toronto Blue Jays right-hander Jose Guzman deep to center field, but Devon White made a sensational catch against the 400-foot marker.

Certain it would be an extra-base hit, Pendleton had rounded second base and passed Sanders. Not realizing the umpires had already called Pendleton out, the Blue Jays relayed the ball to first sacker John Olerud. Amid the chaos, Sanders headed for third base but was eventually chased back to second by Kelly Gruber, who narrowly missed tagging out Sanders for what would have been the first triple play since 1920 in a World Series game.

When the dust had settled TV announcer Sean McDonough informed the viewing audience: "If you're scoring, it's 8-4-3 as they doubled up Pendleton." McDonough was wrong. Pendleton was out the moment he passed Sanders. The throws from White to Blue

Jays second baseman Roberto Alomar to Olerud were meaningless. Pendleton's putout properly went to Toronto shortstop Manny Lee, the closest Blue Jay to Pendleton when he passed Sanders, and there was no assist on the play. But McDonough was not alone in his mistake. The morning after the game several newspapers gave White an assist on the play in their box scores and failed to credit Lee with the putout.

BECAUSE major league games until the early part of this century had only one umpire, fielders could almost literally get away with murder. While an umpire's eyes were busy watching a ball hit down the line to see if it would land fair, the first baseman was free to hold up the batter as he approached the bag while the shortstop tripped the lead runner as he rounded second.

Some third basemen, like John McGraw of the Baltimore Orioles, were only slightly more subtle in their methods. On an outfield fly, while the umpire watched to make sure it was caught, McGraw would grab the belt of the runner on third waiting to tag up and try to score and then release it when the umpire's head whipped around to catch the play at the plate. That split-second holdup was often just enough to prevent a run. One day Honus Wagner was on third base. Wagner was with the Louisville Colonels and had not been in the majors long, but he knew about McGraw. The moment a fly ball was hit to the outfield, he returned to third base and prepared himself as he felt McGraw seize his belt. When the ball was caught, Wagner took off for the plate and made it with ease. Back on third base with his jaw hanging open stood McGraw holding Wagner's belt, which he had loosened while Wagner waited at third to tag up.

As might be expected, the one-umpire system

7.04

Each runner, other than the batter, may without liability to be put out, advance one base when—. . . (d) While he is attempting to steal a base, the batter is interfered with by the catcher or any other fielder.

This rare 19th century action shot from the opening game of the 1889 National League season at Philadelphia shows the lone umpire who worked that game hustling to position himself to make the call at second base on a steal attempt. A year earlier "Honest" John Gaffney had introduced the practice of working behind the pitcher with men on base, but many umpires still preferred to call the entire game from behind the catcher. Transcendental Graphics

also licensed base runners to skirt the rules when they thought an arbiter was not watching them. Among the many tricks reputedly invented by the 1890s Baltimore Orioles was bypassing third base altogether when an umpire's back was to the runner. But in point of fact this shortcut was taken by base runners long before the Orioles became a National League power. One the earliest documented instances of it came in a critical American Association game at Sportsman's Park on September 23, 1883, between the St. Louis Browns and the Philadelphia Athletics.

The two teams had been in a season-long struggle for the AA pennant and the Browns badly needed the game to stay in contention. In the ninth inning St. Louis trailed 9–1 and had two outs. Joe Quest was on first base for the Browns and breaking toward second as a ground ball was hit. Seeing that the play would be made at first base, umpire Charlie Daniels turned his back to the diamond, and Quest wheeled around second and sprinted straight for home. When Philadelphia first sacker Harry Stovey dropped the throw, Quest was able to score. The partisan St. Louis crowd jeered the A's as they protested the run to no avail. However, Quest's tally only narrowed the Philadelphia lead to 9–2, and George Strief, the next batter, made the argument over his teammate's creative bit of baserunning moot when he flied out to end the game.

MUCH OF the history of 7.05 calls for additional research. Fielders in the pre-National Association era on occasion caught balls in their caps. Some threw caps at balls they could not reach. The 1873 season marked the first appearance of a rule that specifically addressed this deed. One base was awarded if a fielder stopped a ball with his hat or cap. No mention was made of a thrown glove because the only gloves worn in the 1870s were protective devices that could not readily be peeled off or detached from the hand.

Beginning in 1876, base runners were awarded two bases if a fielder used his cap or any other part of his attire to interfere with a batted ball. Still no mention was made in the rules of gloves until 1910, when it was decided that if a fielder stopped or caught a batted ball with his cap, glove, or any part of his uniform, while detached from its proper place on his person, the batter and any base runners were entitled to three bases. In 1914 the rule was restructured to make the penalty three bases for a batted ball and two for a thrown ball. The three-base levy was imposed because most violations came when outfielders, despairing of reaching balls hit over their heads or in the gap, flung their

---

7.05

Each runner including the batter-runner may, without liability to be put out, advance— (a) To home base, scoring a run, if a fair ball goes out of the playing field in flight and he touches all bases legally; or if a fair ball which, in the umpire's judgment, would have gone out of the playing field in flight, is deflected by the act of a fielder in throwing his glove, cap, or any article of his apparel; (b) Three bases, if a fielder deliberately touches a fair ball with his cap, mask or any part of his uniform detached from its proper place on his person. The ball is in play and the batter may advance to home base at his peril; (c) Three bases, if a fielder deliberately throws his glove at and touches a fair ball. The ball is in play and the batter may advance to home base at his peril. (d)

(continued)

(continued)

Two bases, if a fielder deliberately touches a thrown ball with his cap, mask or any part of his uniform detached from its proper place on his person. The ball is in play; (e) Two bases, if a fielder deliberately throws his glove at and touches a thrown ball. The ball is in play. . . .

gloves in the hope of knocking them down. Since these hits were almost certain doubles anyway, it was well worth a two-base penalty to throw a glove at them if only to corral those that would otherwise go for triples or even inside-the-park home runs.

There is surprisingly little documentation as to what went on between the early 1880s, when most players first started using gloves, and 1910. With nothing in the rules to prevent it, one can imagine that fielders heaved their gloves at balls they could not reach, but if that had been done with any frequency, surely a preventive measure would have been drafted long before 1910.

Yet we know there were players who took advantage of the absence of a rule, just as players will always take advantage when they see an opening. In the mid 1890s Baltimore Orioles groundskeeper Thomas Murphy was instructed to let the outfield grass grow wild in Orioles Park so that balls could be secreted in it. Rather than give chase when an opponent hit a shot into the gap, Joe Kelley, Steve Brodie, and other Orioles outfielders would scoop up one of the hidden balls and fire it into second base, nailing the shocked runner who had been positive he had at least a standup double. Did Kelley and Brodie resort to tossing their gloves at hits they could not flag down in enemy parks, where the grass did not provide them with a better option? In all likelihood they did, but the proof of it has failed to survive.

Before we return to the manual, note that Rule 7.05 (c) omits mention of any penalty if a fielder throws his glove at and touches a foul ball. This omission might seem insignificant. Why would a fielder hurl his glove at a ball that was going foul anyway? It has been done, however, and for good reason.

In the sixth inning of a game with the St. Louis Browns on July 27, 1947, Boston Red Sox first baseman Jake Jones topped a ball that trickled slowly outside the third base line toward St. Louis third sacker Bob Dillinger. Although the dribbler was foul, Browns pitcher Fred Sanford suddenly realized it might roll fair and Dillinger would be unable to throw Jones out. So Sanford fired his glove at the ball and hit it. Umpire Cal Hubbard promptly awarded Jones a triple.

In 1954 the rule was changed to apply only to fair balls, making it possible now for a pitcher or an infielder to do as Sanford did without penalty.

THERE HAS always been a form of the rule forbidding a catcher to block the plate without having the ball in his possession, but only in recent years has it become a serious issue. Until the early part of this century catchers without the ball were loath to stonewall plate-bound runners, in part because few wore shinguards and cared to risk a needless spiking. Also catcher's interference on a runner bidding to score was called

7.06

When obstruction occurs, the umpire shall call or signal "Obstruction." ... (b) If no play is being made on the obstructed runner, the play shall proceed until no further action is possible. The umpire shall then call "Time" and impose such penalties, if any, as in his judgment will nullify the act of obstruction.... NOTE: The catcher, without the ball in his possession, has no right to block the pathway of the runner attempting to score. The base line belongs to the runner and the catcher should be there only when he is fielding a ball or when he already has the ball in his hand.

Pittsburgh receiver Milt May blocks Jim Beauchamp of the Cardinals from the plate while he awaits the throw home. This moment from a 1971 game occurred soon after catchers were tacitly granted more freedom to block the plate against runners without having the ball in their possession. Transcendental Graphics much more often that it is now. As near as can be determined, most observers think that around the time a second expansion took place in 1969 umpires started being more forgiving of catchers who set up roadblocks several feet up the third-base line and then waited for the ball. In any case, though catchers' violations of Rule 7.06 (b) are often seen now, so few runs are awarded that it almost seems that umpires have been secretly instructed to look the other way while a backstopper wrestles with a runner until help arrives.

THE RULE in the National Association, the first professional league, was quite the opposite with regard to a base bag that broke loose from its moorings. A runner had to hold on to the wayward cushion or else he was subject to being tagged out.

Beginning in 1868, the bag and not the part to which it was fastened was considered to be the base. When a base thief slid so hard he tore the bag out of its socket, he had to chase it down before a fielder got to him with the ball. Likewise, if a runner kicked the bag loose as he rounded it, any runners coming along behind him were obliged to touch the bag, not the spot where it had been. This rule prevailed during the five-year existence of the National Association but was dropped in 1876 as the National League prepared to open play in favor of the pre-1868 edict, which was an ancestor of the current rule that establishes a base at the spot where it is located rather than the bag itself.

A RUNNER has always been subject to being ruled out if he fails to return to his base after a caught fly in fair territory. Before 1880, however, a runner was not obliged to scamper back to his base after a foul fly was caught. Rather, he could return at his leisure.

In either event, a runner was not permitted to tag up and try to advance on a caught fly ball until 1859. Until then an "air" ball was dead as soon as it was caught and remained dead until it was back in the pitcher's hands. But the 1859 amendment merely said that such balls were no longer dead. Four years later the rule put into words that a baserunner had the right to advance after returning to his original base as soon as the ball had been "settled into the hands of a fielder."

For many years the phrase "settled into the hands of a fielder" spelled trouble, especially for umpires who took it to mean that a ball had to be firmly secured before a runner was free to tag up and advance. Some outfielders became deft at juggling routine fly balls in order to hold a runner to his base while they jogged toward the infield until they were close enough to throw the runner out if he attempted to move up. Tommy McCarthy was supposedly a whiz at this trick when he patrolled the outfield with Hugh Duffy for the great Boston Beaneaters teams of the 1890s. But if McCarthy and other gardeners of his era were really so crafty, the question is why the apparent loophole was not sealed up while they were still active. In actuality, it was only in 1920 that the rule was finally altered to allow a runner to advance on a fly ball as soon as it touched a fielder, regardless of whether or not it was held secure.

Since the adoption of the 1920 amendment, on many occasions runners have advanced two and sometimes even three bases on a fly when an outfielder has juggled the ball or else fallen down or crashed into a wall after making a catch. At times a sacrifice fly has scored more than one run even though no errors or mishaps occurred on the play. Rocky Colavito, considered to have one of the strongest arms in history, was once so victimized. Playing right field for Cleveland in the second game of a doubleheader with the Chicago White

Sox on August 30, 1959, Colavito decided to showcase his arm on Barry Latman's fly ball to deep right with Billy Goodman on third base and Al Smith on second. Knowing that Goodman would tag at third and try to score, Colavito put everything he had into a throw home and to his embarrassment saw Smith tally right behind Goodman when his heave rainbowed and seemed to hang in the air forever before it finally descended after both White Sox runners had crossed the plate.

IN THE early days there was a good deal of argument over whether a runner should be declared out when he was hit by a batted ball since it so often was an unavoidable accident. The first effort to address the problem was in 1872, when a rule was created that any player who designedly let a batted or thrown ball hit him was automatically out.

In 1877 the rule became that any base runner, whether his act was by design or not, was out if he was struck by a batted ball before it had passed a fielder. The revision was necessary when it grew apparent that umpires could not be expected to judge whether a runner had intentionally let a ball hit him. Since an official scorer could not be expected to judge either whether the batted ball would have resulted in a hit or an out if a runner had not interfered with it, the vote was to count any batted ball that struck a runner as a single.

The lone exception to this rule occurs when a runner occupying his base is called out for being hit by a ball that has already been ruled an infield fly. No official scorer in major league history has ever been challenged, however, by the following situation.

On the closing day of the season Stroke of the Hawks trails Clout of the Eagles by one percentage point in the race for the league batting title. As luck would have it, the Hawks and the Eagles face each other in the final game. Clout elects to sit out the contest to protect his slim lead. To further aid his teammate's bid for the batting crown, the Eagles pitcher, Flame, intentionally walks Stroke each time he comes to bat.

Stroke's last plate appearance comes with two out in the ninth inning and his team trailing 6–0. So effective has Flame been to this point against the other eight members of the Hawks that he is working on a no-hitter. The gem in the making of course only provides Flame with all the more incentive to purposely pass the dangerous Stroke for the fourth time in the game.

On his way to first base Stroke roundly curses Flame, who merely laughs at him. Stroke seemingly is powerless to do anything to gain revenge against Flame and the Eagles for denying him a fair chance to claim a batting crown, but then, suddenly, an opportunity comes his way. Speed, the Hawks' next batter with two out in the ninth, slices a ground ball toward the second baseman, and Stroke, running to second, makes no effort to avoid being hit by it.

Must the official scorer give Speed a hit on Stroke's contrivance and deprive Flame of a no-hitter? Rules 6.08 (d) and 10.05 both say he does, but happily no official scorer to date has been made to face the unpleasant prospect of ending a no-hit bid on such a rude technicality.

7.08 (H)

Any runner is out when he passes a preceding runner before such runner is out.

HANK AARON cost Milwaukee Braves teammate Joe Adcock a circuit clout in one of the most famous games ever played when he was guilty of mistakenly leaving the base paths after Adcock hit an apparent game-winning home run.

Facing Pittsburgh southpaw Harvey Haddix on May 26, 1959, Aaron and the rest of his mates were set down in order for 12 straight innings. But when the

Pirates were also unable to score off Lew Burdette, Haddix was forced to take the hill again in the bottom of the thirteenth even though he had already retired a single-game record 36 consecutive batters. The Braves 37th batter, Felix Mantilla, led off the thirteenth by reaching first on a throwing error by Pirates third sacker Don Hoak, thereupon ending the longest perfect game in history. After Eddie Mathews bunted Mantilla to second, Aaron was purposely passed to set up a possible inning-ending double play. But Braves first sacker Joe Adcock laced Haddix's second pitch to him over the left-field barrier in Milwaukee's County Stadium for what seemed a game-winning three-run homer. However, Aaron thought the ball had landed in front of the fence. He touched second base and then headed toward the dugout. Adcock, who missed seeing Aaron leave the base paths, was called out when he reached third base, and the final score, instead of being 3–0, was 1–0, as only Mantilla's run counted. Haddix finished the

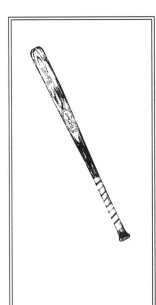

night with a 13-inning one-hit loss and Adcock with the Braves' lone hit, though a double instead of a home run.

Fortunately, Aaron touched second base before he deserted the base paths. If there had been two outs at the time and Aaron had left the field without touching second, he would have been called out at that base for the third out, neither Adcock's hit nor Mantilla's run would have counted, the game might still be in progress, and Aaron would now be as infamous as Fred Merkle—and for much the same reason.

On September 23, 1908, in a game against the Chicago Cubs with the National League pennant hinging on the outcome, New York Giants manager John McGraw chose Merkle to replace regular first sacker Fred Tenney, who was out for the day with an ailing back. Then in his second season with the Giants, Merkle had seen little action but was privileged to sit on the bench beside McGraw, regarded as having one of the keenest minds in the game.

With the score tied in the bottom of the ninth and two outs, the Giants had Moose McCormick on third base and Merkle on first. Al Bridwell then shot a single to center, sending McCormick home with the winning run. As soon as he saw that Bridwell's hit would plate McCormick, Merkle started toward the Giants clubhouse in center field, believing he had no further role in events. But when Cubs second baseman Johnny Evers began clamoring for the ball, Merkle got a sinking feeling that perhaps he had walked off the stage too early.

What happened next will forever be contested. New York sportswriters at the Polo Grounds that afternoon swore that Merkle made for second base at that point and got there ahead of the throw to Evers, and even if he had not beaten it, the ball Evers was fed was not the one that was in play anyway but another ball that was substituted. The game ball, according to some witnesses, somehow wound up in the possession of Giants pitcher Joe McGinnity, who flung it into the left-field bleachers. Chicago correspondents swore that Rube Kroh, a seldom-used Cubs pitcher, wrestled the game ball away from McGinnity and flipped it to Evers long before Merkle arrived at the second base bag. In any event, base umpire Bob Emslie claimed the crowd that had flooded onto the field after Bridwell's hit seemingly won the game blocked him from seeing the play at second, and the onus for making a decision then fell on plate umpire Hank O'Day. After a long delay, O'Day emerged from a conference with Emslie to rule that Merkle had been forced out at second and the game was still tied. Since it was impossible to clear the mob of spectators off the field so the contest could continue, Cubs manager Frank Chance wanted a forfeit victory, but it went into the books as a draw.

When the Giants and the Cubs finished the season deadlocked, the tie game had to be replayed. Three Finger Brown won the makeup contest for Chicago in relief, outdueling Christy Mathewson, and the Cubs went on to best Detroit in the World Series and earn their last World Championship to date.

Merkle's failure to touch second haunted him for the rest of his life, but the real goat may have been John McGraw. The 19-year-old Merkle was only following a lax custom—runners in 1908 often did not bother to touch the next base on a game-winning hit. But on September 4, some three weeks before Merkle's boner, Johnny Evers had endeavored to have Warren Gill of the Pittsburgh Pirates called out by O'Day on a similar play. O'Day demurred at the time but later realized that Evers had a valid argument. Since the Gill incident was widely reported, it should have been incumbent upon McGraw to remind his players of what Evers had tried to do against the Pirates, particularly when a repeat attempt was imminent with two out in the ninth and Giants runners at the corners.

Any runner is out when, after he has acquired legal possession of a base, he runs the bases in reverse order for the purpose of confusing the defense or making a travesty of the game. The umpire shall immediately call "Time" and declare the runner out. . . .

SUPPOSEDLY this rule was triggered by Germany Schaefer, a zany infielder with several American League teams in the early part of the century, but here we have another tale that may be more myth than fact. For one, there are at least two very different versions of the motivating incident.

In *The Glory of Their Times*, Davy Jones insisted it happened in a 1908 game between Detroit and Cleveland. Jones was on third base for the Tigers and Schaefer on first in the late innings of a tie game. Trying to manufacture a run, Schaefer lit out for second, hop-

An early baseball card of Germany Schaefer, credited with being the instigator of the rule that declares a runner out if he runs the bases in reverse order. There are two different reports as to when Schaefer ran the bases backward, but no one can be sure now which version, if either, is true.
Transcendental Graphics

ing to draw a throw from Cleveland catcher Nig Clarke so that Jones could then score. But Clarke refused to bite. Safe at second with an uncontested stolen base, Schaefer reportedly shouted, "Let's try it again," and then raced back to first base. Clarke still did not throw. But when Schaefer again tried to pilfer second on the next pitch, Clarke finally succumbed and threw down to the bag. According to Jones, he took off for home as soon as Clarke let go of the ball, and both he and Schaefer were safe.

Another version had Schaefer on first base and Clyde Milan on third for the Washington Senators in the ninth inning of a 1911 game with the Chicago White Sox. The same sequence of events occurred that Jones reported in his memoirs, except that the Sox catcher steadfastly refused to let go of the ball as Schaefer went through his reverse steal routine and Milan failed to score.

Conceivably, Schaefer pulled his stunt on more than one occasion, in which case both stories may be true. But it seems more likely that neither tale has much substance in fact, for a form of Rule 7.08 (i), prohibiting a runner from running the bases in reverse order to create havoc, was not devised until 1920. By then roughly a decade had passed since Schaefer had reportedly turned the game on its ear with his reverse steal gimmick, far too much time if the rulemakers were really as embarrassed as legend would have us believe.

A RUNNER has always been permitted to overrun first base while trying to beat out a hit as long as he makes no movement toward second base and returns right away to first. If a runner elected to slide, though, in an effort to beat a throw to first, before 1940 he was out if he slid past the bag and was tagged before he could return to it.

7.08 (J)

Any runner is out when he fails to return at once to first base after overrunning or oversliding that base. If he attempts to run to second he is out when tagged. . . .

Any runner is out when, in running or sliding for home base, he fails to touch home base and makes no attempt to return to the base, when a fielder holds the ball in his hand, while touching home base, and appeals to the umpire for the decision. This rule applies only where runner is on his way to the bench and the catcher would be required to chase him. It does not apply to the ordinary play where the runner misses the plate and then immediately makes an effort to touch the plate before being tagged. In that case, runner must be tagged.

RULE 7.08 (к) bids us to inquire what an umpire should do if a player carrying the game-winning run crosses home plate but the opposition fails to realize it. The answer is an umpire should do absolutely nothing. He keeps his mouth shut, gives no signal of any sort as to whether the runner was safe or out, waits for the players in the field to vacate their positions, and then walks off the diamond himself.

That was precisely the way Game 5 of the 1911 World Series ended. The Philadelphia A's and the New York Giants were tied 3–3 in the bottom of the tenth at the Polo Grounds when Fred Merkle of the Giants hit a fly along the rightfield line with Fred Snodgrass on second and Larry Doyle on third. Doyle tagged at third, waited for A's rightfielder Danny Murphy to make the catch, and then scooted home well ahead of the throw and leaped into the arms of joyous teammates, none of whom noticed that Doyle had skipped past the plate without touching it. When catcher Jack Lapp and the rest of the A's also failed to spot Doyle's goof, home plate umpire Bill Klem just smiled to himself, though later he acknowledged to an Associated Press reporter that he would have ruled Doyle out if the A's had appealed. The gift victory extended the Series to a sixth game the following day at Philadelphia's Shibe Park, but when the A's won a 13–2 blowout, Doyle's phantom run became insignificant.

OBSERVE that Rule 7.08, for all the contingencies it covers, has no comment on whether it constitutes interference if a runner deliberately kicks the ball out of the fielder's hand or glove as he is being tagged out on a slide into a base. The key word here is "deliberately." In 1871 the rule became that when a fielder holding the ball tagged a runner who was off a base, the runner was out even if he somehow knocked the ball out of

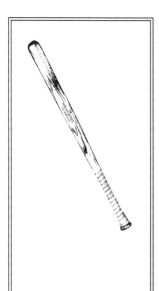

the fielder's hand. This rule was rescinded in 1877, but an umpire could still call a runner out for interference if, in his judgment, an intentional effort was made to dislodge the ball from a fielder's grasp. Without the interference proviso it was felt, rightly, that some runners would stop at nothing to make a fielder drop the ball when a tag play was imminent.

Ty Cobb was notorious for kicking balls out of basemen's gloves without being called on it. A more recent miscreant was Eddie Stanky. On October 6, 1951, at the Polo Grounds, in Game 3 of the World Series, Stanky fired up millions watching on TV as well as his New York Giants teammates with a foot maneuver that, momentarily at least, rattled the seemingly invincible New York Yankees to the core.

In the bottom of the fifth, after Giants pitcher Jim Hearn fanned, Stanky coaxed a walk out of Yankees starter Vic Raschi and then tried to steal second base. Catcher Yogi Berra's throw beat Stanky to the bag, but Stanky kicked the ball out of shortstop Phil Rizzuto's glove with a quick flick of his toe. When the ball rolled away, Stanky took off for third base. Rizzuto was charged with an error on the play rather than registering what should have been the Giants' second out. Umpire Bill Summers turned a deaf ear to Rizzuto's shriek that Stanky's kick constituted interference, nor did he pay any attention to a Yankees protest that Stanky had never touched second base before picking himself up from the ground and darting to third.

Later in the inning Berra dropped a throw home on what ought to have been the third out, and the Giants then broke the game open by scoring five runs in the frame, all of them unearned. The following morning, a Sunday, a headline on the *New York Times* sports page referred to the episode as Stanky's "Field Goal Kick." Much was made of how the play had not only shot the Giants to a 2–1 lead in the Series but had

Yankees shortstop Phil Rizzuto, having just made the tag at second base, still does not realize that Eddie Stanky has kicked the ball out of his glove. An instant later Stanky scrambled to his feet and scooted to third, whereupon Rizzuto began arguing to no avail that the Giants second sacker's "Field Goal Kick" in Game 3 of the 1951 World Series was illegal. AP/Wide World Photos

given them all the momentum and left the Yankees in disarray.

Unhappily for the Giants, the Yankees got lucky. It rained that Sunday, postponing Game 4 at the Polo Grounds and allowing Yankees manager Casey Stengel to send Allie Reynolds to the mound the following afternoon with an extra day's rest. Reynolds hurled a 6–2 win to even the Series and revive the confidence of his teammates. The Yankees went on to win the World Championship 4 games to 2, making Stanky's field goal kick no more than a footnote in Series lore.

THE VAST majority of the time a player who continues to behave as if he were a base runner after he has been called out will be nailed for interference, but there have been notable instances when an umpire chose to rule otherwise. In the bottom of the sixth inning of Game 4 of the 1978 World Series at Yankee Stadium the Yankees trailed 3–0 but had Thurman Munson on second base and Reggie Jackson on first with Lou Piniella batting. Piniella hit a line shot to Los Angeles Dodgers shortstop Bill Russell, who dropped it. There was some question whether Russell dropped the liner on purpose, hoping to set up an easy double play, in which case Piniella would be out according to Rule 6.05 (l) and Munson and Jackson would not be forced to vacate their respective bases. However, second base umpire Joe Brinkman made no call, so the play continued. Russell retrieved the ball, tagged second to force Jackson, and then fired to first expecting to double up Piniella. The ball hit Jackson, however, who was continuing to run, in the hip, and bounced off down the right field line in foul territory. Before the errant peg could be chased down, Munson scored and Piniella reached second.

It then fell on first base umpire Frank Pulli to judge whether Jackson was guilty of interference. Instant replay angles gave the impression that Jackson not only had continued to run after being forced at second but also may have flicked his hip into the path of the throw. Pulli thought otherwise, contending that Jackson neither had intended to interfere with the play by continuing to run or with the throw when he saw it coming toward him. The Dodgers vehemently dissented, but Pulli's call stood and the Yankees eventually scored two runs in the inning and wound up winning the game, 4–3.

Cubs baserunner Ron Campbell struggles to hold his base as Phillies third sacker Richie Allen, tracking a pop fly, tries to push him aside. When the ball dropped safely, Campbell was ruled guilty of interference. The controversial judgment call caused Cubs manager Leo Durocher to play the game under protest. **William Loughman collection**

7.09 (G)

It is interference by a batter or a runner when if, in the judgment of the umpire, a base runner willfully and deliberately interferes with a batted ball or a fielder in the act of fielding a batted ball with the obvious intent to break up a double play, the ball is dead. The umpire shall call the runner out for interference and also call out the batter-runner because of the action of his teammate. In no event may bases be run or runs scored because of such action by a runner.

THE MOST famous beneficiary of this rule was probably Orel Hershiser of the Los Angeles Dodgers. In 1988 Hershiser closed out the regular season with 59 straight scoreless innings to break the old record of 58, set in 1968 by another Dodgers pitching star, Don Drysdale. Like Drysdale, Hershiser needed a controversial umpire's decision to keep his streak alive, and also like Drysdale, the decision came in a game against the San Francisco Giants.

On September 23, 1988, at San Francisco's Candlestick Park, Hershiser allowed Jose Uribe to reach third base and Brett Butler first with one out in the third inning. Ernest Riles then hit a potential double-play grounder but beat the relay to first from Dodgers shortstop Alfredo Griffin as Uribe scored. Hershiser himself was certain the streak had ended after 42 scoreless innings. But when he glanced toward second base, he saw umpire Paul Runge signaling interference on Butler for sliding out of the baseline to hamper Griffin's throw to first. The ruling meant that Riles and Butler were both out on an inning-ending twin killing that canceled Uribe's run.

Hershiser went on to shut out the Giants, 3–0, running his skein to 49 consecutive scoreless innings. He then extended it to 59 against the San Diego Padres on the closing day of the season before being lifted for a reliever after the tenth inning of a 0–0 game that the Padres eventually won 2–1 in 16 frames.

THIS WAS first made a rule in 1914. Embellishments to it came in 1920 and 1949. Not until the latter year, however, was a runner who was touched or physically assisted in any manner by a coach declared out even if no play was made on him. Before 1914 a coach was licensed to tackle a runner if need be to keep him from making what seemed to the coach a foolhardy bid to score.

BOXES FOR base coaches were first established in 1887. Before then the only restriction on coaches was that they could not come within 15 feet of the foul lines to coach base runners. The 15-foot restraining lines were first required to be drawn on all professional fields in 1877, and they appear in many game photos between that year and 1886. The 1877 rule also stipulated that all team members not at bat or on the bases had to stay at least 50 feet outside of the foul lines except for the two base coaches.

The coaches' boxes began 75 feet from the catcher's lines when they were first established in 1887.

7.09 (I)

It is interference by a batter or runner when, in the judgment of the umpire, the base coach at third base, or first base, by touching or holding the runner, physically assists him in returning to or leaving third base or first base.

7.09 (J)

It is interference by a batter or runner when, with a runner on third base, the base coach leaves his box and acts in any manner to draw a throw by a fielder.

According to the new rule, coaches had to stay in their boxes at all times when the ball was in play and were restricted only to coaching runners. If a coach left his box, he could be fined $5 by an umpire unless he was also the team captain and outside the box to appeal a decision that involved a misinterpretation of the rules.

How much money did the National League and the American Association collect in 1887 from coaches who were fined for leaving their boxes? The answer is about as much as they got earlier in that decade from pitchers who were fined for deliberately hitting batters. With all the minds there were in the last century working on refining the rules, there was still only one umpire on the field to act as enforcer. The newly designed coaches' boxes no more kept coaches within their confines than the many interference rules on the books stopped fielders from tripping base runners. Until the early part of this century base coaches were even free to deceive enemy fielders as did Ned Hanlon in a National League game on May 9, 1883, between the Detroit Wolverines and the Chicago White Stockings.

E. HANLON, Center Fielder.

Though only in his fourth major league season, Hanlon had already displayed the ingenuity that would make him one of the game's greatest managers a decade later when he took over the reins of the moribund Baltimore Orioles. As a result, Jack Chapman, the Wolves manager, frequently used Hanlon to coach third base. He was there on that May afternoon with runners at the corners. When the runner on first attempted to steal second, White Stockings catcher Silver Flint rifled the ball to shortstop Tommy Burns, who had moved over to cover the bag. Burns was probably the best shortstop in the game at the time. He nevertheless fell victim to Hanlon. Upon seeing that his teammate would be out at second, Hanlon faked a dash down the third base line as if he were the runner on third trying to score.

Decoyed by the move, Burns held the ball, allowing the runner to slide into second safely.

Hanlon was applauded by the crowd for his fast thinking, but it was not uncommon for a baseball audience in that period to see a base coach act similarly to deceive a fielder. In 1904 a rule was finally introduced to declare a runner at third base out if the third base coach, with less than two out, broke toward the plate on a ground ball to draw an unnecessary throw. Ten years later an addendum also made this true for a fly ball, and the rule has since been refined to make it interference any time a third-base coach leaves his box in an attempt to deke an opponent.

An eerie example of Rule 7.09 (j) in action took place in a Georgia-Florida League game on June 21, 1953, between Fitzgerald and Tifton. Nursing an 8–7 lead in the bottom of the ninth with the bases jammed and two out, Tifton's Bob Badour went to a 3–0 count on Don Stoyle. Badour then threw the next pitch wide, and for a moment it seemed that Stoyle had walked to force in the tying run. But the plate umpire noted that Fitzgerald catcher Tony Fabbio, coaching at third, had faked that he was stealing home on the pitch and properly called the runner on third out to end the game. Along with depriving Stoyle of the game-tying RBI, the decision took away what ought to have been his 100th ribby of the season; he finished with 99.

BEFORE HE died in 1959, Howard Ehmke was the best person to ask if a pitcher could still be credited with a no-hitter if a rival batter stroked a clean hit but was subsequently declared out for missing first base. Pitching for the last-place Boston Red Sox on September 7, 1923, Ehmke twirled a 4–0 no-hitter against the Philadelphia A's that was nearly aborted early in the game when Ehmke's mound rival, Slim Harriss, cracked a liner over the shortstop that rolled all the way

---

7.10

Any runner shall be called out, on appeal, when—...
(b) With the ball in play, while advancing or returning to a base, he fails to touch each base in order before he, or a missed base, is tagged.

to the leftfield wall for an apparent double. But Sox first sacker Joe Harris, spotting that Harriss had missed first, called for the ball, thus preserving Ehmke's no-hit bid.

Four days later the breaks evened out for Ehmke. He lost his shot at becoming the first pitcher in major league history to hurl two consecutive no-hitters when the official scorer ruled that a ground ball Red Sox third baseman Howard Shanks misplayed rated a single. The tainted hit turned out to be the only one Ehmke surrendered in the game.

Many players in the early days lost inside-the-park homers for missing a base, and many in the years since have come away with less than a four-bagger when a teammate ahead of them on the bases either missed a base or mistakenly thought their hit was caught. In 1931 Lou Gehrig would have won the American League home run crown outright rather than sharing it with Babe Ruth if Yankees teammate Lyn Lary had not deprived him of a four-bagger with a base-running gaffe in a game against Washington on April 26. Occupying second base when Gehrig rifled a ball into the centerfield bleachers at Washington's Griffith Stadium, Lary left the base paths after misinterpreting third base coach Joe McCarthy's hand motion to slow down and trot home as a signal that the ball had been caught. Gehrig then passed Lary and was ruled out by umpire Bill McGowan.

No pennant race or World Series has ever turned on a home run that was aborted when its striker missed a base, but all who were either in attendance or watching on TV when Bobby Thomson hit his three-run "Shot Heard 'Round the World" that won the 1951 National League pennant still remember Jackie Robinson of the Dodgers holding his ground at second base and watching carefully to make sure Thomson touched them all before he finally bowed his head to the inevitable and left the field.

OVER THE years the rule dealing with the various ways in which a runner may be ruled out on appeal by the team in the field has created a multitude of thorny situations that have necessitated its frequently being refined. The paragraph pertaining to the possibility of an umpire having to recognize a "fourth out" first appeared in the 1958 manual in an effort to prevent further miscarriages like one that occurred in an International League game on August 30, 1957. On that date the Buffalo Bisons, engaged in a tight struggle with the Toronto Maple Leafs for the IL pennant, hosted the lowly Montreal Royals, destined to finish in the cellar.

Montreal owned a 1–0 lead with one out in the bottom of the seventh, but Russ Sullivan, acquired only days before from Columbus, and all-league second sacker Lou Ortiz then proceeded to reach base for Buffalo. Third baseman Bill Serena followed with a long drive toward the center-field scoreboard. Thinking the blast was ticketed for extra bases, both Sullivan and Ortiz took off at full tilt. But Montreal center gardener Bobby Del Greco made a miraculous last-second grab and then wheeled and fired to first base, easily doubling Ortiz up for the third out. The sad problem for Montreal was that Sullivan crossed the plate before the third out was registered and the insoluble problem confronting umpire Harry Schwarts was that he had to rule Sullivan's run good even though Sullivan hadn't tagged up after Del Greco's catch and would have been subject to being doubled off second base if the Royals had not already recorded their third out of the inning by doubling up Ortiz.

Sullivan's tally knotted the score at 1-all and Buffalo went on to win in 12 innings, 4–2. The Bisons ultimately fell a half game short of the IL pennant in 1957, but the controversy over Sullivan's tainted run and two other similar incidents during the 1957 season led to the Rules Committee drafting a revised section of the

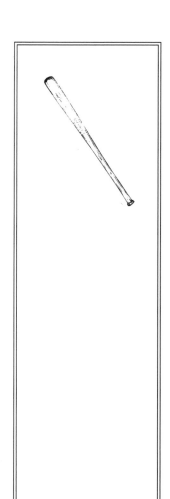

playing code stipulating that an umpire may be required to recognize an apparent "fourth out" when an appeal play on another runner is sustained subsequent to the third out.

The change in the rule meant that in a situation like the one in which Schwarts was forced to award Buffalo a run, the team in the field in the future would not be barred from making an appeal on a play more to its advantage solely because the side had already been retired. If today's rules had prevailed in 1957, Montreal would have been able to appeal Sullivan's run until its defensive corps "left the field" or when the Royals pitcher and all four Montreal infielders had left fair territory on their way to the dugout.

8

THE PITCHER

8.01

Legal pitching delivery. There are two legal pitching positions, the Windup Position and the Set Position, and either position may be used at any time.... (a) The Windup Position. The pitcher shall stand facing the batter, his entire pivot foot on, or in front of and touching and not off the end of the pitcher's plate, and the other foot free. From this position any natural movement associated with his delivery of the ball to the

(continued)

The legal pitching position in 1845 bore little similarity to what it is in 1994. Alexander Cartwright's rules called for a pitcher to stand on a line four yards long, 45 feet from home plate, and drawn at right angles to a line from home plate to second base.

In 1863 a 12 × 3 foot box with its front line 45 feet and its back line 48 feet distant from the plate was introduced. At the moment he released the ball, a pitcher had to have both feet within the box's boundaries. The rear line of the box was moved back one foot in 1866. A year later the size of the pitcher's box was pared to 6 × 4. In 1879 the box's dimensions were changed to 4 × 6. Two years later the front line of the

(continued)

batter commits him to the pitch without interruption or alteration. He shall not raise either foot from the ground, except that in his actual delivery of the ball to the batter, he may take one step backward, and one step forward with his free foot....

box was moved back to 50 feet, but the box's size remained the same until 1886 when it was made 7 × 4. In 1887 the length was reduced to five and a half feet, although the width went unchanged.

The next experiment did not occur until 1893, when the distance was increased to 60 feet, six inches and the box gave way to a mound with a pitcher's plate in the center of it.

Rip Sewell, the creator of the eephus pitch. The unorthodox blooper delivery helped Sewell to win 143 games in the majors after he had slogged along in the minors until he was past 30. **Transcendental Graphics**

Incidentally, a pitcher can still deliver a ball underhand like a slow-pitch softball hurler. But even though there is no limit on the height of a pitch's arc, underhand "moon" balls are eschewed because they would be crushed by major league hitters. Cleverly disguised bloopers are another matter. Rip Sewell and Bobo Newsom in the 1930s and 1940s both developed excellent bloopers that were very effective when mixed in with their other deliveries. Sewell called his the "eephus" ball, after Pittsburgh Pirates teammate Maurice Van Robays said the pitch was eephus, which in baseball parlance at that time meant it was nothing. Sewell's blooper sometimes arced as high as 25 feet, and for years he was able to gloat that no one had ever hit a homer off it. In the 1946 All-Star game at Boston's Fenway Park, Ted Williams ended Sewell's boast by sending one of his eephus balls into orbit.

THE RULE that a pitcher, following his stretch, must come to a complete stop before making his delivery was intended to prevent pitchers from quick-pitching in order to hold runners closer to their bases, but through the years it has meant chaos each time a campaign is waged to enforce it to the letter.

In 1950, when it was first expressly stated that a pitcher had to pause a full second after his stretch with a runner on base, 88 balks were called in the first two weeks of the Pacific Coast League season after there had only been 54 balks in the two major leagues combined the previous year. Another such attempt in the late 1970s saw Frank Tanana set a new American League single-season record for balks in 1978 with eight and Steve Carlton shatter the National League mark the following year by committing 11. In 1984, with enforcement of the complete-stop rule again more relaxed, Tanana tied for the AL lead in balks with just

8.01 (B)

The Set Position. Set Position shall be indicated by the pitcher when he stands facing the batter with his entire pivot foot on, or in front of, and in contact with, and not off the end of the pitcher's plate, and his other foot in front of the pitcher's plate, holding the ball in both hands in front of his body and coming to a complete stop. From such Set Position he may deliver the ball to the batter, throw to a base or step backward off the pitcher's plate with his pivot foot. Before assuming Set Position, the pitcher may elect to make any natural preliminary motion such as that known

(continued)

(continued)

as "the stretch." But if he so elects, he shall come to Set Position before delivering the ball to the batter. . . .

8.01 (D)

If the pitcher makes an illegal pitch with the bases unoccupied, it shall be called a ball unless the batter reaches first base on a hit, an error, a base on balls, a hit batter or otherwise. . . .

---

four and Carlton and Dwight Gooden shared the NL balk title with seven. Four years later, after umpires were told to come down with a vengeance on hurlers who were prone to quick-pitch from the stretch position, no fewer than eight AL pitchers were charged with 10 or more balks, led by Dave Stewart's 16, as umpires socked junior circuit hurlers with an all-time record 558 balks in 1988. The majority were assessed in the early weeks of the season, before officials in both leagues, realizing the situation was rapidly becoming ludicrous, quietly urged the umpires to lighten up a little.

IN ADDITION to having to learn to pitch from inside a box whose dimensions were constantly changing, a pitcher prior to 1893 faced several other restrictions. Most importantly, he had to alter his style of delivery frequently in order to keep pace with the changing rules. Until 1868 a hurler was required to have both feet in contact with the ground when he released the ball, and it had to be delivered with a straight arm swinging parallel to the body or in much the same manner as the delivery of a slow-pitch softball pitcher. In 1872 pitchers for the first time were permitted to deliver the ball with their elbows bent, enabling them to snap their wrists and, thus, throw curveballs as long as they kept their pitching hands below their hips at the point of release. The rule was modified in 1878, requiring pitchers to keep their hands below their waists. A year later it was decreed that a pitcher had to face the batter when he took his position to deliver the ball, thereupon making it easier for an umpire as well as a batter to observe the release point.

The 1883 season marked the next attempt to simplify an umpire's task, as pitchers now could hurl the ball from any angle or height below their shoulders. But when this modification still proved too difficult for

arbiters to monitor, the National League threw up its hands in 1884 and allowed overhand pitching for the first time.

Spalding's Baseball Guide for the 1884 season commented: "The League simply allows what experience has taught them they could not effectively prevent." The surrender to exponents of overhand pitching was a concession that many observers feared would reduce the offensive quotient of the game to near zero. That dire prediction did not prove to be the case, but hitters suffered enough in the 1884 season to cause the National League to restore the ban on overhand pitching the following spring. The prohibition once again was so hard to enforce, though, that a month into the 1885 season the NL reverted to the 1884 rule. Within days the American Association and the other professional circuits also grudgingly lifted all restrictions on the height from which a pitcher could deliver the ball.

But even though overhand pitching was now universally legal, Will White, Tim Keefe, and many more of the game's leading hurlers continued to throw with an underhand wrist snap, both because they felt it saved wear and tear on their arms and because they were too far along in their careers to change. By the early 1890s overhand pitching became the norm as young phenoms like Amos Rusie, Kid Nichols, and Cy Young appeared on the big league scene. All were adolescents in 1885 when the overhand delivery was first legalized for good, still in the formative stages of learning their craft, and so were quickly able to adapt when the last restriction was lifted on the style a pitcher could deploy to deliver the ball to a batter.

Meanwhile, to give batters more of a chance against overhand pitching only 50 feet distant from the plate, in 1887 pitchers for the first time were allowed to take only one step toward the plate as they delivered the ball. Before then many pitchers had launched their

servings after a running start, which was legal as long as their deliveries were begun and ended within the lines of the pitcher's box. Disputes as to whether pitchers exceeded the boundaries were rampant, but with only one arbiter on the scene to detect violations, the argument almost always went against the offensive team. In July 1884 the Cincinnati Red Stockings of the American Association, after complaining all season that Louisville's Guy Hecker was beyond the front line of the box repeatedly when he delivered the ball, finally laid a row of smooth stones in front of the pitcher's box in Cincinnati's American Park so that Hecker would slip on them if he finished his delivery outside it. In retaliation the Louisville club, after grumbling to no avail that Cincinnati ace Will White stood out of bounds when he started his delivery, planted a wall of stones along the right side of the pitcher's box in Eclipse Park.

In 1886, the last year a running start was permitted, Baltimore Orioles rookie left hander Matt Kilroy fanned an all-time record 513 batters and another rookie hurler with Louisville, Toad Ramsey, got 499 hitters to saw the air. The following year, with batters now also given four strikes, Ramsey's whiff total fell to 355 and Kilroy collected just 217 Ks.

Along with abolishing the running start, baseball officials instructed umpires to crack down harder on pitchers who were not obeying the rule to face the batter when they delivered the ball. In the mid-1880s both major leagues had their share of tricksters. Ed Begley of the New York Giants reputedly kept his back to the batter until the last possible instant before he released the ball. Peek-a-Boo Veach employed a similar delivery, explaining his nickname. Larry McKeon evolved all sorts of deceptive tactics to conceal the ball from both the batter and base runners but nevertheless contrived to lose a rookie-record 41 games for Indianapolis in 1884. By the early 1890s all three were long gone from the majors, taking with them the last vestiges of a time when there were nearly as many diverse pitching styles as there were pitchers.

Once the 50-foot pitching distance went the way of the one-bounce out and the fair-foul rule in 1893, many pitchers who fashioned outstanding stats before the distance was increased were unable to make the adjustment when they had to add "legs" to their curves and fastballs, but probably none was more miserable than Charles Leander Jones, best known as "Bumpus." After winning 27 games in the minors earlier in the year, Bumpus Jones was purchased by the Cincinnati Reds in time to hurl the closing contest of the 1892 season. His first game in the majors coincided with the final day that hurlers threw from a rectangular box just 50 feet from the plate. On October 15, 1892, Bumpus Jones inaugurated his career and ushered out the old pitching distance with a feat that has never been duplicated. He twirled a no-hitter in his initial major league game, beating Pittsburgh, 7–1.

Still aglow, Jones reported for spring training with the Reds in 1893 only to find that he would now have to pitch from a mound 60 feet 6 inches from the plate. The transition was beyond him. Seven appearances into the 1893 season, Jones toted a 10.19 ERA, prompting his release. He was never again seen by a major league audience.

BEFORE THE spitball was outlawed a pitcher was free to bring his pitching hand in contact with his mouth anywhere on the diamond. He could even bring the *ball* in contact with his mouth. For a while the Pittsburgh Pirates had a pitcher, Marty O'Toole, who loaded up for a spitter by licking the ball lavishly with his tongue. O'Toole's only season of note was 1912, when he won 15 games. Part of the reason he went

8.02

The pitcher shall not— (a) (1) Bring his pitching hand in contact with his mouth or lips while in the 18 foot circle surrounding the pitching rubber. . . . (2) Apply a foreign substance of any kind to the ball. (3) expectorate on the ball, either hand or his glove.

Luckily for major league officials, Marty O'Toole was gone from the picture by 1920. Had he still been active then, they would have been hard pressed to decide whether to exempt him from Rule 8.02 (a) so he could continue to lick the ball when he wanted to throw a spitter. **National Baseball Library & Archive, Cooperstown, N.Y.**

into a tailspin after 1912 may have come in one of his outings that season against the Philadelphia Phillies when Phils first sacker Fred Luderus found an insidious way to undermine his spitter. Luderus harbored a tube of liniment in his pants pocket and applied a dab of it each time the ball came into his hands. Balls in 1912 often lasted several innings and sometimes even an entire game. By the third inning O'Toole's tongue was so raw he had to be removed from the mound. Pittsburgh manager Fred Clarke, aware of what Luderus was doing, protested. But it went nowhere when Phils skipper Red Dooin pointed out that there was nothing in the rules to prevent it and, furthermore, Luderus was only trying to protect the health of his teammates, who would otherwise be exposed to millions of germs.

The proviso making it illegal for a pitcher to bring his pitching hand in contact with his mouth or lips was not added to the anti-spitball rule until 1968. There was a massive effort at the time to rid the game of the spitter after the majors were given little choice but to acknowledge that many pitchers were using it. The estimates ran as high as 50 or 60, an average of about three pitchers on a team. One hurler, Cal Koonce of the New York Mets, in an almost incredible lapse of candor, admitted in a piece that appeared in the September 2, 1967, issue of *The Sporting News* that the spitter was an important weapon in his arsenal. Subsequently asked if he had really made such an admission, Koonce said, "I don't know what all the fuss is about. A lot of pitchers in the (National) league throw the spitter and everyone knows who they are."

It seems unbelievable, in any case, that for 48 years after the spitball was outlawed the Official Playing Rules Committee failed to stipulate that a pitcher could not spit on his pitching hand. Since 1968 the rule has been amended to allow a pitcher to go to his mouth if he is not on the mound.

8.02 (A)

(5) The pitcher shall not deface the ball in any manner.

WHEN THE spitball was banned, the majors introduced a corollary rule that any player who intentionally discolored or defaced a ball would be kicked out of the game and the ball removed from play. If the umpires were unable to detect a transgressor, then the pitcher would be ejected as soon as the ball was in his possession and socked in addition with a 10-day suspension.

For obvious reasons, this rule didn't fly and was subsequently redrafted so that it was not all bark and no bite. Realizing they were verging on overreacting to the spitball specter and the concomitant bad press that followed Ray Chapman's beaning death, major league rulers privately tempered their stance, even as they continued to rail publicly against pitchers who loaded up the ball. After a livelier type of horsehide was slipped into play during the early 1920s, no one wanted to punish hurlers any more than they were already having to suffer as they watched their ERAs mount alarmingly. In 1922 George Uhle of Cleveland became the first moundsman since the 1890s to win 20 games with an ERA over 4.00. Eight years later Remy Kremer of Pittsburgh became the first pitcher ever to collect 20 wins with an ERA over 5.00.

THE LAST time a pitcher threw a spitball in a major league game without facing the possibility of being penalized for it was in 1934, when Burleigh Grimes was in his final season in the majors. Grimes was the last to remain active of the 17 hurlers who had been given special license in 1920 to continue throwing spitters in the majors until their careers were over. When Grimes notched his 270th and final win on May 30, 1934, by beating Washington 5–4 in a relief role for the New York Yankees, it was the last victory by a hurler legally permitted to throw a spitter.

FOR SOME 24 years after the anti-spitball edict was enacted no pitcher was ejected from a game specifically for violating the rule. Finally, on July 20, 1944, in a night game at St. Louis against the New York Yankees, Nels Potter of the Browns was tossed out by home plate umpire Cal Hubbard. Nearly a quarter cen-

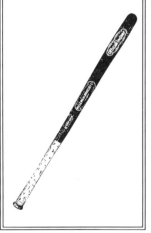

Burleigh Grimes, the last major league pitcher who was legally licensed to go to his mouth wherever and whenever he wanted. Grimes's spitter had batters so psyched out that even when he didn't throw it, he would fake that he was loading up the ball with saliva. **National Baseball Library & Archive, Cooperstown, N.Y.**

tury after the anti-spitball rule went into effect, Potter became its first victim when Hubbard tired of watching him blow on the ball in such a way that it looked like he was spitting on it. Potter insisted he was doing nothing wrong and got huffy with Hubbard. His defiance helped convict him, for it was never proven that he was spraying saliva on the ball when he blew on it.

A few years before the Potter incident, the Yankees were certain that Tommy Bridges of the Detroit Tigers was shutting them down with a spitter. When Yankees skipper Joe McCarthy finally induced umpire Bill McGowan to take a look at the ball, Tigers catcher Mickey Cochrane dropped it as he handed it to McGowan and then rolled it in the dirt down the third base line when he went to pick it up. Cochrane's stratagem has been used time and again ever since 1920 by catchers and infielders when an arbiter has asked to examine a suspicious ball.

ROSIN BAGS were first introduced before the 1926 season, when it was finally acknowledged that pitchers had been operating at an enormous handicap ever since the spitball and other freak deliveries were abolished in 1920. Since no one wanted to encourage hurlers to spit on their hands to get a better grip on the ball, small, finely meshed sealed bags containing rosin were provided by both major leagues for the umpires to hand out to pitchers.

THOUGH the rule does not so specify, it is also illegal for a pitcher to have on his person a jagged fingernail that he can use to nick the surface of a ball. But fingernails are not nearly as much of a worry to umpires as other devices that are at once more disruptive and harder to detect. In a 1987 game Joe Niekro, then with the Minnesota Twins, was caught redhanded with both an emery board and a strip of sandpaper in his hip

---

8.02

... All umpires shall carry with them one official rosin bag. The umpire-in-chief is responsible for placing the rosin bag on the ground back of the pitcher's plate.... A pitcher may use the rosin bag for the purpose of applying rosin to his bare hand or hands. Neither the pitcher nor any other player shall dust the ball with the rosin bag; neither shall the pitcher nor any other player be permitted to apply rosin from the bag to his glove or dust any part of his uniform with the rosin bag.

8.02 (B)

The pitcher shall not have on his person, or in his possession, any foreign substance. For such infraction of this section (b) the penalty shall be immediate ejection from the game.

Twins pitcher Joe Niekro (36) stands convicted with his pockets turned inside out after umpires stopped a 1987 game and found a strip of sandpaper and an emery board in his possession. The discovery seemingly dismayed even Twins manager Tom Kelly (far left).
AP/Wide World Photos

pocket when umpires confronted him on the mound. Niekro was suspended for 10 days, but few pitchers have made it so easy for officials to ferret out their methods for doctoring balls.

During a game at Baltimore's Camden Yards on June 20, 1992, Orioles manager Johnny Oates complained that New York Yankees pitcher Tim Leary was putting "sandpaper scratches" on the ball. The umpires checked Leary's glove and hand and found nothing, but TV cameras showed Leary putting his mouth to his glove after slipping something into his mouth and then spitting something out of his mouth when he reached the Yankees dugout at the end of the inning. Asked later why he only inspected Leary's hand and glove, umpire Dave Phillips said, "It's not my right to look in his mouth and, frankly, I don't want to put my hand into somebody's mouth."

When Steve Carlton was in his prime, sportswrit-
were quite willing to respect his desire not to give in-
iews. The loss to their readers was small, they felt.
lton wasn't very interesting anyway. What was fas-
ating, though, was how he got away year after year
h cutting the ball. No one ever figured out the instru-
nt Carlton used, and he was scarcely about to break
code of silence to convict himself.

But if Leary's and Carlton's techniques for defac-
a ball were too subtle to allow an umpire to indict
m, Los Angeles Dodgers hurler Don Sutton was not
so fortunate. Pitching against the St. Louis Cardinals on
July 14, 1978, Sutton was given the heave in the seventh inning by umpire Doug Harvey after Harvey carefully collected three balls that had become mysteriously
scuffed while in Sutton's hands. Even though Harvey
could not determine how Sutton was doctoring the
balls, he defended his ejection by saying, "I represent
the integrity of the game and I'm going to continue to
do it if necessary." Sutton responded by suing Harvey
for jeopardizing his livelihood.

THE STARTING points for an umpire who has to
decide whether a pitcher is deliberately throwing at
a batter are the pitcher's history, prior events in the
game, and his own intuition. Whether or not the pitcher hits a batter is often irrelevant. In a 1974 game
against the Cincinnati Reds, Doc Ellis of the Pittsburgh
Pirates hit the first three batters he faced in the game—
Pete Rose, Joe Morgan, and Dan Driessen—and then
threw four fastballs high and tight to cleanup hitter
Tony Perez to force in a run. When Ellis nearly nailed
Johnny Bench with his next two pitches, still no one
thought there was malice aforethought in his wild
streak. Finally, though, Pirates manager Danny Mur-
taugh lifted Ellis before anyone was killed. Said Reds

manager Sparky Anderson when asked later for his views on Ellis's performance: "No one would be crazy enough to deliberately hit the first three men. He was so wild he just didn't know where the ball was going."

In contrast, Texas Rangers reliever Bob Babcock was booted from a 1980 game against the California Angels after just one pitch. Babcock entered the fray in the top of the seventh inning following a beanball war during the previous frame that had culminated in a bench-clearing brawl involving both teams. As a consequence the umpires were especially vigilant. When Babcock's first delivery narrowly missed Dan Ford, leading off the inning for the Angels, all four men in blue were convinced he was headhunting on orders from Rangers manager Pat Corrales. Babcock tried to claim his foot had slipped off the rubber as he released the pitch, but no one was about to buy it. He was thumbed from the game almost as soon as the ball whizzed past Ford's head.

A GOOD question here is why pitchers are allowed 20 seconds between deliveries with the bases empty, as dictated by Rule 8.04, rather than 15 seconds or even 10, especially given the vigorous campaign now to speed up games. And, along the same line, why not six warm-up pitches between innings instead of the eight specified in Rule 8.03?

These limitations on pitchers have been part of the game's tradition for so long they are inviolate. How and by whom the 20-second and eight-toss figures were first determined are equally interesting questions, but the answers to them are probably forever beyond our ken now.

For years neither limitation was felt to be necessary, since most pitchers liked to work quickly and relievers were usually players who were already in the game at another position. Even after the modern substitution rule was initiated in 1891 and relievers came off the bench, most needed very little warm-up time. After being summoned into a game, Three Finger Brown would often take just one or two warm-up tosses and then be ready to go to work.

Close observers of the between-innings ritual in the major leagues have noted that umpires nowadays seldom count a pitcher's warm-up tosses. Many hurlers consistently exceed the eight allowed. Much of the reason, no doubt, is that plate umpires have been ordered to fill TV time between innings. As long as commercials are running, everyone is happy to let a pitcher keep throwing.

THE NEXT section deals at considerable length with all the movements a pitcher makes, or fails to make, that constitute a balk. Before we turn to what the balk rules are now, let's take a look at what they used to be.

In 1893, the first year that the pitcher's plate was established at its present distance from home plate, a pitcher was judged to have committed a balk if he did any of the following:

1. Made a motion to deliver the ball to the bat without delivering it;
2. Delivered the ball to the bat while his pivot foot was not in contact with the pitcher's plate;
3. Made a motion to deliver the ball to the bat without having his pivot foot in contact with the pitcher's plate; or
4. Held the ball so long as to delay the game unnecessarily.

Before the 1898 season, three more ways for a pitcher to balk were added:

8.05

If there is a runner, or runners, it is a balk when— (a) The pitcher, while touching his plate, makes any motion naturally associated with his pitch and fails to make such delivery; . . . (b) The pitcher, while touching his plate, feints a throw to first base and fails to complete the throw; (c) The pitcher, while touching his plate, fails to step directly toward a base before throwing to that base; . . . (d) The pitcher, while touching his plate, throws, or feints a throw to an unoccupied base, except for the purpose of making a play; (e) The pitcher makes an illegal pitch; . . . (f) The pitcher delivers the ball to the batter while he is not facing the batter; (g) The pitcher makes any motion naturally associated with his pitch

(continued)

(continued)

while he is not touching the pitcher's plate; (h) The pitcher unnecessarily delays the game; (i) The pitcher, without having the ball, stands on or astride the pitcher's plate or while off the plate, he feints a pitch; (j) The pitcher, after coming to a legal pitching position, removes one hand from the ball other than in an actual pitch, or in throwing to a base; (k) The pitcher, while touching his plate, accidentally or intentionally drops the ball; (l) The pitcher, while giving an intentional base on balls, pitches when the catcher is not in the catcher's box; (m)The pitcher delivers the pitch from Set Position without coming to a stop. . . .

5. Standing in position and making a motion to pitch without having the ball in his possession;

6. Making any motion a pitcher habitually makes to deliver the ball to a batter without immediately delivering it; or

7. Feigning a throw to a base and then not resuming his legal pitching position and pausing momentarily before delivering the ball to the bat.

Proviso No. 6 might seem unnecessary, since even if a pitcher somehow managed to delude a batter into swinging at a phantom pitch, it could not be counted as a strike. The ploy was not an effort to dupe the batter, however, but a base runner for the purpose of getting him to stroll off the bag and then nailing him on the "hidden ball" trick. Before 1898 a pitcher could pantomime his entire delivery routine without having the ball in his possession. Further restrictions on what a pitcher could do while one of his infielders tried to pull off a hidden ball play were imposed in 1920, bringing the rule closer to 8.05 (m)—a (see below), requiring a balk to be called whenever a pitcher stands empty-handed on or astride the rubber.

But though the 1898 balk amendments took a giant step toward the present rule, there was still one more important stride to be made. It was taken in 1899, when for the first time a balk was assessed if a pitcher threw to a base in an attempt to pick off a runner without first stepping toward that base. Prior to then pitchers had been free to do just about as they wished in trying to hold runners close to their bases, including suddenly snapping a throw to a base while looking elsewhere. Helped by the new balk rule, National League teams stole nearly 600 more bases in 1899 than they had the previous year and the Baltimore Orioles set a modern single-season stolen base mark with 364 thefts.

Before 1899 pitchers not only could fake throws to first, they could also twitch their pitching shoulders, swing their legs every which way, and utilize many other maneuvers that are now considered balks. Operating under almost no restrictions, Louisville's Guy Hecker picked Cub Stricker of the Philadelphia A's off first base a record three times in an American Association game on July 29, 1883, to spoil what ought to have been a gala day for Stricker, who went 4-for-4 against one of the top pitchers in the majors at the time.

THERE HAS always been a rule of one sort or another against quick-pitching a batter, though it has not always been deemed a balk. Often it has been simply ruled no pitch. Babe Ruth once benefited enormously from such a judgment. In the final game of the 1928 World Series, the New York Yankees and the St. Louis Cardinals were knotted at 1–all in the top of the seventh when Ruth stepped into the box. Ruth already had one homer on the day, accounting for the Yankees' only run. Willie Sherdel was on the hill for St. Louis. After getting two strikes on Ruth, Sherdel slipped a pitch past the Babe that everyone in St. Louis's Sportsman's Park thought should have been a called third strike. But plate umpire Cy Pfirmin waved it off, saying it had been agreed before the Series that there would be no "quick returns"—pitches that were unacceptable in the American League but condoned by National League arbiters. Given a reprieve, Ruth clubbed a home run and Lou Gehrig followed with another four-bagger to put the game out of the Cardinals' reach.

RULE 8.05 (J) precludes a pitcher from changing to using a different arm to deliver the ball to a batter once he is in his windup or set position. Otherwise he is

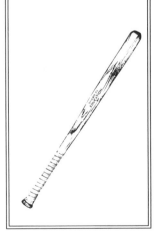

free to switch any time the whim seizes him. There have been several ambidextrous pitchers in the majors, but the only one who had much success with both arms was Tony Mullane. Winner of 284 games between 1881 and 1894, Mullane was not hampered early in his career by having to wear a glove on his non-pitching hand. That freed him to keep the batter guessing from which direction the ball would come until he actually released it.

Mullane was not only a switch-thrower but also a switch-hitter and a fine all-around player. Early in the 1882 season, while playing for Louisville, he became the first American Association performer to steal second, third, and home in a single turn on the bases. With Mullane's departure went one of a kind, and the majors have not seen anything approaching his like since 1894. However, ambidextrous hurlers turn up now and again in minors, usually just to provide a box office attraction, although occasionally with a serious purpose.

In an attempt to stifle Joe Bauman, a legendary left-handed slugger in the low minors who hit a minor loop-record 72 home runs in 1954, Audie Malone, normally a right-hander, resorted to using his left arm when he squared off against Bauman, then with Artesia, in a Longhorn League game on July 4, 1952. Pitching for the Roswell Rockets, Malone got Bauman to fan on a slow curve in the first inning. But Bauman singled in his only other appearance against Malone, who was markedly unsuccessful against the rest of the Artesia lineup. Malone was pelted from the mound in the fourth inning and charged with a 12–8 loss.

For the year Malone posted a 12–16 record and a 5.45 ERA, whereas Bauman led the Texas circuit with 50 homers and 157 RBIs.

BEFORE 1954 the ball was dead as soon as a balk occurred. There were no exceptions. Regardless of what happened, the runner or runners on base moved up one rung, a ball was assessed if the pitch had been released, and that was that.

The old rule cost an offensive team on many occasions but never more dearly than in 1949 when it played a hand in deciding the National League pennant race. In a Saturday night game at St. Louis's Sportsman's Park on August 6, the Cardinals had a runner aboard and cleanup hitter Nippy Jones at bat with two out in the bottom of the first against the New York Giants. On the mound for the Giants was lefty Adrian Zabala, one of the many players banned from Organized Baseball for five years after jumping to the Mexican League at the start of the 1946 season. The ban had been lifted by Commissioner Happy Chandler two months earlier, allowing Zabala to rejoin the Giants, for whom he had last pitched in 1945. During his forced vacation from the majors he had acquired some bad habits while pitching in the outlaw Provincial League. Working out of the stretch with a runner on first, Zabala was caught in a balk by second-base umpire Jocko Conlan as he delivered the ball to the plate. Jones, not seeing the signal, concentrating only on the pitch, proceeded to belt it into the bleachers for an apparent two-run homer. However, the prevailing rule at the time canceled the four-bagger and allowed the runner to advance only from first to second, Forced to bat over, Jones flied out to end the inning.

Zabala was subsequently charged with two more balks that night, giving him three in the game to tie the then-existing major league record. But he was otherwise almost completely in command. The Cardinals managed to scratch out only one tally against him after being robbed of Jones's two-run dinger and lost the game, 3–1. Had that defeat wound up in the victory col-

umn instead, St. Louis would have finished the 1949 season in a flat tie with the Brooklyn Dodgers, forcing a best two-of-three pennant playoff.

In one final note of irony, Zabala won just two games in 1949 and never again pitched in the majors.

FOR ALL the attention lavished on fine-tuning Rule 8.05, we are still left to wonder if a pitcher can be charged with a balk if something totally out of his control occurs to interrupt his delivery with men on base. The perfect pitcher to ask is Stu Miller. In the first of two All-Star games in 1961, on July 11 at San Francisco's Candlestick Park, Miller held a 3–1 lead for the National League stars in the top of the ninth when he ran afoul of the infamous 'Stick wind. With runners on second and third, Miller all of a sudden felt himself being blown off the mound as he prepared to deliver the ball. After the second American League run came home on the balk, the tying tally crossed moments later when the gusting wind spun a roller out of third baseman Ken Boyer's grasp.

The Americans went ahead, 4–3, with another wind-aided run in the top of the tenth but then fell victim themselves to the elements. In the bottom of the frame the NL rallied for two runs when the wind sabotaged Hoyt Wilhelm's knuckleball and made it easy pickings for first Hank Aaron and Willie Mays and then Roberto Clemente, whose single drove home Mays from second with the winning run.

Despite committing the most famous balk in a midsummer classic and giving up three runs in the less-than-two innings he worked in relief, Miller got credit for the victory.

A **FORM** of the rule limiting a manager to one trip to the mound per inning first appeared in the 1967 manual. Its purpose obviously is to prevent managers and pitching coaches from traipsing back and forth endlessly between the dugout and the mound to confer with their batterymen. The one-visit limit helps so much to speed up games that it becomes all the more difficult to believe that in the early part of the century, when managers could hold as many mound powwows as they pleased, contests often took little more than an hour.

8.06

A professional league shall adopt the following rule pertaining to the visit of the manager or coach to the pitcher: (a) This rule limits the number of trips a manager or coach may make to any one pitcher in any one inning; (b) A second trip to the same pitcher in the same inning will cause this pitcher's automatic removal. . . .

THE UMPIRE

9.01 (A)

The league president shall appoint one or more umpires to officiate at each league championship game. The umpires shall be responsible for the conduct of the game in accordance with these official rules and for maintaining discipline and order on the playing field during the game.

Currently each major league has a staff of 32 umpires. In 1883, when umpires first became salaried representatives of their respective major leagues, both the National League and the American Association carried just four arbiters. At the time the NL and the AA were both eight-team loops, meaning that there were a maximum of four playing sites in each circuit on a given day. One umpire was assigned to each site, and it was up to him to make his own travel arrangements, book his own hotel accommodations, pay for cleaning his uniform, and so on. The four AA arbiters at the beginning of the 1883 season were John Kelly, William H. Becannon, Charlie Daniels, and Benjamin Sommers. Kelly was the prize

of the four; *Sporting Life* described him as "prompt, decided, energetic...possessed of excellent judgment." Daniels was the most experienced, having previously served five seasons in the National League. Yet the terse assessment in *Sporting Life* of him was: "He is not a professional."

In 1883 the AA paid its umpires $140 a month, plus $3 per diem for travel expenses. Meager as this salary might seem, it was more than the NL paid, and the AA accordingly had a better quality of officiating. Of the four umpires the NL hired in 1883, one was a college student who was fired a few weeks into the season, and by 1885 only Stuart Decker was still a member of the senior loop's staff.

In the 1880s, if an umpire took sick or was unable to work for some other reason, one of three things could occur. If an experienced umpire who was acceptable to both teams just happened to be at the ballground that day, he would be pressed into service. If the visiting team had a player not in its starting lineup whom the home club was willing to let officiate, the job was his for the day. When neither of these options came through, a substitute player or a knowledgeable spectator umped the game and it was deemed an exhibition contest.

As an example, the scheduled American Association game on May 3, 1883, between the Philadelphia Athletics and the Pittsburgh Alleghenys became an exhibition when umpire Charlie Daniels took ill and no good substitute for him was on hand. The crowd of around 1200 was unaware of the change in the game's status until they had bought tickets and were in their seats. They then saw something considerably less than they had paid for as Frank McLaughlin, normally a shortstop, took the box for Pittsburgh and opposed Lon Knight, the A's regular right fielder, with Pittsburgh winning 15–2.

One question that naturally arises here is: Why would a home team agree to accept an opposition player as an umpire? The answer is: So that the game would be a championship contest. For all games that counted in the standings except those that took place on Sundays or holidays, the visiting club received an appearance fee—as little as $65 per game in the American Association until 1888—and the home team then got to keep all the money that was collected at the gate. If the game was declared an exhibition, the two teams split the take down the middle.

Sometimes fans would sit through an entire game without learning until days later whether it was an exhibition or a regular contest. When rookie umpire John Valentine missed his train and failed to show up for an American Association game between Louisville and the New York Metropolitans on June 21, 1884, both teams stewed over whether or not to play an exhibition contest. Meanwhile, the Louisville crowd howled that they'd paid good money to see a championship affair. Finally, Mets manager Jim Mutrie hit upon a compromise. He made it known his club would play a game that would count in the standings but only if he could choose the umpire. He then designated pitcher Tim Keefe, since Keefe had the day off anyway because Jack Lynch was slated to hurl.

Louisville acceded to Mutrie, but after the Mets won the game the Falls City club filed a protest, claiming Keefe was not a fit umpire for a championship contest. Mutrie eventually agreed to have the game thrown out, even though it deprived his club of a victory, in return for half of the day's gate receipts. Later in the season AA officials reversed their position again and decided the count the game in the standings.

It can come as no surprise to learn that there were a multitude of protests in the 1880s questioning the fitness of an umpire. Likewise, there were frequent protests questioning his honesty. In 1882 Dick Higham, a National League umpire and a former player, was banned from baseball for betting on games at which he officiated. Higham was assigned by the senior loop to work a string of games involving the Detroit Wolverines. When Wolves president W. G. Thompson, who also happened to be the mayor of Detroit, began complaining that all of Higham's close decisions seemed to go against his club, he was ignored at first. But when the pattern persisted the league met in executive session to hear Thompson's grievance. His case was so persuasive that a full-scale investigation was conducted. It took remarkably little sleuthing to unmask Higham as a crook. An inspection of his mail revealed that much of it was in code, and not a particularly sophisticated one. From the phraseology Higham used, it was easy to deduce that he was in collusion with gamblers who were making a tidy sum, owing to his guaranteed assistance in each game, by betting against Detroit.

Higham's duplicity and the suspicion that surrounded the work of several other umpires in that era made the National League adopt Rule 67, which stated:

> "Any League umpire who shall in the judgment of the President of the League be guilty of ungentlemanly conduct or of selling, or offering to sell, a game in which he is umpire, shall thereupon be removed from his official capacity and placed under the same disabilities inflicted upon expelled players by the Constitution of the League."

By the mid-1890s umpires were better paid, helping to make their honesty no longer a constant question, and Rule 67 was eliminated.

9.01 (c)

Each umpire has authority to rule on any point not specifically covered in these rules.

EVEN THOUGH the game has existed in more or less its present form for a century and a half, virtually every umpire who has worked at his craft for any length of time has run into a situation the rulemakers have still not satisfactorily addressed.

Umpire Wesley Curry rose to an unanticipated challenge in an American Association skirmish at Eclipse Park in Louisville on July 9, 1887, between the Falls City club and Brooklyn. With the Brooks ahead 4–2, Louisville loaded the bases. Reddy Mack then scored from third on an infield boot and hovered near the plate to coach teammate Bill White as White raced to beat the throw home from shortstop Germany Smith. Seeing that Brooklyn catcher Bob Clark would get the ball before White arrived, Mack intentionally jostled Clark, preventing him from tagging the sliding Louisville runner. While Mack and Clark continued to thrash around, Joe Werrick proceeded to tally what fans thought was the third run on the play, putting the local club up 5–4.

But Curry declared White out at the plate and also disallowed Werrick's run, claiming that Mack had illegally obstructed Clark. Although Curry's ruling seems now to have been the only possible verdict under the circumstances, at the time it triggered a storm of protest when Brooklyn ended up winning the game, 4–3. In 1887 there was still absolutely nothing in the rulebook dealing with the problem that had forced itself on Curry. The dilemma was that only a base runner could be guilty of obstructing a fielder in the 1887 manual, and the moment Mack crossed the plate he was by definition no longer a base runner.

Curry's decision, though it was reviled in Louisville and condemned even by many impartial observers, ultimately was seen to have been entirely reasonable and resulted in the creation of an ancestor to Rule 7.09 (e) that considers any member of an offensive team who stands around any base and hinders a fielder guilty of interference.

In a 1977 game at Minnesota between the Twins and the Cleveland Indians four American League umpires were confronted with a problem that has yet to be definitively resolved by the rulebook. With the bases loaded and two out in the bottom of the eleventh inning, a 3-and-1 pitch to Butch Wynegar got away from Cleveland reliever Jim Kern and sailed past the Tribe receiver. As the winning run raced home from third on the wild pitch, plate umpire Vic Voltaggio called it ball four, giving Wynegar a walk that would have forced home the winning run in any event.

But rather than go to first base, Wynegar joined the celebration at the plate. Rule 4.09 (b) says that when the winning run in a game is forced home on a walk, "the umpire shall not declare the game ended until the runner forced to advance from third has touched home base and the batter-runner has touched first base." Upon seeing that Wynegar had failed to go to first as is necessary before the winning run can become official, Cleveland manager Jeff Torborg called the oversight to Voltaggio's attention. When Voltaggio said the wild pitch took precedence and eliminated Wynegar's need to go to first, Torborg accepted the explanation.

Later it developed that Voltaggio was really winging it and that the American League would have been caught in an inescapable web if Torborg had pushed the issue by lodging a formal protest. There is still nothing in the rulebook to support Voltaggio's contention that a wild pitch obviates a batter's obligation to touch first base on a game-ending walk. Nor is there any provision for how the Indians could have gone about retiring Wynegar for failing to comply with Rule 6.08 (a), which entitles a batter to first base without liability to be put out, provided he advances to and touches first base. Credit Voltaggio for imagination and *chutzpah*, but had Torborg been more resourceful and the Indians and the Twins contenders in 1977, Wynegar could have become a goat of the first order.

THE ADDENDUM to Rule 9.02 (c) is a comparatively recent innovation. For over half a century after the major leagues began using at least two umpires in a game in the early 1900s, the team on defense had no recourse if a home plate umpire's vision was blocked or some other circumstance prevented him from gauging whether a batter swung at a pitch and he refused to consult with a colleague who might have had a better view. Now a defensive team can force the issue simply by signaling that it wants a second opinion.

THIS PARAGRAPH makes it clear that a runner has no grounds to protest if he is thrown out when he sets off for second base after the plate umpire has called a fourth ball on the batter, only to have a base umpire, on appeal, rule it a checked-swing strike. Nor, for that matter, could the catcher protest if the runner made second uncontested before the base umpire called the pitch a strike. In a 1906 game between the Pittsburgh Pirates and the Chicago Cubs, Pirates player-manager Fred Clarke occupied third base with the bags loaded and a 3-and-1 count on the batter. When the umpire said nothing and gave no sign on the next pitch, Clarke assumed it was ball four, forcing him home, and started trotting toward the plate. Both the catcher and the batter also thought it was a free pass. As the catcher tossed the ball back to the pitcher and the batter headed for first, Clarke touched the plate. Suddenly the umpire erupted and cried, "Strike two!" When everyone looked at him in amazement, he sheepishly admitted that he'd been unable to speak right away because something had been caught in his throat.

Since time had not been called, the umpire had no choice but to rule that Clarke's run counted. The official scorer in turn had to credit Clarke with a steal of home, albeit unintentional.

9.02 (D)

No umpire may be replaced during a game unless he is injured or becomes ill.

IN THE EVENT a replacement is not available for an umpire who is injured or becomes ill during a game, the umpiring crew works the rest of the game a man short. This is a fairly common occurrence nowadays and not much of a hardship, with four-man crews the norm in regular season games, and six in postseason clashes. Fifty years ago, however, sometimes only two umpires were assigned to a game and a player occasionally had to fill in when an arbiter was idled. Hall of Fame umpire Jocko Conlan got his start in this way.

In 1935 Conlan was a backup outfielder with the Chicago White Sox. One torrid afternoon late in July the Sox were playing twin bill with the St. Louis Browns at Sportsman's Park. At the close of the first game umpire Red Ormsby was overcome by the heat, leaving his partner, Harry Geisel, to handle the second game alone. Since he was out of action anyway with a sprained thumb, Conlan volunteered to help out Geisel by working the bases. When Ormsby was still too weak to officiate the following day, Conlan subbed for him again and was paid $50 by the American League.

Conlan discovered that he liked the job. At the close of the 1935 season, when it grew evident to him that his playing days in the majors were numbered, he accepted an offer to umpire the following year in the New York-Pennsylvania League for $300 a month. In 1941, after a five-year apprenticeship in the minors, Conlan was hired as a regular umpire by the National League. He stayed at the job for 25 years, distinguishing himself not only for his officiating skills but for making all signals with his left hand and wearing a bow tie during games.

9.03 (B)

If there are two or more umpires, one shall be designated umpire-in-chief and the others field umpires.

ALTHOUGH it's not a formal rule that umpires must rotate their jobs, working the plate one day, first base the next, and so on, it has become a sacrosanct tradition, and the umpires' union would swiftly take issue if either major league were to decide that one

of its umps was so good behind the plate that he should be permanently assigned to calling balls and strikes. Time was, though, when a league could do just that with an umpire's consent. Bill Klem was so esteemed that he was a National League arbiter for 16 years before he deigned to begin rotating the crew-chief role with his fellow umpires by working the bases.

THE NATIONAL LEAGUE and the American League have not always had the same rules regarding the responsibilities a home plate umpire has as opposed to a base umpire. As one example, the balk incident cited in Chapter 8 that may have cost the St. Louis Cardinals the National League pennant in 1949 could not have happened in the same way that year in the American League. Originally, it was reported in accounts of the game that plate umpire Bill Stewart called the balk. But actually second base umpire Jocko Conlan cited Giants pitcher Adrian Zabala for the infraction

9.04 (A)

The umpire-in-chief shall stand behind the catcher. (He usually is called the plate umpire.) His duties shall be to: (1) Take full charge of, and be responsible for, the proper conduct of the game; (2) Call and count balls and strike; (3) Call and declare fair balls and fouls except those commonly called by

(continued)

(continued)

field umpires; (4) Make all decisions on the batter; (5) Make all decisions except those commonly reserved for the field umpires; (6) Decide when a game shall be forfeited; (7) If a time limit has been set, announce the fact and the time set before the game starts; (8) Inform the official scorer of the official batting order, and any changes in the lineups and batting order, on request; (9) Announce any special ground rules, at his discretion.

that forced Nippy Jones to bat over again. In the National League any umpire in 1949 could nail a hurler for failing to pause in his stretch before delivering a pitch, whereas the only American League official permitted to pass that judgment was the home plate ump.

IN THE EARLY years when an umpire worked a game alone he generally stood in back of the catcher, even though most catchers then played so far behind the plate positioning himself behind them put an umpire at a sizable distance from the batter. In the late 1880s "Honest" John Gaffney introduced umping in the center of the diamond or behind the pitcher with men on base. Most arbiters quickly grew to prefer working there for safety reasons.

When catching equipment improved, enabling receivers to move closer to the plate, umpires accordingly began to get behind catchers again when the bases were clear, albeit with great reluctance. Even though a mask by then had become a standard part of an umpire's apparel, the face-gear most arbiters wore provided scant protection. In a Union Association game at Wilmington on September 8, 1884, umpire Pat Dutton nearly became the first on-the-field fatality in major league history when a foul tip off the bat of Cincinnati's Jack Glasscock hit him in the throat. Dutton went down as if he had been poleaxed and lay so still that Glasscock and Wilmington catcher Tony Cusick thought he was dead. But, luckily, there was a Doctor Frantz among the crowd at the game. Frantz rushed out on the field and discovered that Dutton had ceased breathing because a broken bone in his lower jaw was pressing on his windpipe. The doctor was able to manipulate the bone back into place, and Dutton soon regained consciousness. But when he was unable to resume umpiring, the game was stopped at that point.

Injuries like the one Dutton suffered discouraged many umpires from working in back of the plate whenever it could be avoided, but standing behind the pitcher was not necessarily a refuge either. It put an umpire's back to four infielders and three outfielders, all of whom could make his job miserable even when he could keep them under surveillance. Lacking eyes in the back of his head, an arbiter often failed to note that a first sacker had dislodged the first base bag and begun inching it backward until the distance to it had grown mysteriously to 95 feet, or that a batter had fanned because the second baseman was standing in his line of vision and waving a white handkerchief.

BECAUSE AN umpire in the early days worked alone and the rulemakers recognized that he could not hope to see everything, before 1881 he could reserve a decision on a matter of judgment until he had taken a poll of spectators and players who might have had a better view of a play than he, or reverse a decision he had already rendered if the testimony of a witness to a play was convincing enough to change his mind.

In 1887, when batsmen for the first time were given their base in both major leagues if they were hit by a pitch, the rule was amended, restoring an umpire's right to consult with a player before rendering a decision. Behind the revision was an awareness that the newly adopted rule would make it necessary on occasion for umpires, particularly when they were calling the game from behind the pitcher, to confer with batters and catchers before deciding if a hitter was struck by a pitch and a free base should be awarded. By 1897 an umpire was no longer permitted to ask a player for help in making a decision. In fact, umpires were instructed not to reverse any decisions in which the sole question involved was whether there had been an error of judgment.

9.04 (c)

If different decisions should be made on one play by different umpires, the umpire-in-chief shall call all the umpires into consultation, with no manager or player present. After consultation, the umpire-in-chief (unless another umpire may have been designated by the league president) shall determine which decision shall prevail, based on which umpire was in best position and which decision was most likely correct. Play shall proceed as if only the final decision had been made.

ALTHOUGH THE crew chief has the final word if two or more umpires disagree on a rule interpretation or a matter of judgment, if he is outweighed by the majority of his staff, he will usually go with the consensus point of view. Since umpires are afforded the same protection as jurors, the baseball public never learns how the opinion fell on a thorny play unless one of the arbiters chooses to talk for the record.

A case in point was a ball hit at Shea Stadium by rookie outfielder Dave Augustine of the Pittsburgh Pirates against the New York Mets in the top of the thirteeth inning on September 20, 1973. Of the four umpires working the game, at least one is believed to have adamantly maintained Augustine's blow had struck the top of the fence and should be a two-run homer, but the consensus was that it had bounced off the facing of the fence, allowing Mets left fielder Cleon Jones to retrieve the ball and relay it to third baseman Wayne Garrett, who fired it home to Jerry Grote in time to nail Richie Zisk, representing the potential winning run.

The Mets won the game with a tally in the bottom of the thirteenth and went on to win the National League East title in 1973 by a two and a half game margin over the Pirates. Had Augustine been credited with a home run and the Pirates held on to win this disputed game, the two clubs would have finished the season half a game apart, necessitating that the Mets make up a postponed game. A New York defeat in the makeup game would have left the Mets, Pirates, and St. Louis Cardinals all tied with an 81–81 record, setting up a three-way playoff for the division crown, but because Augustine only got a double on the hit, the Pirates will always feel they were robbed of a chance to play in the 1973 World Series and Augustine will always feel an added sense of loss. However differently he may believe, the record book says he never hit a home run in a major league game.

NO MAJOR league player has ever been barred for life for fighting with an umpire, although down through the years there have been numerous physical confrontations with umpires that could have been grounds for permanent banishment. Ty Cobb's pugnacious temperament got him into a multitude of fistfights with fans and fellow players, and even on at least one occasion with an umpire. Billy Evans, the most fastidious and also generally the most mild-mannered arbiter of his day, nevertheless locked horns with Cobb during a contest he was officiating. The argument grew so heated that Cobb challenged Evans to meet him under the stands after the game.

To Cobb's surprise and pleasure, Evans accepted. The few witnesses to the bout later characterized it as quick and brutal, with Cobb, as expected, administering a sound thrashing to Evans. Following the custom of the times, Evans chose not to report the incident to the American League office, now a violation of Rule 9.05 (a) that would probably earn his immediate suspension, if not dismissal.

Evans was not the only umpire in the early 1900s to engage in fistcuffs with a player, but he was among the last. By the time Judge Landis took office as baseball's first commissioner in 1920, umpires were no longer fair game for irate players whenever they rendered an unpopular decision. Had Landis been made to review an incident like the one in July 1911 involving Phillies outfielder Sherry Magee and rookie National League umpire Bill Finneran, he might well have banished Magee for life. Magee slugged Finneran after

he was thrown out of a game for disputing a call. For what was described as his "brutal and unprovoked assault," Magee was suspended for the rest of the season and fined $200.

However, league president Tom Lynch, himself a former umpire, lifted the suspension after Magee had been out of uniform just 36 days, in part because there was testimony that Magee, who suffered from epilepsy, might have been in the throes of a seizure when he decked Finneran.

In the 1890s Magee's action would probably not even have merited a suspension. During a game on July 22, 1897, Cincinnati Reds pitcher Pink Hawley floored umpire Jack Sheridan with a punch to the jaw; Sheridan contented himself with ejecting Hawley. In another game that season, Cincinnati catcher Heinie Peitz charged umpire Tim Hurst. When Hurst fended Peitz off with his mask, Peitz clouted him in the mouth, but this incident was one of the rare times that Hurst was on the receiving end. Asked once why he became a major league umpire, a job that required him to work a game alone and endure virulent abuse from players, fans, owners, and even, on occasion, reporters, Hurst said, "It's a hard life, lads, but you can't beat the hours." Hurst, a boxing referee on the side, seemed to thrive on jobs that were laden with conflict. If a player questioned one of his calls too vehemently, Hurst would put his mouth close to the protestor's ear and offer the key to his hotel room, where everything was "nice and quiet" and there would be no witnesses when the player got his jaw broken so that he couldn't bellyache about an umpire's decision for the rest of the season. No one ever took Hurst's offer.

But not all umpires in Hurst's day were as bellicose as he. Many who were not quickly found themselves unable to keep control of a game. Consequently, few men lasted at the job. Half a season, a year at most,

was about the average tenure. In the 1895 campaign alone 59 different men served as umpires in regular season games, and National League president Nick Young grew so desperate to fill the constant vacancies in his ranks that he hired most of his arbiters sight unseen or else gave the post to ex-players with no officiating experience who were down on their luck. One such was Hank O'Day, who had pitched with Washington of the National League in the late 1880s to a young catcher named Connie Mack. By the mid-1890s, when O'Day became an NL arbiter, Mack was managing the Pittsburgh Pirates. Revered for his almost ecclesiastical demeanor when he later piloted the Philadelphia A's for half a century, Mack was not always the gentlemen in the rollicking 1890s. He and O'Day clashed so fiercely one afternoon that the umpire was forced to eject his former batterymate and then summon a policeman when Mack refused to leave. The job O'Day and others were called on to perform was so stressful that Boston sportswriter Tim Murnane, himself an ex-player, observed, "The time will soon come when no person above the rank of garrotter can be secured to umpire a game."

At the turn of the century, about the only weapon an umpire had, apart from his fists, was the authority to fine players. In 1895 a rule was inserted allowing umpires to assess fines of $25 to $100 for specified misconduct. The following year the sanction was broadened so that umpires could also fine players $25 for vulgar or indecent language; but even this power could not help an umpire when an entire team got on his case.

In a doubleheader at Louisville on July 10, 1897, umpire Tom Lynch heaved two New York Giants players, George Davis and Willie Clark, out of the first game and then refused to work the second contest after the opener ended in a near brawl. Jimmy Wolf, an

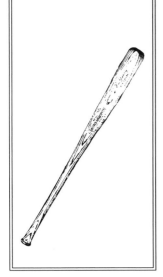

ex-Louisville outfielder, volunteered to sub in the nightcap. With New York ahead 7–2 in the ninth, Giants starter Mike Sullivan hit a wild streak and reliever Amos Rusie was no improvement. Ball after ball was called by Wolf until Tom McCreary walked to force in the tying run. The Giants then surrounded Wolf, and the crowd surged onto the field to protect him. Eventually the police had to haul several Giants players off the field so that the game could continue.

During the last century there were also occasions when the police had to escort umpires to safety after a game. In an American Association contest between Cincinnati and Washington on May 31, 1884, umpire Terry Connell forfeited the game to Cincinnati when Washington manager Holly Hollingshead tired of watching every decision Connell made go against his men and pulled them off the field with the Ohio club ahead, 6–0. Connell no sooner announced the forfeit than the crowd in the nation's capital swarmed onto the diamond to vent their wrath.

Immediately finding himself surrounded, Connell gave ground to the throng and backpedaled toward the outfield. To help him get out of the park alive, the Cincinnati club secreted its carriage behind a gate in the ballpark fence. At a prearranged signal, the gate was flung open and several policemen pushed the terrified umpire through it and lifted him into the carriage. With the crowd in mad pursuit and the driver frantically whipping the horses, Connell fled down the street in a cloud of dust.

What finally gave an umpire enough protection to make his job bearable was not so much a change in the rules as a change in a custom. Before the 1898 season the National League acknowledged the possibility that the one-umpire system might have lived too long by drawing up the responsibilities each umpire would have in a game where two officials were assigned, but

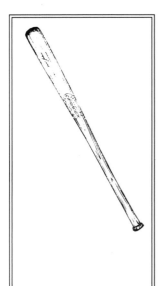

most games still had only one man in blue. Toward the end of the first decade of the 20th century, largely upon the lead of the American League, both major leagues began using two umpires in every game, thereby providing more protection as well as better coverage of the action. Three became the norm by the 1920s, and in the early 1950s fans began to grow accustomed to seeing four umpires on the field.

Why, then, did major league owners wait so long to begin using two umpires in each game? The obvious answer is to save money, but an equally important reason was that the owners of the stronger teams during the 1890s preferred the way games could be manipulated into victories with only one umpire officiating to improving the quality of their product. The players knew better. A players' rebellion when salary restrictions were imposed after the 1889 season ended in the players forming their own league, called fittingly the Players League. Among the innovations the players made in their loop was to schedule two umpires to work every game, one behind the bat and the other on the bases. Unfortunately, the lesson was lost on the owners after the Players League rebellion was suppressed and the mutineers returned to the fold.

Another innovation the players tried fared somewhat better. Realizing the 50-foot pitching distance was too short and gave hurlers too much advantage, the players experimented by moving the forward line of the pitcher's boxes in their parks a foot and a half farther away from the plate. But when that change seemed too little, there was a campaign to adjust the line again, putting it back another foot and a half. Given the direction the players were headed, had the Players League survived, by 1893, when the National League finally established the pitcher's plate at its present distance, the forward line in the players' loop would have been at 54½ feet, or only about six inches short of the point where a pitcher typically lets go of the ball now when he delivers it to the plate. Too, the players' way of going about the change, adding eighteen inches at a time, would have made the transition easier for most pitchers and probably would have saved a few careers.

THERE IS NO limit to the amount of time an umpiring crew can take to "decide a knotty problem." Long before the rulebook stated that the first requisite for an umpire is to get decisions right, arbiters recognized it as an unwritten principle of their profession. In a 1922 game involving the St. Louis Browns and the New York Yankees that had considerable bearing on the American League pennant race, an umpires' conference resulted in a decision change that bade play to continue after virtually everyone on the scene thought the contest was over. Trailing 2–1 with two out in the top of the ninth, the Browns had Chick Shorten on second base, Pat Collins at first, and Johnny Tobin at the plate. Tobin hit a routine grounder to Yankees first sacker Wally Pipp, who tossed to pitcher Sam Jones, racing over to cover. When Jones crossed the bag ahead of Tobin, base umpire Ollie Chill gave the out signal and the Yankees started to leave the field. Shorten rounded third base and kept running, however, as Browns manager Lee Fohl, coaching at first, began arguing with Chill that Jones had not had the ball in his possession but rather had been juggling it as he tagged the bag. Because his view was blocked by Jones, Chill missed seeing that the ball was not held securely, but when Fohl then appealed to plate umpire Brick Owens, Owens agreed that Tobin should have been ruled safe.

Before the dispute ran its course, Shorten crossed the plate and many of the 49,152 in attendance left the Polo Grounds, then the home the Yan-

9.05

...GENERAL INSTRUCTIONS TO UMPIRES...Do not allow criticism to keep you from studying out bad situations that may lead to protested games. Carry your rule book. It is better to consult the rules and hold up the game ten minutes to decide a knotty problem than to have a game thrown out on protest and replayed....

kees shared with the New York Giants. Most of the players meanwhile adjourned to their respective clubhouses. Finally, after a 20-minute delay, Chill reversed his call and both teams were ordered to return to the field and resume play. The Browns went on to win the game, 7–2, but nevertheless ended the season in second place, one game behind the Yankees.

THESE INSTRUCTIONS help explain why an umpire will refuse to confer with the other members of his crew even when every player, fan, and TV camera at the stadium is morally certain that he blew a critical judgment call. Their gist dissuades an umpire from consulting with his colleagues unless he is willing to admit he is not sure of his decision. An umpire who admits this too often is not long for his job.

In the bottom of the ninth inning of Game 6 of the 1985 World Series, just about no one in the country except first base umpire Don Denkinger believed Kansas City pinch hitter Jorge Orta beat the throw to first on his grounder. St. Louis manager Whitey Herzog begged Denkinger to get help, but Denkinger stuck to his guns, maintaining it was his play to call and he had gotten it right. Later Denkinger insisted St. Louis first baseman Jack Clark had pulled his foot off the bag, a miscue that eluded everyone else in the stadium as well as several dozen TV cameras. Many Mound City fans still think they were jobbed out of the 1985 World Championship by an umpire's bad call, but more impartial observers also remembered the pop foul Clark missed later in the inning that could have taken much of the onus off Denkinger if it had been caught.

In any event, Denkinger's handling of the situation was regarded by fellow umpires as exemplary, even if his decision may always cause him to be vilified in St. Louis.

NOTE THAT masculine pronouns still are used throughout Section 9.00 in every reference to an umpire or his duties. Although that has been the case ever since the first rule book was written, there has never been a time when female umpires have been expressly prohibited from serving in the major leagues. Although women arbiters have only recently begun to break the unwritten sex barrier in organized baseball, distaff umpires have been working for pay in all-male games for nearly a century. One of the earliest and best at her trade was Amanda Clement, who once held the woman's record of 275 feet for throwing a baseball.

A resident of Hudson, South Dakota, Clement played first base for the town team in the early 1900s

Anyone could be forgiven for believing this proper-looking, middle-aged woman was an educator. For that was Amanda Clement's profession when she posed for this photo. But in her younger days Clement had been the greatest distaff umpire of her time. David Nemec collection

and gained recognition not only for her playing prowess but also for her knowledge of the rules. Soon she began getting assignments to officiate local semipro games for pay. After Clement worked the South Dakota semipro championship clash without incident, invitations began coming her way from neighboring North Dakota. Before she retired from the game to become a physical education director at Wyoming University, Clement called balls and strikes for some six seasons in the Dakotas, Nebraska, Iowa, and Minnesota. Because slacks were taboo for women 90 years ago, Clement umpired in a long, full skirt, white blouse, dark tie, and peaked cap.

10

THE OFFICIAL SCORER

League presidents were first required by rule to appoint official scorers in 1957. Not until 1950 was it even stated in the rulebook that an official scorer was an accredited representative of the league although by then he had been long recognized as such.

For many years teams customarily awarded official scorers' jobs to favored sportswriters who could use the extra money the assignment paid. In the last century a club was not required to divulge the identity of its official scorer. It was felt that shrouding the position in secrecy would protect the scorer from players and fans who might otherwise assail his decisions. During the 1890s the Chicago White Stockings kept the name of their official scorer a mystery. Later it emerged that Elisa Green Williams, a friend of the White Stockings' owner Al Spalding, had been awarding hits and errors in all the team's home games. Williams would sit primly between two players' wives, seemingly no more than a fan, although she secretly was keeping careful score of every play. After each game her son would mail her scoresheets to the National League office, unaware of what the envelope contained.

G **IVEN THE** fact that their job was a sinecure and subject to the whims of the club that paid them, official scorers, particularly in the last century, were frequently accused of favoring home-team players in their rulings. Here is what one reporter had to say about Baltimore Orioles outfielder Willie Keeler's march to the National League batting crown in 1897:

> John Heydler, who is one of the best known baseball scribes in the business, says exception should be taken to this over generous scoring and that Keeler's figure of .432 will not agree with any private accounts. Frank Houseman of St. Louis also has objections to Baltimore scoring methods. He says: 'Down in Baltimore, one day, Keeler sent two flies to Lally (leftfielder Dan Lally of the St. Louis Cardinals), who muffed both of them. Then he hit to Hartman (Cards third baseman Fred Hartman) and the latter fumbled and then threw wild. Then Keeler made a good single. The next morning four hits appeared to Keeler's credit in the Baltimore papers. Talk about Cleveland stuffing Burkett's average, why, they are not in it with the oyster scribes of Baltimore.'

Keeler's batting average was reduced later to .424 when discrepancies were discovered in his hit and at bat totals. Yet to be done is a comparison of his home and road batting stats in 1897, which will help determine whether even his .424 mark was deserved or rather was padded in all likelihood by Baltimore's official scorer.

10.02

The official score report prescribed by the league president shall make provisions for entering the information listed below, in a form convenient for the compilation of permanent statistical records: (a) The following records for each batter and runner: (1) Number of times he batted, except that no time at bat shall be charged against a player when (i) He hits a sacrifice bunt or sacrifice fly (ii) He is awarded first base on four called balls (iii) He is hit by a pitched ball (iv) He is awarded first base because of interference or obstruction.

DURING THE National League's inaugural season of 1876 a batter was socked with a turn at bat every time he walked. Punished most by the rule was free pass leader Jim O'Rourke, who collected 20 walks and thus 20 extra times at bat. The rule was rescinded in 1877 but then resurrected ten years later in 1887. The upside in 1887, however, was that each walk was also scored as a hit. This bonus swelled batting averages to astronomical proportions. Tip O'Neill topped the American Association with a .492 mark and Cap Anson's .421 figure paced the National League.

In 1968 the Special Baseball Records Committee voted to treat a base on balls as neither a hit nor a time at bat and made their judgment retroactive to 1876. This ruling meant statisticians had to recalculate batting averages for both the 1876 and 1887 seasons after bases on balls were deducted from the at bat totals for each player. In the former year averages jumped, though not a lot because there were very few walks issued in the 1870s; Jim O'Rourke, who stood to gain the most, went from .312 to .362. But in the 1887 season averages were shaved in some cases as much as 60 or 70 points. Tip O'Neill's .492 mark, for one, dropped to .435.

Many baseball historians are still upset by the committee's 1968 ruling, believing that it affects the historical integrity of the game to act as if today's rules are better than those of the past. Dennis Bingham convincingly argues that what we want from the past, above all, is an accurate account of what happened, and that by allowing a "special committee" to change a scoring rule of the past, we have in a very real sense changed what occurred. Certainly in 1887 the entire baseball community accepted that O'Neill hit .492, and his mark remained the all-time single-season record for nearly 80 years.

One further point of interest: Had the 1887 rule been in effect in 1941, Ted Williams would have batted .540.

10.02 (N) †

The official score report shall make provisions for entering the time required to play the game, with delays for weather or light failure deducted.

THIS ITEM has always been included in major league box scores, but a century ago no one paid much attention to how long a game took to play and official scorers did not need to be precise. Most would round off the time of a game, usually to the nearest five minutes. A game that took an hour and eight minutes would thus be recorded as having lasted an hour and ten minutes. Few games, in any event, took longer than an hour and a half.

During the 1887 season when bases on balls were counted as hits and many players went up to the plate looking for walks, causing some games to drag on for over two hours, *Sporting Life* found the development so revolting that it predicted "the public will call a halt (to the new rule) by refusing to attend games." When club owners also began noticing that fans were leaving their parks in the seventh or eighth inning, they took quick heed. The new rule was scrapped after only a one-season trial, and the average time of a game again fell to well under two hours.

10.03 (A)

In compiling the official score report, the official scorer shall list each player's name and his fielding posi-

(continued)

THESE examples to many modern fans may seem more like something that would occur in a softball game than a baseball game, but they were chosen for good reason. Against Ernie Lombardi, who was slow as an ox and hit murderous top-spin ground balls and liners that could fell an elephant, teams often played their

(continued)

tion or positions in the order in which the player batted, or would have batted if the game ends before he gets to bat. NOTE: When a player does not exchange positions with another fielder but is merely placed in a different spot for a particular batter, do not list this as a new position. EXAMPLES: (1) Second baseman goes to the outfield to form a four-man outfield. (2) Third baseman moves to a position between shortstop and second baseman.

10.03 (B)

Any player who enters the game as a substitute batter or substitute runner, whether or not he continues in the game thereafter, shall be identified in the batting order by a special symbol which shall refer to a separate record of substitute batters and runners. . . .

middle infielders back on the outfield grass, creating four- and sometimes even five-man outfields. It was felt that even at that distance a ball Lombardi hit would get to a fielder so fast that there would still be time to retire the slew-footed slugger.

The shift devised in 1946 by Cleveland player-manager Lou Boudreau to combat Ted Williams of the Boston Red Sox packed three infielders on the right side of the diamond and left only third sacker Ken Keltner to the left of second base. However, Boudreau was not really the inventor of the "Williams Shift." A similar alignment had been used by managers as far back as 1922 against lefty pull-hitters Cy Williams of the Philadelphia Phillies and Ken Williams of the St. Louis Browns, both of whom thrived on the short right-field porches in their home parks.

Official scorers at games where the Lombardi alignment or the various Williams shifts were deployed took no cognizance of the defensive alterations in compiling their score reports.

BEFORE 1907 American League official scorers did not always credit players with a game played if they appeared only as pinch hitters, pinch runners, or defensive replacements. The National League continued not to require that these types of substitute appearances be reported until 1912. As a result, many players who got into games only fleetingly never saw their names in major league box scores and some even failed to be included in the early editions of the Macmillan *Baseball Encyclopedia*, before researchers confirmed their existence.

Mistakes and omissions in early-day box scores are still being unearthed. Not long ago baseball historian Dick Thompson established that Ivan Bigler, for many years believed to be a "phantom" player whose name appeared in a 1917 St. Louis Browns box score through a typographical error, actually participated in the game in question as a pinch runner.

THE RATIONALE for sticking a pitcher with a loss in a forfeited game that goes at least five innings if his team is trailing when the infraction occurs owes to the fact that in most instances a forfeit grows out of events that make the guilty team fairly certain it is going to lose the game anyway. Likewise, the pitcher on the team benefiting by the forfeit in some cases gets a gift win.

In rare cases a pitcher is deprived of a win that should have been his when his team is saddled with a forfeit loss at a juncture when it was leading in the game. Perhaps the most unjust example came in the last major league game played in Washington on September 30, 1971, when a crowd riot ended the game with two out in the top of the ninth and the Senators leading the New York Yankees, 7–5. Paul Lindblad was one out away from recording his eighth victory of the season. Instead he received no decision for his day's work, as did Yankees hurler Jack Aker, who was about to be tagged with his fifth defeat.

The stats for the 1971 season credit Yankees pitchers with only 81 of their team's 82 wins but balance because an asterisk makes it clear that one victory came by forfeit. In the last century official scorers and team statisticians were not always so careful, even though forfeits were much more common then. For many years, the stats for a number of teams during the 1880s and 1890s failed to balance in the Macmillan *Baseball Encyclopedia* partly because forfeit wins and losses were not taken into account. In addition pitchers in forfeited games were often erroneously credited with wins or losses that have since been deducted.

ALTHOUGH the RBI did not become an official statistic until 1920, many sportswriters kept track of RBIs on an informal basis prior to then. As far back as 1879, a Buffalo paper recorded RBIs in box scores of the Buffalo Bisons' National League games. In the mid-1880s Henry Chadwick, the father of baseball writers, urged the inclusion of the RBI feature in all box scores. Finally, by the early 1890s, Chadwick carried his point and National League official scorers grudgingly obeyed instructions to catalog RBIs. But most found it a burden and the practice was soon abandoned. In 1907 the *New York Press* revived the RBI, but it did not become an official statistic again until the Baseball Writers of America encouraged its adoption in 1920.

RBI figures for most of the pre-1920 seasons have since been reconstructed from box scores and game accounts, but several American Association seasons in the 1880s are still missing, as is the 1884 Union Association campaign.

DURING the 1980s an official scorer was also required to furnish his league's office with the name of the player who collected the game-winning RBI in each game. The experimental category lasted just nine seasons before it was given a quiet burial in 1989. At that it endured much longer and was much better received by the baseball public than several other experimental categories over the years. The most interesting one may have been an official scorer's nightmare that was labeled "Total Bases Run." This invention survived all of one season, the 1880 campaign. That year National League official scorers were made to include in their game reports the number of bases each player touched safely. The totals were then computed to determine the Total Bases Run champion for the season. Since the category had only a one-year life span, there was only one champion. The winner was Abner Dalrymple of the Chicago White Stockings with 501 bases safely touched.

AN OFFICIAL scorer on occasion is obliged to award a hit even when the defensive team does not make an ordinary effort to retire a batter. The most common situation occurs in a tie game with the home team at bat in the bottom of the ninth or an extra inning with a runner on third and less than two out. Often when a batter hits a long fly ball at this point that will inevitably allow the winning run to tag up and score, the defensive team will make no attempt to catch it. The official scorer customarily awards the batter a single in these cases.

Probably the most famous hit that an official scorer was forced to award owing to defensive indifference was on October 3, 1976, when two Kansas City Royals teammates third baseman George Brett, who is white, and designated hitter Hal McRae, who is black, went down to their final at bats of the season in a game against the Minnesota Twins virtually deadlocked in their battle for the American League batting crown.

In the top of the ninth Brett hit a fly ball that dropped in front of Twins left fielder Steve Brye and then bounced over Brye's head and rolled to the wall. Before Brye could chase down the ball and relay it home, Brett tallied an inside-the-park home run, enabling him to finish the season with a .333 batting average.

McRae then stepped to the plate also at .333, albeit a fraction of a point lower than Brett's mark. When he hit a ground ball that was obviously going to result in his being thrown out, McRae began shouting at Twins manager Gene Mauch as he ran toward first base. McRae's wrath swiftly brought Mauch out of the dugout, and the two confronted each other. A fight nearly ensued when McRae accused Mauch of ordering Brye to let Brett's fly ball drop safely, citing a racial motivation.

Mauch repeatedly denied that he had coaxed his players to steer the batting crown Brett's way if the chance arose, but Brett joined in McRae's grievance when he went on record with a statement that his fly ball definitely should have been caught. Brye meanwhile waffled, saying at first that he had just misjudged the ball but eventually acknowledging that most American League players preferred to see Brett rather than McRae win the batting crown if only because Brett was a full-time player while McRae served as no more than a designated hitter.

THIS SPECIAL note triggers the question if it applies with equal force when a no-hitter is in the making, especially in light of the commonly held belief that an official scorer is obliged to follow a rule that the first hit of a game should always be a clean one. Even though there has never been any such rule, there have been several occasions when an official scorer has gone far out of his way to rule a hit an error, sometimes even long after the fact, in order to preserve a no-hitter.

One of the most egregious instances came at St. Louis's Sportsman's Park on May 5, 1917, when Browns southpaw Ernie Koob won a 1–0 no-hitter over the Chicago White Sox. The official scorer, John Sheridan, was late that day getting to the park and so missed seeing Buck Weaver's hot shot in the first inning that eluded Browns second sacker Ernie Johnson. Many of the other writers at the game, both home and visiting, thought it was a hit. But when Sheridan arrived and had time to realize what was at stake, he took a poll of his fellow writers when the game ended and then elected to charge Johnson with an *ex post facto* error on the play.

10.05 (F)

...NOTE: In applying the above rules, always give the batter the benefit of the doubt. A safe course to follow is to score a hit when exceptionally good fielding of a ball fails to result in a putout.

10.08

A stolen base shall be credited to a runner whenever he advances one base unaided by a hit, a putout, an error, a force-out, a fielder's choice, a passed ball, a wild pitch or a balk. . . .

Sheridan's handling of the situation resulted in a pledge by both Chicago and St. Louis baseball writers to guard the game against any more such mercurial scorer's decisions in the future. The pledge was largely forgotten, however, by the following afternoon when Bob Groom of the Browns shut out the White Sox 3–0 and duplicated Koob's no-hit feat in the process to mark the only time in history that two pitchers on the same team have registered no-nos on successive days.

THIS INTRODUCTION explains why when Rickey Henderson stole 130 bases in 1982 to break the modern record, the "modern" qualifier was added. In 1886 official scorers were instructed to credit a runner with a stolen base for every extra base he advanced of his own volition. Beginning that year, any time a runner went from first to third on a single or advanced a base on a fly ball he earned a theft that was worth every bit as much as a steal he made on the pitcher. A runner was also credited then with a stolen base even if he ran beyond or overslid the bag he was trying for and was subsequently tagged out.

In 1887 two players in the National League and four in the American Association swiped over 100 bases, led by Hugh Nicol of the Cincinnati Red Stockings with 138, still the all-time record. There is no way now of determining how many of Nicol's steals fit the current definition, but it is probably significant that he averaged more than one a game and had more thefts than hits. In 125 contests Nicol collected just 102 hits and posted a .215 batting average, lending considerable weight to the theory that he garnered a lot of steals via the old standard since he had relatively few base-running opportunities.

In 1892 a proviso was added to the stolen base rule, spelling out that a theft would only be credited to a runner if there was either a possible chance or a palpable effort made to retire him. Eliminated were instances where a runner moved up a base on fly ball too deep for an outfielder even to make a throw or where a runner went from first to third on a hit into the gap while the batter loafed to a single. But there was still a lack of uniformity among official scorers. Some continued to bestow a stolen base whenever a runner hustled while others went by the letter of the rule. As a result, the 1892 proviso was dropped before the 1897 season.

Finally, in 1898 the modern stolen base rule was adopted, removing credit for any extra bases advanced on a batted ball.

BEFORE 1909 a runner earned a theft even if a teammate at the front or the back end of an attempted double or triple steal was nabbed.

10.08 (G)

No stolen base shall be scored when a runner advances solely because of the defensive team's indifference to his advance. Score as a fielder's choice.

10.09 (D)

Do not score a sacrifice bunt when, in the judgment of the scorer, the batter is bunting primarily for a base hit and not for the purpose of advancing a runner or runners. Charge the batter with a time at bat. . . .

UNTIL 1920 a runner could be awarded a stolen base when a defensive team was indifferent to his advance. One point must be made here: Failing to try to nail a runner attempting to steal is not automatically characterized as indifference. Former Baltimore Orioles catcher Gus Triandos, the only player with a perfect 1.000 steal percentage in over 1000 games, profited from this rule. Triandos's only career steal attempt in a 1958 game between Baltimore and the New York Yankees was successful when the Yankees were so surprised that no throw was made. But the official scorer ruled correctly that a theft should be awarded because the situation called for a throw.

HAVING TO judge whether a batter is trying to sacrifice or bunting for a base hit has been a problem for official scorers ever since 1893, when it first became a rule not to charge a player with a time at bat on a sacrifice bunt, although the rule was not universally applied until 1897. Because the note to Rule 10.09 (d) says the batter must be given the benefit of the doubt, many times an official scorer has no option but to award a sacrifice, even though the situation clearly calls for a batter to be hitting away.

In Game 38 of Joe DiMaggio's 56-game hitting streak, with the New York Yankees comfortably ahead, Tommy Henrich was reluctantly credited with a sacrifice when he bunted with one out in the bottom of the eighth and a runner on first to stay out of a potential double play so that DiMaggio, hitless on the day, would be assured of getting one more at bat. It paid off when DiMaggio laced a two-out double to keep his streak alive. Late in the 1961 season American League official scorers were similarly hamstrung as Jimmy Piersall bunted time after time when he came up with runners on even though they were reasonably certain that he was only sacrificing to avoid being charged with a time at bat so he could assure that his batting average would remain above .300. Piersall finished at .322, far and away a career high.

RULE 10.09 (E) has had a mercurial history. The 1908 season was the first in which a player was not assessed with a time at bat if he advanced a teammate at least one base with a fly ball. No distinction was made, though, between sacrifice flies and sacrifice bunts until 1920, when the RBI was made an official statistic and it became important to determine how many RBIs were the result of fly ball outs. In 1931 a decision was made to eliminate the sacrifice fly rule and charge a player with a time at bat. Batting averages dropped accordingly but stayed so high during the 1930s that the rule change was little noticed.

In 1939 the sacrifice fly was revived on an experimental basis but only in cases where a fly-out scored a runner. For reasons that are impossible to fathom now, the experiment was judged such a failure that it lasted only one season. In 1940 the sacrifice fly was again abolished and the rule remained dormant until 1954, when it was once more hauled out of mothballs and given another trial. Since then the rule has endured with only one significant change. In 1974 an addendum made it clear that a sacrifice fly should be scored if a batter hit a fly ball that brought home a run after it was caught by an infielder running into the outfield to chase a pop fly. Many official scorers had already been giving sacrifice flies in such cases, as well as on foul flies caught by infielders that allowed a runner to score.

10.09 (E)

Score a sacrifice fly when, before two are out, the batter hits a fly ball or a line drive handled by an outfielder or an infielder running in the outfield which (1) is caught, and a runner scores after the catch, or (2) is dropped, and a runner scores, if in the scorer's judgment the runner could have scored after the catch had the fly been caught. NOTE: Score a sacrifice fly in accordance with 10.09 (e) (2) even though another runner is forced out by reason of the batter becoming a runner.

FOR THE most part the rules for crediting fielders with putouts and assists have always been much the same as they are now, but there have been some notable differences. The 1878 season was the first in which an official scorer was authorized to credit an assist to a fielder if a batted or thrown ball bounced off him to another fielder who then made an assist or a putout. Until the late 1880s pitchers were generally given an assist every time they struck out a batter. Before 1931 a pitcher was also given an assist if a catcher snared a pitched ball in time to nail a runner trying to steal home. That same year the rule was first drafted to credit a putout to the fielder closest to the play when a runner is hit by a batted ball.

One of the scoring rules for 1877 mandated giving an assist to any fielder who made a play in time to put out a batter even if a subsequent error by another fielder prevented the out from being recorded. This rule was an ancestor of the current rule to the same purpose and allowed official scorers in the last century to credit assists to pitchers even on strikeouts that went awry. Interestingly, however, while the pitcher might get an assist on such a play, he would not always receive credit for a strikeout. The most remarkable example of this ironical rule in action occurred on July 7, 1884, in a Union Association fray between Boston and Chicago. In the box for Chicago that day, with everything working for him, was One Arm Daily. Daily not only shut down the Boston Unions 5–0 on just one hit, a three-bagger by Beantown catcher Ed Crane, but he fanned 19 batters to tie Charlie Sweeney's then-existing major league record, set only a month to the day earlier. In actuality, though, Daily should have had 20 strikeouts. One was lost to a third-strike passed ball by Chicago receiver Bill Krieg. The Union Association, in its lone year as a major league, refused to assign a pitcher a whiff unless the batter was retired. On another missed third strike in Daily's dream game, Krieg managed to toss out the batter at first in the nick of time. Krieg thus had 18 putouts on the day and one assist. Daily meanwhile notched 22 assists, all but two of them on strikeouts or, in one instance, a miscarried strikeout.

Since 1889 a third strike has been scored as a strikeout but not an assist in every league even if it results in a wild pitch or a passed ball that permits a batter to get to first base.

ALTHOUGH it has yet to happen on the major league level, a pitcher could conceivably toss a perfect game in which his team made an infinite number of errors. Rule 10.13 (a) explains how it can be done; every muffed foul fly that extends a batter's time at the plate is an error regardless of whether or not the batter subsequently reaches base.

THE **1904** season was the first in which an official scorer was licensed to charge a fielder with an error for failing to cover a base that he should have. Previously the error had always been given to the fielder who threw the ball—i.e., the catcher on a steal attempt —even when the throw would have been on target if a teammate had been where he was supposed to be.

MANY followers of the game are curious why there isn't a rule that charges a team with an error rather than an individual player—or in some cases no one at all—in situations where an error of omission or an error in judgment occurs, such as when two or more fielders allow a pop fly to drop untouched between them. For one year, and one year only, there

10.13 (A)

An error shall be charged against any fielder when he muffs a foul fly, to prolong the time at bat of a batter whether the batter subsequently reaches first base or is put out.

10.13 (E)

An error shall be charged against any fielder whose failure to stop, or try to stop, an accurately thrown ball permits a runner to advance, providing there was occasion for the throw. If such throw be made to second base, the scorer shall determine whether it was the duty of the second baseman or the shortstop to stop the ball, and an error shall be charged to the negligent player. . . .

was such a rule. In 1888 all batted balls that allowed a player to reach base safely but were neither hits nor errors that could be readily assigned to a fielder were deemed "unaccepted chances." In part because the new department could not conveniently be fit into box scores it was dumped after the 1888 season, but there is no reason it could not be resurrected. Every pitcher who has been charged with an earned run owing to a play that should have been made but could not be labeled an error will agree that the notion of an unaccepted chance makes perfect sense.

UNTIL 1912 pitchers' earned run averages were compiled only on an informal basis. That year the National League for the first time made the ERA an official statistic. The following season the American League hopped on the bandwagon. At that time an earned run was assessed to a pitcher every time a player scored by the aid of base hits, sacrifice hits, walks, hit batters, wild pitches, and balks before enough fielding chances had been offered a defensive team to record three outs. In 1917 stolen bases were added to the list of permissible aids to the scoring of an earned run.

Before the 1931 season, runners who reached base on catcher's interference were added to passed balls and the other types of errors that exempted a pitcher from being charged with an earned run. The 1931 rule reemphasized, however, that a run emanating from a batter who reached first on a wild-pitch third strike was earned even though the pitcher was charged with an error on the play because the wild pitch was solely the pitcher's fault. All other errors that allowed a batter to reach base or prolonged his turn at bat exempted the pitcher from being saddled with an earned run, including errors committed by him.

Pitchers' ERAs before the 1912 season in many

cases have been reconstructed, sometimes only after laboriously poring over old box scores and game accounts. In other cases a statistic that was computed over a century ago was taken as fact for the lack of any method to verify it. No one can really be sure now that Tim Keefe, by present scoring rules, really posted an all-time record low 0.86 ERA for the Troy Trojans in 1880. Certainly it seems hard to imagine that Keefe could have allowed only 10 earned runs in 105 innings and yet lost six of his twelve decisions, whereas Troy's other pitcher, Mickey Welch, won more than half his games despite a 2.54 ERA that was .17 runs above the National League average that season.

Even Dutch Leonard's 20th century record low 0.96 ERA in 1914 has been scaled downward from 1.01 in recent years as new information has come to light, revealing that Leonard hurled 224.2 innings that season rather than 222.2, the total with which he was credited for well over half a century. Indeed, the career and single season ERAs for virtually every pitcher active prior to 1920 have undergone some adjustments since the first Macmillan *Baseball Encyclopedia* appeared in 1968.

Incidentally, the career and single season ERAs for even some contemporary pitchers differ from one record book to another. Tommy John is a good example. The 1993 edition of the *Baseball Encyclopedia* lists him with 4708.1 career innings pitched and ERAs of 2.97 in 1979 and 2.64 in 1981. The 1993 edition of *Total Baseball* meanwhile credits John with 4710.1 career innings and ERAs of 2.96 in 1979 and 2.63 in 1981.

A mistake on some editor's part? Not at all. To simplify the math work, between the seasons of 1976 and 1982 major leagues statisticians were directed to round off the innings a pitcher worked to the nearest whole inning, only to revert in 1982 to the original rule that counted each third of an inning. *Total Baseball* incorporated all the thirds of an inning John had lost to the new ruling in his career and single season stats, whereas the *Baseball Encyclopedia* deducted a third of an inning from John's stats in six different seasons. The discrepancy has yet to be resolved. Even though John did indeed hurl 4710.1 career innings, major league officialdom still puts his total at 4708.1.

ONE OF THE more intriguing complexities of the formula for determining when to charge a relief pitcher with an earned run is that it makes it possible for a reliever to be assessed an earned run for a tally that is unearned in his team's totals. If, say, a reliever enters in an inning when all the runs his predecessor allowed are unearned because of errors and then promptly gives up a home run to the first batter he faces, the dinger is charged as an earned run to his account but an unearned run to the team's. Consequently, in many instances a team will have a season ERA that is lower than the aggregate season ERAs of its pitchers.

THE 1950 RULEBOOK was the first to formalize what previously had only been a custom not to award a starting pitcher a victory unless he worked at least five innings in all games that went six or more innings. Before then exceptions had occasionally been made, especially when a pitcher had to be removed after being injured.

In the last century, when teams often had only one standout pitcher, mainline hurlers were also commonly removed whenever they held a seemingly insurmountable lead. But removing a pitcher at that time meant having him swap positions with another player, who would then finish the game in the box. Sometimes a pitcher would be lifted long before the fifth inning and

---

10.18 (G)

When pitchers are changed during an inning, the relief pitcher shall not be charged with any run (earned or unearned) scored by a runner who was on base at the time he entered the game, nor for runs scored by any runner who reaches base on a fielder's choice which puts out a runner left on base by the preceding pitcher....

10.19 (A)

Credit the starting pitcher with a game won only if he has pitched at least five complete innings and his team not only is in the lead when he is replaced but remains in the lead the remainder of the game.

sent to first base or right field on the premise that he could always be brought back into the box if the complexion of the game changed. No thought was given then to denying a hurler a win in such cases. In reviewing old records, however, some researchers have taken it upon themselves to deduct victories whenever a starting pitcher made only a token appearance. As one example where this effort to rewrite history has been allowed to happen, Hoss Radbourn is listed now in several record books with only 59 wins in 1884 rather than 60, an all-time mark that for over a century went unchallenged.

UNTIL WELL into this century it was customary for an official scorer to stick a starting pitcher with a defeat when his team lost even if he left the game with his club ahead. Likewise, a pitcher sometimes would collar a win in a game that he left while his team was trailing. In 1912 Jeff Tesreau of the New York Giants got one such victory that seemed insignificant at the time but turned out to be of monumental importance. Tesreau was relieved by Rube Marquard in the top of the ninth inning of a game in which the Giants were trailing. When the Giants rallied in the bottom of the frame, the official scorer put a "W" beside Tesreau's name. Nowadays the win would go to Marquard, who was in the game when the winning run scored. Had Marquard garnered that extra victory, it would have enabled him to launch the 1912 season by winning his first 20 decisions. Instead he had to settle for 19 straight wins, tying the all-time single season record.

There is a strong temptation now among baseball historians to correct these apparent injustices. As a result, the career won and lost totals of many pitchers, including several Hall of Famers, have undergone a considerable reshuffling in the past two decades. It be-

---

10.19 (E)

Regardless of how many innings the first pitcher has pitched, he shall be charged with the loss of the game if he is replaced when his team is behind in the score, or falls behind because of runs charged to him after he is replaced, and his team thereafter fails either to tie the score or gain the lead.

comes almost a matter of personal taste whether Tom Hughes had 16 wins for the Boston Braves in 1915 (as per the 1993 *Baseball Encyclopedia*) or 20 wins (as per the 1982 edition). Hughes is by no means an extreme example. In any event, many decisions made by official scorers over a span of some 50 years have since been rescinded in an effort to bring a historical uniformity to all records.

10.19 (F)

No pitcher shall be credited with pitching a shutout unless he pitches the complete game, or unless he enters the game with none out before the opposing team has scored in the first inning, puts out the side without a run

(continued)

THIS RULE might almost have been individually tailored for Ernie Shore, owner of the greatest one-game relief stint in history. On June 23, 1917, in the first game of a doubleheader at Fenway Park, Shore relieved Red Sox starter Babe Ruth after Ruth was booted by home-plate umpire Brick Owens for arguing a ball four call to Washington Senators leadoff hitter Ray Morgan. Sox catcher Pinch Thomas was also tossed for objecting to the call. Thomas's replacement, Sam Ag-

(continued)

scoring and pitches all the rest of the game. When two or more pitchers combine to pitch a shutout a notation to that effect should be included in the league's official pitching records.

10.20

Credit a pitcher with a save when he meets all three of the following conditions: (1) He is the finishing pitcher in a game won by his club; and (2) He is not the winning pitcher; and (3) He qualifies under one of the following conditions: (a) He enters the game with a lead of no more than three runs and pitches for at least one inning; or (b) He enters the game, regardless of the count, with the potential tying run either on base, or at bat, or on deck (that is, the potential tying run is either already on base or is one of the first two batsmen he faces); or (c) He pitches effectively for at least three innings....

new, gunned down Morgan trying to steal second, and Shore then retired the next 26 batters in a row and received credit for both a shutout and a perfect game. The perfect-game honor is still the subject of controversy—many feel no pitcher can have a perfecto for hurling what, technically, is not even a complete game—but the shutout stands firm, according to the rulebook.

UNTIL 1969 the term "save" was not even an official part of the game's lexicon. That season major league rulemakers first paid formal acknowledgement to a facet of relief pitching that many publications, *The Sporting News* among them, had already long since recognized. But what *The Sporting News* deemed a save and what is now considered a save are not at all the same. In 1967, for example, *The Sporting News* named Minnie Rojas of the California Angels the American League "Fireman of the Year" for his 22 saves, whereas Ted Abernathy of the Chicago Cubs got the National League trophy for netting 26 saves.

Most record books now list Rojas with 27 saves in 1967 and Abernathy with 28. The reason for the disparity is because *The Sporting News* granted a save only when a reliever faced the tying or lead run during his mound stint or else began the final inning with no more than a two-run lead and then pitched a perfect inning. In contrast, both major leagues gave a save in 1969, the year the term got its official baptism, if a reliever merely entered the game with his team in front and held the lead for the remainder of the game. In other words, by *The Sporting News*'s definition, in 1967 a reliever who came into a game with his team ahead 4–1 and worked three perfect innings would not get a save, but the major league rule in 1969 gave a save to a reliever who worked just the final inning of a 10–0 blowout.

Over the years this sort of inequity has been eliminated. In 1973 the rule was amended to give a reliever a save if he either found the potential tying or winning run on base or at the plate during his stint or else worked at least three effective innings. Two years later the current save rule was adopted.

In determining saves after the fact for pitchers active before the concept was birthed researchers have applied the current rule. Hence Ed Walsh and Slim Sallee, the major league save leaders in 1912, achieved their 10 and six saves, respectively, in much the same fashion as Bobby Thigpen notched his record 57 saves in 1990.

BEFORE EACH major league had an official statistician, tabulation errors were often made that resulted in the wrong players being awarded batting titles, stolen base crowns, etc. The most flagrant error was perpetrated by an unidentified statistician, probably one from Philadelphia, in 1884. From the data furnished them at the close of that season, American Association officials eventually awarded the loop batting crown to Philadelphia A's first baseman Harry Stovey with a .404 average. Stovey's heady figure stood uncontested for a century until researchers in the 1980s made a close study of the 1884 AA season and discovered that his true mark was .326 and that the real winner of the 1884 AA bat crown was Dave Orr with a .354 average. A blunder so enormous seems as if it must have been deliberate, a calculated attempt to steer the honor to Stovey, one of the AA's most popular and most highly esteemed players. But several mistakes that occurred after 1884, though as far-reaching, were probably unintentional, resulting only from carelessness.

In 1901, at the close of the American League's inaugural season as a major league, Nap Lajoie was

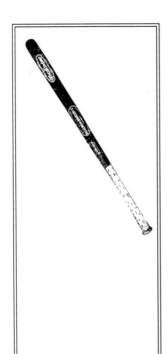

designated the fledgling loop's batting leader with a .422 average on 220 hits in 543 at bats. A statistician noticed in 1918 that 220 hits in 543 at bats produced only a .405 mark, and all the record books then reduced Lajoie's 1901 average to the lower figure. Following a story on Lajoie in *The Sporting News* in 1953, attention was again drawn to his 1901 season. The official American League records for that year had long since been destroyed, but baseball historian John Tattersall revealed that his check of the 1901 box scores had unearthed 229 hits for Lajoie in 543 at bats. Tattersall's research again restored Lajoie's average to .422, where it remained until another dig through the 1901 box scores in the 1980s confirmed that Lajoie had actually collected 232 hits in 544 at bats that year for a 20th-century record .426 average. Among the three newly discovered hits were a triple and a home run that also raised Lajoie's slugging percentage for 1901 to .643, a 13-point hike.

To the question whether it is safe now to assume that all serious discrepancies in batting, pitching, and fielding records have been eliminated, the answer still must be no. In fact, Nap Lajoie's .426 batting average in 1901 has yet to gain universal acceptance, and at least two other significant discrepancies that have been unearthed remain unchanged in record books sanctioned by the major leagues.

One is the 1910 American League batting race, for years food for violent controversy, which was seemingly resolved a few years ago when it was incontrovertibly established that Ty Cobb hit .383 rather than .385, giving the crown to Nap Lajoie with a .384 mark.

The problem stemmed from a Detroit box score that had inadvertently been included twice in the season-end calculations, a duplication that credited Cobb with three extra at bats and two unearned hits. However, major league officials continue to recognize Cobb as the 1910 American League batting leader, believing that history should not be rewritten. Many baseball analysts concur, though for a different reason. In a doubleheader on the last day of the 1910 season, to help Lajoie overtake the unpopular Cobb, St. Louis Browns manager Jack O'Connor ordered his rookie third baseman Red Corriden to play deep on Lajoie, enabling Lajoie to bunt down the third-base line at will and collect six "baby" hits in the twinbill. Cobb still won the bat title by a single point—or so it was then thought—but O'Connor and Browns coach Harry Howell were later banned from the majors for their role in the effort to deprive Cobb of his honor.

National League statisticians also have a long-standing cross to bear. In 1912 Chicago Cubs third baseman Heinie Zimmerman was awarded the Triple Crown when he seemingly paced the senior loop with a .372 batting average, 14 home runs, and 103 RBIs. It has since developed that Zimmerman had only 99 RBIs that year, leaving him three behind Honus Wagner, the true leader with 102. But the *Baseball Encyclopedia* continues to claim that Zimmerman had 103 RBIs in 1912, although other major reference books credit him with only two legs of the Triple Crown—batting average and home runs.

JUST ONCE in major league history has a player been denied a batting crown even though he met the minimum performance standards then in existence. In 1938 rookie Washington Senators outfielder Taffy Wright hit .350 in exactly 100 games. At the time a player had to appear in at least 100 games to be eligible for a batting title. But because Wright collected just 263 at bats, an exception was made and the crown went instead to Boston Red Sox first baseman Jimmie Foxx, who finished a point behind Wright at .349.

Because there was no at-bat minimum in 1938, Wright theoretically could have won the crown with just one at bat as long as he somehow got into 100 games. The 100-game minimum became the standard in 1920 and remained in effect until 1945, when a 400 at-bat minimum was introduced. For the next dozen seasons the rule for determining batting and slugging leaders fluctuated wildly, with a new twist being added almost yearly. In 1957 the major leagues at last adopted the current standard that a player must have 3.1 plate appearances per every game his team plays to qualify as a batting or slugging leader.

TAFFY WRIGHT was denied the American League batting title in 1938 because Jimmie Foxx finished right on his tail. If no other hitter had been within 30 points of Wright's .350 mark, in all likelihood he would have been the first rookie in American League history to wear a batting crown.

As evidence of this is the fact that several other batting leaders prior to 1957 who would not have qualified for their crowns under the current rules were allowed to reign largely because their averages stood alone at the head of the pack. Amazingly, there were no pretenders to the throne in the last century, although there was a brief campaign to award Pittsburgh outfielder Jake Stenzel the 1893 National League bat title with a .409 average in just 60 games. The push for Stenzel died out, especially when it emerged that he really hit only .362. Since 1901, however, both major leagues have crowned five batting champs with suspect credentials. The two American League winners who would not qualify now are Ty Cobb in 1914 and Dale Alexander in 1932. The three National League champs with fewer than 3.1 plate appearances per game their teams played are Bubbles Hargrave in 1926, Debs Garms in 1940,

(continued)

on balls, times hit by pitcher, sacrifice hits, sacrifice flies and times awarded first base because of interference or obstruction.

and Ernie Lombardi in 1942. Lombardi won with just 309 at bats, and Hargrave at 326 had only a few more. Both were catchers, accounting somewhat for the willingness to overlook their skimpy plate totals. Because of the harsh demands of the position, catchers have always been given special dispensation with respect to appearance requirements in determining league leaders, whether it be in a batting or a fielding category.

Since Lombardi's triumph in 1942, no catcher has won a major league batting title. But had the same 100-game-minimum rule that governed in 1942 still been in operation a dozen years later, the 1954 National League bat crown would have gone to Smokey Burgess, a backstopper with the Philadelphia Phillies. In 108 games and 345 at bats, Burgess swatted .368, 23 points better than Willie Mays, the recognized leader in 1954.

The 1954 season saw another batting-title first when a player who would have won his league's batting title under the current rule failed to qualify under the standard then in existence. On the surface, this seems an impossibility. How could a player accumulate 3.1 plate appearances for every game his team played and yet fail to get into enough games or have enough at bats to qualify as a leader? And yet, incredibly, it happened.

In 1952 a rule was passed that a player had to have 2.6 official at bats for every game his team played to win a hitting title. The rule was still on the books in 1954 when Ted Williams posted a .345 batting average, slugged at a .635 pace, and had a .516 on-base percentage after he collected 136 walks in just 117 games. But because Williams got so many free passes, he had just 386 at bats. His total was 20 short of the 406 he needed to give him 2.6 at bats for each of the 156 games the Red Sox played, and the crown went instead to Cleveland's Bobby Avila with a .341 batting average.

Officially, Ted Williams won six batting titles, exactly half the number that Ty Cobb collected. By present-day rules, however, Williams would have had seven hitting crowns and Cobb only ten. National Baseball Library & Archive, Cooperstown, N.Y.

Williams was awarded the slugging title, however, because his .635 mark was 100 points higher than runner-up Minnie Minoso.

When Williams's walks, sacrifice hits, and hit by pitches in 1954 are combined with his at bats, his total number of plate appearances is far in excess of the number needed in 1994, let alone in 1954 when the schedule was eight games shorter.

But although Williams must have felt an injustice had been done him, few members of the baseball public were aware of it at the time. By 1954 most fans were thoroughly befuddled as to what credentials a player needed to win a batting title. The confusion persisted until expansion lengthened the schedule to 162 games and made it imperative that a player accumulate at least 502 plate appearances to qualify as a leader. In 1959 many in Cleveland were baffled when Tito Francona of the Indians entered the last day of the season with the highest average in the American League and yet was said by the media to have no chance to win the batting title even though he was just a couple of at bats shy of 400. Only then did Tribe fans discover that at some point (back in 1957 to be exact) the rule had been changed from 400 at bats to 3.1 plate appearances for every scheduled game. Francona finished with 399 at bats and a .363 batting average, 10 points above winner Harvey Kuenn, but he needed some 30 more plate appearances to meet the minimum standard.

BEFORE 1951, to qualify as an ERA leader a pitcher needed only to hurl 10 complete games. Generally, any hurler who had 10 complete games also worked at least 154 innings, the number equaling the amount of games played up until expansion in 1961, but sometimes the ERA champ would be a real eye-opener.

In 1940, after being called up from the minors with less than eight weeks to go in the season, Tiny Bonham of the New York Yankees tossed 10 complete games in 12 starts and notched a 1.90 ERA, easily good enough to win the crown until someone pointed out he had pitched only 99.1 innings. A number of record books recognized Bonham anyway (and some still do), whereas others gave the honor to Bob Feller with a 2.63 ERA. The complete-game minimum of 10 was firm, however, before 1951. Just once was an exception made—in 1927 when New York Yankees rookie Wilcy Moore, working as a combination starter-reliever, posted a 2.28 ERA in 213 innings but had just six complete games in his 12 starts. The Moore case pointed up the most serious flaw in the old rule; a pure relief pitcher had no chance to win the award because, regardless of how many innings he pitched, he could never collect a sufficient number of complete games. Sure enough, in 1952, only the second season the new

---

10.23 (B)

The individual pitching champion shall be the pitcher with the lowest earned-run average, provided that he has pitched at least as many innings as the number of games scheduled for each club in his league that season. EXCEPTION: However, pitchers in National Association leagues shall qualify for the pitching championship by having the lowest earned-run average and having pitched at least as many innings as 80% of the number of games scheduled for each club in his league that season.

Many record books still refuse to recognize Wilcy Moore as the American League ERA champ in 1927 even though he had a 2.28 ERA in 213 innings. Because Moore collected only six complete games, four short of the minimum standard then, some consider the leader to have been Waite Hoyt with a 2.63 ERA. National Baseball Library & Archive, Cooperstown, N.Y.

rule was in effect, the National League ERA crown went to Hoyt Wilhelm with a 2.43 ERA in 159.1 innings and 71 games, all in relief.

Along with taking into account the increasing importance of relief pitching, the new rule in 1951 showed a certain prescience in another way when it made a minimum number of innings pitched the only requirement. Were 10 complete games still the standard, only about three pitchers in any given season would vie for the ERA crown nowadays.

CONSECUTIVE-GAME HIT-
TING STREAKS. A consecu-
tive-game hitting streak shall
not be terminated if all the
player's plate appearances
(one or more) result in a base
on balls, hit batsman, defensive interference or a sacrifice bunt. The streak shall
terminate if the player has a
sacrifice fly and no hit. The
player's individual consecutive-game hitting streak shall
be determined by the con-
secutive games in which the
player appears and is not determined by his club's
games.

CONSECUTIVE PLAYING
STREAK. A consecutive-
game playing streak shall be
extended if the player plays
one half-inning on defense,
or if he completes a time at
bat by reaching base or being
put out. A pinch-running

(continued)

RULE 10.24 (B) answers whether Joe DiMaggio's 56-game hitting streak in 1941 would have been terminated if he had been injured and unable to play in a game. The skein would simply have been put on hold and then resumed when DiMaggio returned to action regardless of how many games he missed. Some other significant hitting streaks have nearly gone unrecognized, though, when their perpetrators sat out games, but owing to public inattention rather than an interruption. In 1922 first baseman Ray Grimes of the Chicago Cubs set an all-time major league record when he collected at least one RBI in 17 consecutive games. No one was aware of it at the time, not even in Chicago, because the streak did not come in a continuous 17-game stretch. Actually, Grimes had to sit it out for nine days in the middle of his skein when his back acted up. But even if his feat had been accomplished in a single 17-game burst, it still might have gone unremarked until long after the fact. In 1922 the RBI had only been an official statistic for two seasons, and as yet few cared much about records anyway. When Pete Rose established a new record for career base hits in 1985, virtually the whole world was aware of it, but Ty Cobb's landmark 4000th hit in 1927 received so little publicity that even Cobb failed to realize what he had done until he read about it in the newspaper the following day.

THIS COULD almost be called "The Lou Gehrig Rule." In Gehrig's day there was no formal rule regarding the minimum amount of time a player had to appear in a game to extend a consecutive-game playing streak beyond that his name had to appear in the box score. The present rule was drawn up before the 1974 season in conjunction with legislation on what terminates a hitting streak.

One has to think that the rulemakers had

(continued)

appearance only shall not extend the streak. If a player is ejected from a game by an umpire before he can comply with the requirements of this rule, his streak shall continue.

Between 1925 and 1939 Lou Gehrig's presence broke the spirit of every first baseman in the New York Yankees' farm chain. Once the "Iron Horse" embarked on his record for consecutive games played, the only other Yankee to play more than ten games at the first sack during that 14-year span was Jack Saltzgaver with 18—most of them in late-inning relief of Gehrig. National Baseball Library & Archive, Cooperstown, N.Y.

Gehrig's shadow on their minds when they decreed that a single plate appearance, even in a pinch-hitting role, would not terminate a consecutive-games-played streak but a pinch-running appearance would. Obviously a pinch runner is often in a game longer than a pinch hitter, who may be around for only a single pitch. Gehrig, however, had a day in 1934 when his back hurt so much after an injury the previous afternoon that

it seemed his streak was at an end. But fortunately New York was on the road, allowing Yankees manager Joe McCarthy to find an ingenious way around Gehrig's temporary disability. On his lineup card that afternoon McCarthy penciled in Gehrig as the Yankees shortstop and leadoff hitter in place of Frank Crosetti.

The record books thus show Gehrig as having played one game at shortstop in 1934, making him one of the rare lefthanders to play a keystone position, even though he never actually served as a shortfielder. After opening the game with a single, Gehrig was removed for a pinch runner as soon as he touched first base. His streak was thereby preserved, never to be seriously jeopardized again until early in the 1939 season when he began showing advanced symptoms of the neuro-muscular disease that would soon claim his life.

OFFICIAL BASEBALL RULES

DIVISIONS OF THE CODE

1.00—Objectives of the Game, the Playing Field, Equipment.
2.00—Definition of Terms.
3.00—Game Preliminaries.
4.00—Starting and Ending the Game.
5.00—Putting the Ball in Play, Dead Ball and Live Ball (in Play).
6.00—The Batter.
7.00—The Runner.
8.00—The Pitcher.
9.00—The Umpire.
10.00—The Official Scorer.

RECODIFIED, AMENDED AND ADOPTED BY PROFESSIONAL BASEBALL OFFICIAL PLAYING RULES COMMITTEE AT NEW YORK CITY, DECEMBER 21, 1949; AMENDED AT NEW YORK CITY, FEBRUARY 5, 1951; TAMPA, FLA., MARCH 14, 1951; CHICAGO, ILL., MARCH 3, 1952; NEW YORK CITY, NOVEMBER 4, 1953; NEW YORK CITY, DECEMBER 8, 1954; CHICAGO, ILL., NOVEMBER 20, 1956; TAMPA, FLA., MARCH 30–31, 1961; TAMPA, FLA., NOVEMBER 26, 1961; NEW YORK CITY, JANUARY 26, 1963; SAN DIEGO, CALIF., DECEMBER 2, 1963; HOUSTON, TEX., DECEMBER 1, 1964; COLUMBUS, O., NOVEMBER 28, 1966; PITTSBURGH, PA., DECEMBER 1, 1966; MEXICO CITY, MEXICO, NOVEMBER 27, 1967; SAN FRANCISCO, CALIF., DECEMBER 3, 1968; NEW YORK CITY, JANUARY 31, 1969; FORT LAUDERDALE, FLA., DECEMBER 1, 1969; LOS ANGELES, CALIF., NOVEMBER 30, 1970; PHOENIX, ARIZ., NOVEMBER 29, 1971; ST. PETERSBURG, FLA., MARCH 23, 1972; HONOLULU, HAWAII, NOVEMBER 27, 1972; HOUSTON, TEX., DECEMBER 3 AND 7, 1973; NEW ORLEANS, LA., DECEMBER 8, 1975; HOLLYWOOD, FLA., DECEMBER 8, 1975; LOS ANGELES, CALIF., DECEMBER 6, 1976; HONOLULU, HAWAII, DECEMBER 5, 1977; ORLANDO, FLA., DECEMBER 4, 1978; TORONTO, ONTARIO, CANADA, DECEMBER 3, 1979; DALLAS, TEX., DECEMBER 8, 1980; HOLLYWOOD, FLA., DECEMBER 7, 1981; HONOLULU, HAWAII, DECEMBER 5, 1982; NASHVILLE, TN., DECEMBER 5, 1983; NEW YORK, N.Y., JANUARY 8, 1985; NEW YORK, N.Y., MARCH 27, 1986; HOLLYWOOD, FLA., DECEMBER 9, 1986; NEW YORK CITY, NOVEMBER 23, 1987; NEW YORK CITY, JANUARY 26, 1989; CHICAGO, ILL., DECEMBER 3, 1990; MIAMI, FLA., DECEMBER 5, 1991; LOUISVILLE, KY., DECEMBER 4, 1992.

Foreword

This code of rules is written to govern the playing of baseball games by professional teams of the American League of Professional Baseball Clubs, the National League of Professional Baseball Clubs, and the leagues which are members of the National Association of Professional Baseball Leagues.

We recognize that many amateur and non-professional organizations play their games under professional rules, and we are happy to make our rules available as widely as possible. It is well to remember that specifications as to fields, equipment, etc., may be modified to meet the needs of each group.

Money fines, long-term suspensions and similar penalties imposed by this code are not practicable for amateur groups, but officers and umpires of such organizations should insist on strict observance of all the rules governing the playing of the game.

Baseball not only has maintained its position as the National Game of the United States, but also has become an International Game being played in seventy-seven countries. Its popularity will grow only as long as its players, managers, coaches, umpires and administrative officers respect the discipline of its code of rules.

THE OFFICIAL PLAYING RULES COMMITTEE

William A. Murray—Chairman

Bill White	Tom Grieve	Joseph J. Buzas
John McHale	Pat Gillick	Jimmy Bragan
Bill Giles	Robert Brown, M.D.	George Sisler, Jr.

AMATEUR BASEBALL ADVISORY MEMBERS

Raoul Dedeaux   Ronald Tellefsen

OFFICIAL BASEBALL RULES

The Official Playing Rules Committee has adopted no changes for the 1993 season.

Important Note

The Official Playing Rules Committee at its December 1977 meeting, voted to incorporate the Notes-Case Book-Comments section directly into the Official Playing Rules at the appropriate places. Basically, the Case Book interprets or elaborates on the basic rules and in essence have the same effect as rules when applied to particular sections for which they are intended.

This arrangement is designed to give quicker access to any written language pertaining to an Official Rule and does not require a reader to refer to different sections of the Official Playing Rules book in considering the application of a particular rule.

Case Book material is printed in smaller type than the rule language.

1.00—OBJECTIVES OF THE GAME.

1.01 Baseball is a game between two teams of nine players each, under direction of a manager, played on an enclosed field in accordance with these rules, under jurisdiction of one or more umpires.

1.02 The objective of each team is to win by scoring more runs than the opponent.

1.03 The winner of the game shall be that team which shall have scored, in accordance with these rules, the greater number of runs at the conclusion of a regulation game.

1.04 THE PLAYING FIELD. The field shall be laid out according to the instructions below, supplemented by Diagrams No. 1, No. 2 and No. 3 on adjoining pages.

The infield shall be a 90-foot square. The outfield shall be the area between two foul lines formed by extending two sides of the square, as in Diagram 1. The distance from home base to the nearest fence, stand or other obstruction on fair territory shall be 250 feet or more. A distance of 320 feet or more along the foul lines, and 400 feet or more to center field is preferable. The infield shall be graded so that the base lines and home plate are level. The pitcher's plate shall be 10 inches above the level of home plate. The degree of slope from a point 6 inches in front of the pitcher's plate to a point 6 feet toward home plate shall be 1 inch to 1 foot, and such degree of slope shall be uniform. The infield and outfield, including the boundary lines, are fair territory and all other area is foul territory.

It is desirable that the line from home base through the pitcher's plate to second base shall run East-Northeast.

It is recommended that the distance from home base to the backstop, and from the base lines to the nearest fence, stand or other obstruction on foul territory shall be 60 feet or more. See Diagram 1.

When location of home base is determined, with a steel tape measure 127 feet, 3-3/8 inches in desired direction to establish second base. From home base, measure 90 feet toward first base; from second base, measure 90 feet toward first base; the intersection of these lines establishes first base. From home base, measure 90 feet toward third base; from second base, measure 90 feet toward third base; the intersection of these lines establishes third base. The distance between first base and third base is 127 feet, 3-3/8 inches. All measurements from home base shall be taken from the point where the first and third base lines intersect.

The catcher's box, the batters' boxes, the coaches' boxes, the three-foot first base lines and the next batter's boxes shall be laid out as shown in Diagrams 1 and 2.

The foul lines and all other playing lines indicated in the diagrams by solid black lines shall be marked with wet, unslaked lime, chalk or other white material.

The grass lines and dimensions shown on the diagrams are those used in many fields, but they are not mandatory and each club shall determine the size and shape of the grassed and bare areas of its playing field.

NOTE **(a)** Any Playing Field constructed by a professional club after June 1, 1958, shall provide a minimum distance of 325 feet from home base to the nearest fence, stand or other obstruction on the right and left field foul lines, and a minimum distance

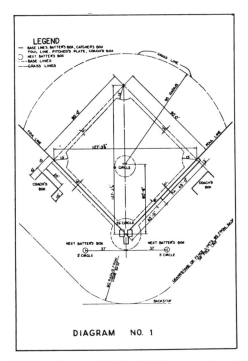

DIAGRAM NO. 1

than twenty-five feet from the base lines. They shall be roofed and shall be enclosed at the back and ends.

1.09 The ball shall be a sphere formed by yarn wound around a small core of cork, rubber or similar material, covered with two stripes of white horsehide or cowhide, tightly stitched together. It shall weigh not less than five nor more than 5-1/4 ounces avoirdupois and measure not less than nine nor more than 9-1/4 inches in circumference.

1.10 (a) The bat shall be a smooth, round stick not more than 2-3/4 inches in diameter at the thickest part and not more than 42 inches in length. The bat shall be one piece of solid wood.

NOTE: No laminated or experimental bats shall be used in a professional game (either championship season or exhibition games) until the manufacturer has secured approval from the Rules Committee of his design and methods of manufacture.

(b) Cupped Bats. An indentation in the end of the bat up to one inch in depth is permitted and may be no wider than two inches and no less than one inch in diameter. The indentation must be curved with no foreign substance added. **(c)** The bat handle, for not more than 18 inches from its end, may be covered or treated with any material or substance to improve the grip. Any such material or substance, which extends past the 18 inch limitation, shall cause the bat to be removed from the game.

NOTE: If the umpire discovers that the bat does not conform to (c) above until a time during or after which the bat has been used in play, it shall not be grounds for declaring the batter out, or ejected from the game.

of 400 feet to the center field fence. **(b)** No existing playing field shall be remodeled after June 1, 1958, in such manner as to reduce the distance from home base to the foul poles and to the center field fence below the minimum specified in paragraph **(a)** above.

1.05 Home base shall be marked by a five-sided slab of whitened rubber. It shall be a 17-inch square with two of the corners removed so that one edge is 17 inches long, two adjacent sides are 8-1/2 inches and the remaining two sides are 12 inches and set at an angle to make a point. It shall be set in the ground with the point at the intersection of the lines extending from home base to first base and to third base; with the 17-inch edge facing the pitcher's plate, and the two 12-inch edges coinciding with the first and third base lines. The top edges of home base shall be beveled and the base shall be fixed in the ground level with the ground surface. (See drawing D in Diagram 2.)

1.06 First, second and third bases shall be marked by white canvas bags, securely attached to the ground as indicated in Diagram 2. The first and third base bags shall be entirely within the infield. The second base bag shall be centered on second base. The bags shall be 15 inches square, not less than three nor more than five inches thick, and filled with soft material.

1.07 The pitcher's plate shall be a rectangular slab of whitened rubber, 24 inches by 6 inches. It shall be set in the ground as shown in Diagrams 1 and 2, so that the distance between the pitcher's plate and home base (the rear point of home plate) shall be 60 feet, 6 inches.

1.08 The home club shall furnish players' benches, one each for the home and visiting teams. Such benches shall not be less

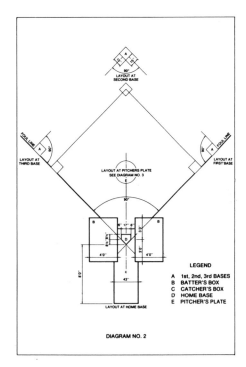

	LEGEND
A	1st, 2nd, 3rd BASES
B	BATTER'S BOX
C	CATCHER'S BOX
D	HOME BASE
E	PITCHER'S PLATE

DIAGRAM NO. 2

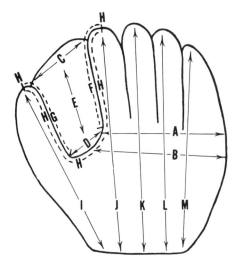

(A) Palm width—7¾''	**(H)** Crotch seam—13¾''
(B) Palm width—8''	**(I)** Thumb top to bottom edge—7¾''
(C) Top opening of web—4½'' (webbing not to be wider than 4½'' at any point)	**(J)** 1st finger top to bottom edge—12''
(D) Bottom opening of web—3½''	**(K)** 2nd finger top to bottom edge—11¾''
(E) Web top to bottom—5¾''	**(L)** 3rd finger top to bottom edge—10¾''
(F) 1st finger crotch seam—5½''	**(M)** 4th finger top to bottom edge—9''
(G) Thumb crotch seam—5½''	

(d) No colored bat may be used in a professional game unless approved by the Rules Committee.

1.11 (a) (1) All players on a team shall wear uniforms identical in color, trim and style, and all players' uniforms shall include minimal six-inch numbers on their backs. **(2)** Any part of an undershirt exposed to view shall be of a uniform solid color for all players on a team. Any player other than the pitcher may have numbers, letters, insignia attached to the sleeve of the undershirt. **(3)** No player whose uniform does not conform to that of his teammates shall be permitted to participate in a game. **(b)** A league may provide that **(1)** each team shall wear a distinctive uniform at all times, or **(2)** that each team shall have two sets of uniforms, white for home games and a different color for road games. **(c) (1)** Sleeve lengths may vary for individual players, but the sleeves of each individual player shall be approximately the same length. **(2)** No player shall wear ragged, frayed or slit sleeves. **(d)** No player shall attach to his uniform tape or other material of a different color from his uniform. **(e)** No part of the uniform shall include a pattern that imitates or suggests the shape of a baseball. **(f)** Glass buttons and polished metal shall not be used on a uniform. **(g)** No player shall attach anything to the heel or toe of his shoe other than the ordinary shoe plate or toe plate. Shoes with pointed spikes similar to golf or track shoes shall not be worn. **(h)** No part of the uniform shall include patches or designs relating to commercial advertisements. **(i)** A league may provide that the uniforms of its member teams include the names of its players on their backs. Any name other than the last name of the player must be approved by the League President. If adopted, all uniforms for a team must have the names of its players.

1.12 The catcher may wear a leather mitt not more than thirty-eight inches in circumference, nor more than fifteen and one-half inches from top to bottom. Such limits shall include all lacing and any leather band or facing attached to the outer edge of the mitt. The space between the thumb section and the finger section of the mitt shall not exceed six inches at the top of the mitt and four inches at the base of the thumb crotch. The web shall measure not more than seven inches across the top or more than six inches from its top to the base of the thumb crotch. The web may be either a lacing or lacing through leather tunnels, or a center piece of leather which may be an extension of the palm, connected to the mitt with lacing and constructed so that it will not exceed any of the above mentioned measurements.

1.13 The first baseman may wear a leather glove or mitt not more than twelve inches long from top to bottom and not more than eight inches wide across the palm, measured from the base of the thumb crotch to the outer edge of the mitt. The space between the thumb section and the finger section of the mitt shall not exceed four inches at the top of the mitt and three and one-half inches at the base of the thumb crotch. The mitt shall be constructed so that this space is permanently fixed and cannot be enlarged, extended, widened, or deepened by the use of any materials or process whatever. The web of the mitt shall measure not more than five inches from its top to the base of the thumb crotch. The web may be either a lacing, lacing through leather tunnels, or a center piece of leather which may be an extension of the palm connected to the mitt with lacing and constructed so that it will not exceed the above mentioned measurements. The webbing shall not be constructed of wound or wrapped lacing or deepened to make a net type of trap. The glove may be of any weight.

1.14 Each fielder, other than the first baseman or catcher, may use or wear a leather glove. The measurements covering size of glove shall be made by measuring front side or ball receiving side of glove. The tool or measuring tape shall be placed to contact the surface or feature of item being measured and follow all contours in the process. The glove shall not measure more than 12'' from the tip of any one of the 4 fingers, through the ball pocket to the bottom edge or heel of glove. The glove shall not measure more than 7-3/4'' wide, measured from the inside seam at base of first finger, along base of other fingers, to the outside edge of little finger edge of glove. The space or area between the thumb and first finger, called crotch, may be filled with leather webbing or back stop. The webbing may be constructed of two plies of standard leather to close the crotch area entirely, or it may be constructed of a series of tunnels made of leather, or a series of panels of leather, or of lacing leather thongs. The webbing may not be constructed of wound or wrapped lacing to make a net type of trap. When webbing is made to cover entire crotch area, the webbing can be constructed so as to be flexible. When constructed of a series of sections, they must be joined together. These sections may not be so constructed to allow depression to be developed by curvatures in the section sides. The webbing shall be made to control the size of the crotch opening. The crotch opening shall measure not more than 4-1/2'' at the top, not more than 5-3/4'' deep, and shall be 3-1/2'' wide at its bottom. The opening of

Suggested Layout of Pitching Mound

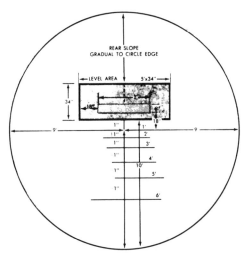

REAR SLOPE
GRADUAL TO CIRCLE EDGE

LEVEL AREA   5'x34''

34''

9'   9'

1''   1''
11''   2'
1''   3'
1''   4'
10'
1''   5'
1''
6'

The degree of slope from a point 6'' in front of the pitcher's plate to a point 6' toward home plate shall be 1'' to 1', and such degree of slope shall be uniform.

crotch shall not be more than 4-1/2'' at any point below its top. The webbing shall be secured at each side, and at top and bottom of crotch. The attachment to be made with leather lacing, these connections to be secured. If they stretch or become loose, they shall be adjusted to their proper condition. The glove can be of any weight.

1.15 (a) The pitcher's glove shall be uniform in color, including all stitching, lacing and webbing. The pitcher's glove may not be white or gray. **(b)** No pitcher shall attach to his glove any foreign material of a color different from the glove.

1.16 A Professional League shall adopt the following rule pertaining to the use of helmets: **(a)** All players shall use some type of protective helmet while at bat. **(b)** All players in National Association Leagues shall wear a double ear-flap helmet while at bat. **(c)** All players entering the Major Leagues commencing with the 1983 championship season and every succeeding season thereafter must wear a single ear-flap helmet (or at the player's option, a double ear-flap helmet), except those players who were in the Major League during the 1982 season, and who, as recorded in that season, objected to wearing a single ear-flap helmet. **(d)** All catchers shall wear a catcher's protective helmet, while fielding their position. **(e)** All bat/ball boys or girls shall wear a protective helmet while performing their duties.

If the umpire observes any violation of these rules, he shall direct the violation to be corrected. If the violation is not corrected within a reasonable time, in the umpire's judgment, the umpire shall eject the offender from the game, and disciplinary action, as appropriate, will be recommended.

1.17 Playing equipment including but not limited to the bases, pitcher's plate, baseball, bats, uniforms, catcher's mitts, first baseman's gloves, infielders and outfielders gloves and protective helmets, as detailed in the provisions of this rule, shall not contain any undue commercialization of the product. Designations by the manufacturer on any such equipment must be in good taste as to the size and content of the manufacturer's logo or the brand name of the item. The provisions of this Section 1.17 shall apply to professional leagues only.

NOTE: Manufacturers who plan innovative changes in baseball equipment for professional baseball leagues should submit same to the Official Playing Rules Committee prior to production.

2.00—DEFINITIONS OF TERMS.

(All definitions in Rule 2.00 are listed alphabetically.)

ADJUDGED is a judgment decision by the umpire.

An APPEAL is the act of a fielder in claiming violation of the rules by the offensive team.

A BALK is an illegal act by the pitcher with a runner or runners on base, entitling all runners to advance one base.

A BALL is a pitch which does not enter the strike zone in flight and is not struck at by the batter.

If the pitch touches the ground and bounces through the strike zone it is a "ball." If such a pitch touches the batter, he shall be awarded first base. If the batter swings at such a pitch after two strikes, the ball cannot be caught, for the purposes of Rule 6.05 **(c)** and 6.09 **(b)**. If the batter hits such a pitch, the ensuing action shall be the same as if he hit the ball in flight.

A BASE is one of four points which must be touched by a runner in order to score a run; more usually applied to the canvas bags and the rubber plate which mark the base points.

A BASE COACH is a team member in uniform who is stationed in the coach's box at first or third base to direct the batter and the runners.

A BASE ON BALLS is an award of first base granted to a batter who, during his time at bat, receives four pitches outside the strike zone.

A BATTER is an offensive player who takes his position in the batter's box.

BATTER-RUNNER is a term that identifies the offensive player who has just finished his time at bat until he is put out or until the play on which he became a runner ends.

The BATTER'S BOX is the area within which the batter shall stand during his time at bat.

The BATTERY is the pitcher and catcher.

BENCH OR DUGOUT is the seating facilities reserved for players, substitutes and other team members in uniform when they are not actively engaged on the playing field.

A BUNT is a batted ball not swung at, but intentionally met with the bat and tapped slowly within the infield.

A CALLED GAME is one in which, for any reason, the umpire-in-chief terminates play.

A CATCH is the act of a fielder in getting secure possession in his hand or glove of a ball in flight and firmly holding it; providing he does not use his cap, protector, pocket or any other part of his uniform in getting possession. It is not a catch, however, if simultaneously or immediately following his contact with the ball, he collides with a player or a wall, or if he falls down, and as a result of such collision or falling, drops the ball. It is not a catch if a fielder touches a fly ball which then hits a member of the offensive team or an umpire and then is caught by another defensive player. If the fielder has made the catch and drops the ball while in the act of making a throw following the catch, the ball shall be adjudged to have been caught. In establishing the validity of the catch, the fielder shall hold the ball long enough to prove that he has complete control of the ball and that his release of the ball is voluntary and intentional.

A catch is legal if the ball is finally held by any fielder, even though juggled, or held by another fielder before it touches the ground. Runners may leave their bases the instant the first fielder touches the ball. A fielder may reach over a fence, railing, rope or other line of demarcation to make a catch. He may jump on top of a railing, or canvas that may be in foul ground. No interference should be allowed when a fielder reaches over a fence, railing, rope or into a stand to catch a ball. He does so at his own risk.

If a fielder, attempting a catch at the edge of the dugout, is "held up" and kept from an apparent fall by a player or players of either team and the catch is made, it shall be allowed.

The CATCHER is the fielder who takes his position back of the home base.

The CATCHER'S BOX is that area within which the catcher shall stand until the pitcher delivers the ball.

THE CLUB is a person or group of persons responsible for assembling the team personnel, providing the playing field and required facilities, and representing the team in relations with the league.

A COACH is a team member in uniform appointed by the manager to perform such duties as the manager may designate, such as but not limited to acting as base coach.

A DEAD BALL is a ball out of play because of a legally created temporary suspension of play.

The DEFENSE (or DEFENSIVE) is the team, or any player of the team, in the field.

A DOUBLE-HEADER is two regularly scheduled or rescheduled games, played in immediate succession.

A DOUBLE PLAY is a play by the defense in which two offensive players are put out as a result of continuous action, providing there is no error between putouts. **(a)** A force double play is one in which both putouts are force plays. **(b)** A reverse force double play is one in which the first out is a force play and the second out is made on a runner for whom the force is removed by reason of the first out. Examples of reverse force plays: runner on first, one out; batter grounds to first baseman, who steps on first base (one out) and throws to second baseman or shortstop for the second out (a tag play).

Another example: bases loaded, none out; batter grounds to third baseman, who steps on third base (one out); then throws to catcher for the second out (tag play).

DUGOUT (See definition of BENCH)

A FAIR BALL is a batted ball that settles on fair ground between home and first base, or between home and third base, or that is on or over fair territory when bounding to the outfield past first or third base, or that touches first, second or third base, or that first falls on fair territory on or beyond first base or third base, or that, while on or over fair territory touches the person of an umpire or player, or that, while over fair territory, passes out of the playing field in flight.

A fair fly shall be judged according to the relative position of the ball and the foul line, including the foul pole, and not as to whether the fielder is on fair or foul territory at the time he touches the ball.

If a fly ball lands in the infield between home and first base, or home and third base, and then bounces to foul territory without touching a player or umpire and before passing first or third base, it is a foul ball; or if the ball settles on foul territory or is touched by a player on foul territory, it is a foul ball. If a fly ball lands on or beyond first or third base and then bounces to foul territory, it is a fair hit.

Clubs, increasingly, are erecting tall foul poles at the fence line with a wire netting extending along the side of the pole on fair territory above the fence to enable the umpires more accurately to judge fair and foul balls.

FAIR TERRITORY is that part of the playing field within, and including the first base and third base lines, from home base to the bottom of the playing field fence and perpendicularly upwards. All foul lines are in fair territory.

A FIELDER is any defensive player.

FIELDER'S CHOICE is the act of a fielder who handles a fair grounder and, instead of throwing to first base to put out the batter-runner, throws to another base in an attempt to put out a preceding runner. The term is also used by scorers **(a)** to account for the advance of the batter-runner who takes one or more extra bases when the fielder who handles his safe hit attempts to put out a preceding runner; **(b)** to account for the advance of a runner (other than by stolen base or error) while a fielder is attempting to put out another runner; and **(c)** to account for the advance of a runner made solely because of the defensive team's indifference (undefended steal).

A FLY BALL is a batted ball that goes high in the air in flight.

A FORCE PLAY is a play in which a runner legally loses his right to occupy a base by reason of the batter becoming a runner.

Confusion regarding this play is removed by remembering that frequently the "force" situation is removed during the play. Example: Man on first, one out, ball hit sharply to first baseman who touches the bag and batter-runner is out. The force is removed at that moment and runner advancing to second must be tagged. If there had been a runner on third or second, and either of these runners scored before the tag-out at second, the run counts. Had the first baseman thrown to second and the ball then had been returned to first, the play at second was a force out, making two outs, and the return throw to first ahead of the runner would have made three outs. In that case, no run would score.

Example: Not a force out. One out. Runner on first and third. Batter flies out. Two out. Runner on third tags up and scores. Runner on first tries to retouch before throw from fielder reaches first baseman, but does not get back in time and is out. Three outs. If, in umpire's judgment, the runner from third touched home before the ball was held at first base, the run counts.

A FORFEITED GAME is a game declared ended by the umpire-in-chief in favor of the offended team by the score of 9 to 0, for violation of the rules.

A FOUL BALL is a batted ball that settles on foul territory between home and first base, or between home and third base, or that bounds past first or third base on or over foul territory, or that first falls on foul territory beyond first or third base, or that, while on or over foul territory, touches the person of an umpire or player, or any object foreign to the natural ground.

A foul fly shall be judged according to the relative position of the ball and the foul line, including the foul pole, and not as to whether the infielder is on foul or fair territory at the time he touches the ball.

A batted ball not touched by a fielder, which hits the pitcher's rubber and rebounds into foul territory, between home and first, or between home and third base is a foul ball.

FOUL TERRITORY is that part of the playing field outside the first and third base lines extended to the fence and perpendicularly upwards.

A FOUL TIP is a batted ball that goes sharp and direct from the bat to the catcher's hands and is legally caught. It is not a foul tip unless caught and any foul tip that is caught is a strike, and the ball is in play. It is not a catch if it is a rebound, unless the ball has first touched the catcher's glove or hand.

A GROUND BALL is a batted ball that rolls or bounces close to the ground.

The HOME TEAM is the team on whose grounds the game is played, or if the game is played on neutral grounds, the home team shall be designated by mutual agreement.

ILLEGAL (or ILLEGALLY) is contrary to these rules.

An ILLEGAL PITCH is (1) a pitch delivered to the batter when the pitcher does not have his pivot foot in contact with the pitcher's plate; (2) a quick return pitch. An illegal pitch when runners are on base is a balk.

An INFIELDER is a fielder who occupies a position in the infield.

An INFIELD FLY is a fair fly ball (not including a line drive nor an attempted bunt) which can be caught by an infielder with ordinary effort, when first and second, or first, second and third bases are occupied, before two are out. The pitcher, catcher and any outfielder who stations himself in the infield on the play shall be considered infielders for the purpose of this rule.

When it seems apparent that a batted ball will be an Infield Fly, the umpire shall immediately declare "Infield Fly" for the benefit of the runners. If the ball is near the baselines, the umpire shall declare "Infield Fly, if Fair."

The ball is alive and runners may advance at the risk of the ball being caught, or retouch and advance after the ball is touched, the same as on any fly ball. If the hit becomes a foul ball, it is treated the same as any foul.

If a declared Infield Fly is allowed to fall untouched to the ground, and bounces foul before passing first or third base, it is a foul ball. If a declared Infield Fly falls untouched to the ground outside the baseline, and bounces fair before passing first or third base, it is an Infield Fly.

On the infield fly rule the umpire is to rule whether the ball could ordinarily have been handled by an infielder—not by some arbitrary limitation such as the grass, or the base lines. The umpire must rule also that a ball is an infield fly, even if handled by an outfielder, if, in the umpire's judgment, the ball could have been as easily handled by an infielder. The infield fly is in no sense to be considered an appeal play. The umpire's judgment must govern, and the decision should be made immediately.

When an infield fly rule is called, runners may advance at their own risk. If on an infield fly rule, the infielder intentionally drops a fair ball, the ball remains in play despite the provisions of Rule 6.05 (l). The infield fly rule takes precedence.

IN FLIGHT describes a batted, thrown, or pitched ball which has not yet touched the ground or some object other than a fielder.

IN JEOPARDY is a term indicating that the ball is in play and an offensive player may be put out.

An INNING is that portion of a game within which the teams alternate on offense and defense and in which there are three putouts for each team. Each team's time at bat is a half-inning.

INTERFERENCE (a) Offensive interference is an act by the team at bat which interferes with, obstructs, impedes, hinders or confuses any fielder attempting to make a play. If the umpire declares the batter, batter-runner, or a runner out for interference, all other runners shall return to the last base that was in the judgment of the umpire, legally touched at the time of the interference, unless otherwise provided by these rules.

In the event the batter-runner has not reached first base, all runners shall return to the base last occupied at the time of the pitch. (b) Defensive interference is an act by a fielder which hinders or prevents a batter from hitting a pitch. (c) Umpire's interference occurs (1) When an umpire hinders, impedes or prevents a catcher's throw attempting to prevent a stolen base, or (2) When a fair ball touches an umpire on fair territory before passing a fielder. (d) Spectator interference occurs when a spectator reaches out of the stands, or goes on the playing field, and touches a live ball.

On any interference the ball is dead.

THE LEAGUE is a group of clubs whose teams play each other in a pre-arranged schedule under these rules for the league championship.

THE LEAGUE PRESIDENT shall enforce the official rules, resolve any disputes involving the rules, and determine any protested games. The league president may fine or suspend any player, coach, manager or umpire for violation of these rules, at his discretion.

LEGAL (or LEGALLY) is in accordance with these rules.

A LIVE BALL is a ball which is in play.

A LINE DRIVE is a batted ball that goes sharp and direct from the bat to a fielder without touching the ground.

THE MANAGER is a person appointed by the club to be responsible for the team's actions on the field, and to represent the team in communications with the umpire and the opposing team. A player may be appointed manager. (a) The club shall designate the manager to the league president or the umpire-in-chief not less than thirty minutes before the scheduled starting time of the game. (b) The manager may advise the umpire that he has delegated specific duties prescribed by the rules to a player or coach, and any action of such designated representative shall be official. The manager shall always be responsible for his team's conduct, observance of the official rules, and deference to the umpires. (c) If a manager leaves the field, he shall designate a player or coach as his substitute, and such substitute manager shall have the duties, rights and responsibilities of the manager. If the manager fails or refuses to designate his substitute before leaving, the umpire-in-chief shall designate a team member as substitute manager.

OBSTRUCTION is the act of a fielder who, while not in possession of the ball and not in the act of fielding the ball, impedes the progress of any runner.

If a fielder is about to receive a thrown ball and if the ball is in flight directly toward and near enough to the fielder so he must occupy his position to receive the ball he may be considered "in the act of fielding a ball." It is entirely up to the judgment of the umpire as to whether a fielder is in the act of fielding a ball. After a fielder has made an attempt to field a ball and missed, he can no longer be in the "act of fielding" the ball. For example: an infielder dives at a ground ball and the ball passes him and he continues to lie on the ground and delays the progress of the runner, he very likely has obstructed the runner.

OFFENSE is the team, or any player of the team, at bat.

OFFICIAL SCORER. See Rule 10.00.

An OUT is one of the three required retirements of an offensive team during its time at bat.

An OUTFIELDER is a fielder who occupies a position in the outfield, which is the area of the playing field most distant from home base.

OVERSLIDE (or OVERSLIDING) is the act of an offensive player when his slide to a base, other than when advancing from home to first base, is with such momentum that he loses contact with the base.

A PENALTY is the application of these rules following an illegal act.

The PERSON of a player or an umpire is any part of his body, his clothing or his equipment.

A PITCH is a ball delivered to the batter by the pitcher.

All other deliveries of the ball by one player to another are thrown balls.

A PITCHER is the fielder designated to deliver the pitch to the batter.

The pitcher's PIVOT FOOT is that foot which is in contact with the pitcher's plate as he delivers the pitch.

"PLAY" is the umpire's order to start the game or to resume action following any dead ball.

A QUICK RETURN pitch is one made with obvious intent to catch a batter off balance. It is an illegal pitch.

REGULATION GAME. See Rules 4.10 and 4.11.

A RETOUCH is the act of a runner in returning to a base as legally required.

A RUN (or SCORE) is the score made by an offensive player who advances from batter to runner and touches first, second, third and home bases in that order.

A RUN-DOWN is the act of the defense in an attempt to put out a runner between bases.

A RUNNER is an offensive player who is advancing toward, or touching, or returning to any base.

"SAFE" is a declaration by the umpire that a runner is entitled to the base for which he was trying.

SET POSITION is one of the two legal pitching positions.

SQUEEZE PLAY is a term to designate a play when a team, with a runner on third base, attempts to score that runner by means of a bunt.

A STRIKE is a legal pitch when so called by the umpire, which— (a) Is struck at by the batter and is missed; (b) Is not struck at, if any part of the ball passes through any part of the strike zone; (c) Is fouled by the batter when he has less than two strikes; (d) Is bunted foul; (e) Touches the batter as he strikes at it; (f) Touches the batter in flight in the strike zone; or (g) Becomes a foul tip.

The STRIKE ZONE is that area over home plate the upper limit of which is a horizontal line at the midpoint between the top of the shoulders and the top of the uniform pants, and the lower level is a line at the top of the knees. The Strike Zone shall be determined from the batter's stance as the batter is prepared to swing at a pitched ball.

A SUSPENDED GAME is a called game which is to be completed at a later date.

A TAG is the action of a fielder in touching a base with his body while holding the ball securely and firmly in his hand or glove; or touching a runner with the ball, or with his hand or

Top of shoulders

Mid point

Top of pants

Strike Zone

Top of knees

glove holding the ball, while holding the ball securely and firmly in his hand or glove.

A THROW is the act of propelling the ball with the hand and arm to a given objective and is to be distinguished, always, from the pitch.

A TIE GAME is a regulation game which is called when each team has the same number of runs.

"TIME" is the announcement by an umpire of a legal interruption of play, during which the ball is dead.

TOUCH. To touch a player or umpire is to touch any part of his body, his clothing or his equipment.

A TRIPLE PLAY is a play by the defense in which three offensive players are put out as a result of continuous action, providing there is no error between putouts.

A WILD PITCH is one so high, so low, or so wide of the plate that it cannot be handled with ordinary effort by the catcher.

WIND-UP POSITION is one of the two legal pitching positions.

3.00—GAME PRELIMINARIES.

3.01 Before the game begins the umpire shall—**(a)** Require strict observance of all rules governing implements of play and equipment of players; **(b)** Be sure that all playing lines (heavy lines on Diagrams No. 1 and No. 2) are marked with lime, chalk or other white material easily distinguishable from the ground or grass; **(c)** Receive from the home club a supply of regulation baseballs, the number and make to be certified to the home club by the league president. Each ball shall be enclosed in a sealed package bearing the signature of the league president, and the seal shall not be broken until just prior to game time when the umpire shall open each package to inspect the ball and remove its gloss. The umpire shall be the sole judge of the fitness of the balls to be used in the game; **(d)** Be assured by the home club that at least one dozen regulation reserve balls are immediately available for use if required; **(e)** Have in his possession at least two alternate balls and shall require replenishment of such supply of alternate balls as needed throughout the game. Such alternate balls shall be put in play when—**(1)** A ball has been batted out of the playing field or into the spectator area; **(2)** A ball has become discolored or unfit for further use; **(3)** The pitcher requests such alternate ball.

The umpire shall not give an alternate ball to the pitcher until play has ended and the previously used ball is dead. After a thrown or batted ball goes out of the playing field, play shall not be resumed with an alternate ball until the runners have reached the bases to which they are entitled. After a home run is hit out of the playing grounds, the umpire shall not deliver a new ball to the pitcher or the catcher until the batter hitting the home run has crossed the plate.

3.02 No player shall intentionally discolor or damage the ball by rubbing it with soil, rosin, paraffin, licorice, sand-paper, emery-paper or other foreign substance.

PENALTY: The umpire shall demand the ball and remove the offender from the game. In case the umpire cannot locate the offender, and if the pitcher delivers such discolored or damaged ball to the batter, the pitcher shall be removed from the game at once and shall be suspended automatically for ten days.

3.03 A player, or players, may be substituted during a game

at any time the ball is dead. A substitute player shall bat in the replaced player's position in the team's batting order. A player once removed from a game shall not re-enter that game. If a substitute enters the game in place of a player-manager, the manager may thereafter go to the coaching lines at his discretion. When two or more substitute players of the defensive team enter the game at the same time, the manager shall, immediately before they take their positions as fielders, designate to the umpire-in-chief such players' positions in the team's batting order and the umpire-in-chief shall so notify the official scorer. If this information is not immediately given to the umpire-in-chief, he shall have authority to designate the substitutes' places in the batting order.

A pitcher may change to another position only once during the same inning; e.g. the pitcher will not be allowed to assume a position other than a pitcher more than once in the same inning.

Any player other than a pitcher substituted for an injured player shall be allowed five warm-up throws. (See Rule 8.03 for pitchers.)

3.04 A player whose name is on his team's batting order may not become a substitute runner for another member of his team.

This rule is intended to eliminate the practice of using so-called courtesy runners. No player in the game shall be permitted to act as a courtesy runner for a teammate. No player who has been in the game and has been taken out for a substitute shall return as a courtesy runner. Any player not in the lineup, if used as a runner, shall be considered as a substitute player.

3.05 (a) The pitcher named in the batting order handed the umpire-in-chief, as provided in Rules 4.01 **(a)** and 4.01 **(b)**, shall pitch to the first batter or any substitute batter until such batter is put out or reaches first base, unless the pitcher sustains injury or illness which, in the judgment of the umpire-in-chief, incapacitates him from pitching. **(b)** If the pitcher is replaced, the substitute pitcher shall pitch to the batter then at bat, or any substitute batter, until such batter is put out or reaches first base, or until the offensive team is put out, unless the substitute pitcher sustains injury or illness which, in the umpire-in-chief's judgment, incapacitates him for further play as a pitcher. **(c)** If an improper substitution is made for the pitcher, the umpire shall direct the proper pitcher to return to the game until the provisions of this rule are fulfilled. If the improper pitcher is permitted to pitch, any play that results is legal. The improper pitcher becomes the proper pitcher as soon as he makes his first pitch to the batter, or as soon as any runner is put out.

If a manager attempts to remove a pitcher in violation of Rule 3.05 (c) the umpire shall notify the manager of the offending club that it cannot be done. If, by chance, the umpire-in-chief has, through oversight, announced the incoming improper pitcher, he should still correct the situation before the improper pitcher pitches. Once the improper pitcher delivers a pitch he becomes proper pitcher.

3.06 The manager shall immediately notify the umpire-in-chief of any substitution and shall state to the umpire-in-chief the substitute's place in the batting order.

Players for whom substitutions have been made may remain with their team on the bench or may "warm-up" pitchers. If a manager substitutes another player for himself, he may continue to direct his team from the bench or the coach's box. Umpires should not permit players for whom substitutes have been made, and who are permitted to remain on the bench, to address any remarks to any opposing player or manager, or to the umpires.

3.07 The umpire-in-chief, after having been notified, shall immediately announce, or cause to be announced, each substitution.

3.08 (a) If no announcement of a substitution is made, the substitute shall be considered as having entered the game when—**(1)** If a pitcher, he takes his place on the pitcher's plate; **(2)** If a batter, he takes his place in the batter's box; **(3)** If a fielder, he reaches the position usually occupied by the fielder he has replaced, and play commences; **(4)** If a runner, he takes the place of the runner he has replaced. **(b)** Any play made by, or on, any of the above mentioned unannounced substitutes shall be legal.

3.09 Players in uniform shall not address or mingle with spectators, nor sit in the stands before, during, or after a game. No manager, coach or player shall address any spectator before or during a game. Players of opposing teams shall not fraternize at any time while in uniform.

3.10 (a) The manager of the home team shall be the sole judge as to whether a game shall be started because of unsuitable weather conditions or the unfit condition of the playing field, except for the second game of a doubleheader. EXCEPTION: Any league may permanently authorize its president to suspend the application of this rule as to that league during the closing weeks of its championship season in order to assure that the championship is decided each year on its merits. When the postponement of, and possible failure to play, a game in the final series of a championship season between any two teams might affect the final standing of any club in the league, the president, on appeal from any league club, may assume the authority granted the home team manager by this rule. **(b)** The umpire-in-chief of the first game shall be the sole judge as to whether the second game of a doubleheader shall not be started because of unsuitable weather conditions or the unfit condition of the playing field. **(c)** The umpire-in-chief shall be the sole judge as to whether and when play shall be suspended during a game because of unsuitable weather conditions or the unfit condition of the playing field; as to whether and when the play shall be resumed after such suspension; and as to whether and when a game shall be terminated after such suspension. He shall not call the game until at least thirty minutes after he has suspended play. He may continue the suspension as long as he believes there is any chance to resume play.

The umpire-in-chief shall at all times try to complete a game. His authority to resume play following one or more suspensions of as much as thirty minutes each shall be absolute and he shall terminate a game only when there appears to be no possibility of completing it.

3.11 Between games of a doubleheader, or whenever a game is suspended because of the unfitness of the playing field, the umpire-in-chief shall have control of ground-keepers and assistants for the purpose of making the playing field fit for play.

PENALTY: For violation, the umpire-in-chief may forfeit the game to the visiting team.

3.12 When the umpire suspends play he shall call "Time." At the umpire's call of "Play," the suspension is lifted and play resumes. Between the call of "Time" and the call of "Play" the ball is dead.

3.13 The manager of the home team shall present to the umpire-in-chief and the opposing manager any ground rules he thinks necessary covering the overflow of spectators upon the playing field, batted or thrown balls into such overflow, or any other contingencies. If these rules are acceptable to the opposing manager they shall be legal. If these rules are unacceptable to the opposing manager, the umpire-in-chief shall make and enforce any special ground rules he thinks are made necessary by ground conditions, which shall not conflict with the official playing rules.

3.14 Members of the offensive team shall carry all gloves and other equipment off the field and to the dugout while their team is at bat. No equipment shall be left lying on the field, either in fair or foul territory.

3.15 No person shall be allowed on the playing field during a game except players and coaches in uniform, managers, news photographers authorized by the home team, umpires, officers of the law in uniform and watchmen or other employees of the home club. In case of unintentional interference with play by any person herein authorized to be on the playing field (except members of the offensive team participating in the game, or a coach in the coach's box, or an umpire) the ball is alive and in play. If the interference is intentional, the ball shall be dead at the moment of the interference and the umpire shall impose such penalties as in his opinion will nullify the act of interference.

NOTE: See Rule 7.11 for individuals excepted above, also see Rule 7.08 (b).

The question of intentional or unintentional interference shall be decided on the basis of the person's action. For example: a bat boy, ball attendant, policeman, etc., who tries to avoid being touched by a thrown or batted ball but still is touched by the ball would be involved in unintentional interference. If, however, he kicks the ball or picks it up or pushes it, that is considered intentional interference, regardless of what his thought may have been.

PLAY: Batter hits ball to shortstop, who fields ball but throws wild past first baseman. The offensive coach at first base, to avoid being hit by the ball, falls to the ground and the first baseman on his way to retrieve the wild thrown ball, runs into the coach; the batter-runner finally ends up on third base. The question is asked whether the umpire should call interference on the part of the coach. This would be up to the judgment of the umpire and if the umpire felt that the coach did all he could to avoid interfering with the play, no interference need be called. If it appeared to the umpire that the coach was obviously just making it appear he was trying not to interfere, the umpire should rule interference.

3.16 When there is spectator interference with any thrown or batted ball, the ball shall be dead at the moment of interference and the umpire shall impose such penalties as in his opinion will nullify the act of interference.

APPROVED RULING: If spectator interference clearly prevents a fielder from catching a fly ball, the umpire shall declare the batter out.

There is a difference between a ball which has been thrown or batted into the stands, touching a spectator thereby being out of play even though it rebounds onto the field and a spectator going onto the field or reaching over, under or through a barrier and touching a ball in play or touching or otherwise interfering with a player. In the latter case it is clearly intentional and shall be dealt with as intentional interference as in Rule 3.15. Batter and runners shall be placed where in the umpire's judgment they would have been had the interference not occurred.

No interference shall be allowed when a fielder reaches over a fence, railing, rope or into a stand to catch a ball. He does so at his own risk. However, should a spectator reach out on the playing field side of such fence, railing or rope, and plainly prevent the fielder from catching the ball, then the batsman should be called out for the spectator's interference.

Example: Runner on third base, one out and a batter hits a fly ball deep to the outfield (fair or foul). Spectator clearly interferes with the outfielder attempting to catch the fly ball. Umpire calls the batter out for spectator interference. Ball is dead at the time of the call. Umpire decides that because of the distance the ball was hit, the runner on third base would have scored after the catch if the fielder had caught the ball which was interfered with, therefore, the runner is permitted to score. This might not be the case if such fly ball was interfered with a short distance from home plate.

3.17 Players and substitutes of both teams shall confine themselves to their team's benches unless actually participating in the play or preparing to enter the game, or coaching at first or third base. No one except players, substitutes, managers, coaches, trainers and bat boys shall occupy a bench during a game.

PENALTY: For violation the umpire may, after warning, remove the offender from the field.

Players on the disabled list are permitted to participate in pregame activity and sit on the bench during a game but may not take part in any activity during the game such as warming up a pitcher, bench-jockeying, etc. Disabled players are not allowed to enter the playing surface at any time or for any purpose during the game.

3.18 The home team shall provide police protection sufficient to preserve order. If a person, or persons, enter the playing field during a game and interfere in any way with the play, the visiting team may refuse to play until the field is cleared.

PENALTY: If the field is not cleared in a reasonable length of time, which shall in no case be less than fifteen minutes after the visiting team's refusal to play, the umpire may forfeit the game to the visiting team.

4.00—STARTING AND ENDING A GAME.

4.01 Unless the home club shall have given previous notice that the game has been postponed or will be delayed in starting, the umpire, or umpires, shall enter the playing field five minutes before the hour set for the game to begin and proceed directly to home base where they shall be met by the managers of the opposing teams.

In sequence—**(a)** First, the home manager shall give his batting order to the umpire-in-chief, in duplicate. **(b)** Next, the visiting manager shall give his batting order to the umpire-in-chief, in duplicate. **(c)** The umpire-in-chief shall make certain that the original and copies of the respective batting orders are identical, and then tender a copy of each batting order to the opposing manager. The copy retained by the umpire shall be the official batting order. The tender of the batting order by the umpire shall establish the batting orders. Thereafter, no substitutions shall be made by

either manager, except as provided in the rules. **(d)** As soon as the home team's batting order is handed to the umpire-in-chief the umpires are in charge of the playing field and from that moment they shall have sole authority to determine when a game shall be called, suspended or resumed on account of weather or the condition of the playing field.

Obvious errors in the batting order, which are noticed by the umpire-in-chief before he calls "Play" for the start of the game, should be called to the attention of the manager or captain of the team in error, so the correction can be made before the game starts. For example, if a manager has inadvertently listed only eight men in the batting order, or has listed two players with the same last name but without an identifying initial and the errors are noticed by the umpire before he calls "play," he shall cause such error or errors to be corrected before he calls "play" to start the game. Teams should not be "trapped" later by some mistake that obviously was inadvertent and which can be corrected before the game starts.

4.02 The players of the home team shall take their defensive positions, the first batter of the visiting team shall take his position in the batter's box, the umpire shall call "Play" and the game shall start.

4.03 When the ball is put in play at the start of, or during a game, all fielders other than the catcher shall be on fair territory. **(a)** The catcher shall station himself directly back of the plate. He may leave his position at any time to catch a pitch or make a play except that when the batter is being given an intentional base on balls, the catcher must stand with both feet within the lines of the catcher's box until the ball leaves the pitcher's hand.

PENALTY: Balk.

(b) The pitcher, while in the act of delivering the ball to the batter, shall take his legal position; **(c)** Except the pitcher and the catcher, any fielder may station himself anywhere in fair territory; **(d)** Except the batter, or a runner attempting to score, no offensive player shall cross the catcher's lines when the ball is in play.

4.04 The batting order shall be followed throughout the game unless a player is substituted for another. In that case the substitute shall take the place of the replaced player in the batting order.

4.05 (a) The offensive team shall station two base coaches on the field during its term at bat, one near first base and one near third base. **(b)** Base coaches shall be limited to two in number and shall **(1)** be in team uniform, and **(2)** remain within the coach's box at all times.

PENALTY: The offending base coach shall be removed from the game, and shall leave the playing field.

It has been common practice for many years for some coaches to put one foot outside the coach's box or stand astride or otherwise be slightly outside the coaching box lines. The coach shall not be considered out of the box unless the opposing manager complains, and then, the umpire shall strictly enforce the rule and require all coaches (on both teams) to remain in the coach's box at all times.

It is also common practice for a coach who has a play at his base to leave the coach's box to signal the player to slide, advance or return to a base. This may be allowed if the coach does not interfere with the play in any manner.

4.06 (a) No manager, player, substitute, coach, trainer or batboy shall at any time, whether from the bench, the coach's box or on the playing field, or elsewhere—**(1)** Incite, or try to incite, by word or sign a demonstration by spectators; **(2)** Use language which will in any manner refer to or reflect upon opposing players, an umpire, or any spectator; **(3)** Call "Time," or employ any other word or phrase or commit any act while the ball is alive and in play for the obvious purpose of trying to make the pitcher commit a balk. **(4)** Make intentional contact with the umpire in any manner. **(b)** No fielder shall take a position in the batter's line of vision, and with deliberate unsportsmanlike intent, act in a manner to distract the batter.

PENALTY: The offender shall be removed from the game and shall leave the playing field, and, if a balk is made, it shall be nullified.

4.07 When a manager, player, coach or trainer is ejected from a game, he shall leave the field immediately and take no further part in that game. He shall remain in the club house or change to street clothes and either leave the park or take a seat in the grandstand well removed from the vicinity of his team's bench or bullpen.

If a manager, coach or player is under suspension he may not be in the dugout or press box during the course of a game.

4.08 When the occupants of a player's bench show violent disapproval of an umpire's decision, the umpire shall first give warning that such disapproval shall cease. If such action continues—

PENALTY: The umpire shall order the offenders from the bench to the club house. If he is unable to detect the offender, or offenders, he may clear the bench of all substitute players. The manager of the offending team shall have the privilege of recalling to the playing field only those players needed for substitution in the game.

4.09 HOW A TEAM SCORES. **(a)** One run shall be scored each time a runner legally advances to and touches first, second, third and home base before three men are put out to end the inning. EXCEPTION: A run is not scored if the runner advances to home base during a play in which the third out is made **(1)** by the batter-runner before he touches first base; **(2)** by any runner being forced out; or **(3)** by a preceding runner who is declared out because he failed to touch one of the bases. **(b)** When the winning run is scored in the last half-inning of a regulation game, or in the last half of an extra inning, as the result of a base on balls, hit batter or any other play with the bases full which forces the runner on third to advance, the umpire shall not declare the game ended until the runner forced to advance from third has touched home base and the batter-runner has touched first base.

An exception will be if fans rush onto the field and physically prevent the runner from touching home plate or the batter from touching first base. In such cases, the umpires shall award the runner the base because of the obstruction by the fans.

PENALTY: If the runner on third refuses to advance to and touch home base in a reasonable time, the umpire shall disallow the run, call out the offending player and order the game resumed. If, with two out, the batter-runner refuses to advance to and touch first base, the umpire shall disallow the run, call out the offending player, and order the game resumed. If, before two are out, the batter-runner refuses to advance to and touch first base, the run shall count, but the offending player shall be called out.

Approved Ruling: No run shall score during a play in which the third out is made by the batter-runner before he touches first base. Example: One out, Jones on second, Smith on first. The batter, Brown, hits safely. Jones scores. Smith is out on the throw to the plate. Two outs. But Brown missed first base. The ball is thrown to first, an appeal is made, and Brown is out. Three outs. Since Jones crossed the plate during a play in which the third out was made by the batter-runner before he touched first base, Jones' run does not count.

Approved Ruling: Following runners are not affected by an act of a preceding runner unless two are out.

Example: One out, Jones on second, Smith on first, and batter, Brown, hits home run inside the park. Jones fails to touch third on his way to the plate. Smith and Brown score. The defense holds the ball on third, appeals to umpire, and Jones is out. Smith's and Brown's runs count.

Approved Ruling: Two out, Jones on second, Smith on first and batter, Brown, hits home run inside the park. All three runs cross the plate. But Jones missed third base, and on appeal is declared out. Three outs. Smith's and Brown's runs are voided. No score on the play.

Approved Ruling: One out, Jones on third, Smith on second. Batter Brown flies out to center. Two out. Jones scores after catch and Smith scores on bad throw to plate. But Jones, on appeal, is adjudged to have left third before the catch and is out. Three outs. No runs.

Approved Ruling: Two out, bases full, batter hits home run over fence. Batter, on appeal, is declared out for missing first base. Three outs. No run counts.

Here is a general statement that covers:

When a runner misses a base and a fielder holds the ball on a missed base, or on the base originally occupied by the runner if a fly ball is caught, and appeals for the umpire's decision, the runner is out when the umpire sustains the appeal; all runners may score if possible, except that with two out the runner is out at the moment he misses the bag, if an appeal is sustained as applied to the following runners.

Approved Ruling: One out, Jones on third, Smith on first, and Brown flies out to right field. Two outs. Jones tags up and scores after the catch. Smith attempted to return to first but the right fielder's throw beat him to the base. Three outs. But Jones scored before the throw to catch Smith reached first base, hence Jones' run counts. It was not a force play.

4.10 (a) A regulation game consists of nine innings, unless extended because of a tie score, or shortened **(1)** because the home team needs none of its half of the ninth inning or only a fraction of it, or **(2)** because the umpire calls the game. EXCEPTION: National Association leagues may adopt a rule providing that one or both games of a doubleheader shall be seven innings in length. In such games, any of these rules applying to the ninth inning shall apply to the seventh inning. **(b)** If the score is tied after nine completed innings play shall continue until **(1)** the visiting team has scored more total runs than the home team at the end of a completed inning, or **(2)** the home team scores the winning run in an uncompleted inning. **(c)** If a game is called, it is a regulation game: **(1)** If five innings have been completed; **(2)** If the home team has scored more runs in four or four and a fraction half-innings than the visiting team has scored in five completed half-innings; **(3)** If the home team scores one or more runs in its half of the fifth inning to tie the score. **(d)** If each team has the same number of runs when the game ends, the umpire shall declare it a "Tie Game." **(e)** If a game is called before it has become a regulation game, the umpire shall declare it "No Game." **(f)** Rain checks will not be honored for any regulation or suspended game which has progressed to or beyond a point of play described in 4.10(c).

4.11 The score of a regulation game is the total number of runs scored by each team at the moment the game ends. **(a)** The game ends when the visiting team completes its half of the ninth inning if the home team is ahead. **(b)** The game ends when the ninth inning is completed, if the visiting team is ahead. **(c)** If the home team scores the winning run in its half of the ninth inning (or its half of an extra inning after a tie), the game ends immediately when the winning run is scored. EXCEPTION: If the last batter in a game hits a home run out of the playing field, the batter-runner and all runners on base are permitted to score, in accordance with the base-running rules, and the game ends when the batter-runner touches home plate.

APPROVED RULING: The batter hits a home run out of the playing field to win the game in the last half of the ninth or an extra inning, but is called out for passing a preceding runner. The game ends immediately when the winning run is scored.

(d) A called game ends at the moment the umpire terminates play. EXCEPTION: If the game is called while an inning is in progress and before it is completed, the game becomes a SUSPENDED game in each of the following situations: **(1)** The visiting team has scored one or more runs to tie the score and the home team has not scored; **(2)** The visiting team has scored one or more runs to take the lead and the home team has not tied the score or retaken the lead.

National Association Leagues may also adopt the following rules for suspended games in addition to 4.11 **(d)** **(1)** & **(2)** above. (If adopted by a National Association League, Rule 4.10 (c) (d) & (e) would not apply to their games.): **(3)** The game has not become a regulation game (4-1/2 innings with the home team ahead, or 5 innings with the visiting club ahead or tied). **(4)** Any regulation game tied at the point play is stopped because of weather, curfew or other reason. **(5)** If a game is suspended before it becomes a regulation game, and is continued prior to another regularly scheduled game, the regularly scheduled game will be limited to seven innings. **(6)** If a game is suspended after it is a regulation game, and is continued prior to another regularly scheduled game, the regularly scheduled game will be a nine inning game.

EXCEPTION: The above sections **(3)**, **(4)**, **(5)** & **(6)** will not apply to the last scheduled game between the two teams during the championship season, or League Playoffs.

Any suspended game not completed prior to the last scheduled game between the two teams during the championship season, will become a called game.

4.12 SUSPENDED GAMES. **(a)** A league shall adopt the following rules providing for completion at a future date of games terminated for any of the following reasons: **(1)** A curfew imposed by law; **(2)** A time limit permissible under league rules; **(3)** Light failure or malfunction of a mechanical field device under control of the home club. (Mechanical field device shall include automatic tarpaulin or water removal equipment). **(4)** Darkness, when a law prevents the lights from being turned on. **(5)** Weather, if the game is called while an inning is in progress and before it is completed, and one of the following situations prevails: **(i)** The visiting team has scored one or more runs to tie the score, and the home team has not scored. **(ii)** The visiting team has scored one or more runs to take the lead, and the home team has not tied the score or retaken the lead. **(b)** Such games shall be known as suspended games. No game called because of a curfew, weather, or a time limit shall be a suspended game unless it has progressed far enough to have been a regulation game under the provisions of Rule 4.10. A game called under the provisions of 4.12**(a)**, **(3)** or **(4)** shall be a suspended game at any time after it starts.

NOTE: Weather and similar conditions—4.12 **(a)** (1 through 5)—shall take precedence in determining whether a called game shall be a suspended game. A game can only be considered a suspended game if stopped for any of the five **(5)** reasons specified in Section **(a)**. Any regulation game called due to weather with the score tied (unless situation outlined in 4.12 **(a)** **(5)** **(i)** prevails) is a tie game and must be replayed in its entirety. **(c)** A suspended game shall be resumed and completed as follows:

(1) Immediately preceding the next scheduled single game between the two clubs on the same grounds; or **(2)** Immediately preceding the next scheduled doubleheader between the two clubs on the same grounds, if no single game remains on the schedule; or **(3)** If suspended on the last scheduled date between the two clubs in that city, transferred and played on the grounds of the opposing club, if possible; **(i)** Immediately preceding the next scheduled single game, or **(ii)** Immediately preceding the next scheduled doubleheader, if no single game remains on the schedule. **(4)** If a suspended game has not been resumed and completed on the last date scheduled for the two clubs, it shall be a called game. **(d)** A suspended game shall be resumed at the exact point of suspension of the original game. The completion of a suspended game is a continuation of the original game. The lineup and batting order of both teams shall be exactly the same as the lineup and batting order at the moment of suspension, subject to the rules governing substitution. Any player may be replaced by a player who had not been in the game prior to the suspension. No player removed before the suspension may be returned to the lineup.

A player who was not with the club when the game was suspended may be used as a substitute, even if he has taken the place of a player no longer with the club who would not have been eligible because he had been removed from the lineup before the game was suspended.

If immediately prior to the call of a suspended game, a substitute pitcher has been announced but has not retired the side or pitched until the batter becomes a baserunner, such pitcher, when the suspended game is later resumed may, but is not required to start the resumed portion of the game. However, if he does not start he will be considered as having been substituted for and may not be used in that game.

(e) Rain checks will not be honored for any regulation or suspended game which has progressed to or beyond a point of play described in 4.10 **(c)**.

4.13 RULES GOVERNING DOUBLEHEADERS. **(a)(1)** Only two championship games shall be played on one date. Completion of a suspended game shall not violate this rule. **(2)** If two games are scheduled to be played for one admission on one date, the first game shall be the regularly scheduled game for that date. **(b)** After the start of the first game of a doubleheader, that game shall be completed before the second game of the doubleheader shall begin. **(c)** The second game of a doubleheader shall start twenty minutes after the first game is completed, unless a longer interval (not to exceed thirty minutes) is declared by the umpire-in-chief and announced to the opposing managers at the end of the first game. EXCEPTION: If the league president has approved a request of the home club for a longer interval between games for some special event, the umpire-in-chief shall declare such longer interval and announce it to the opposing managers. The umpire-in-chief of the first game shall be the timekeeper controlling the interval between games. **(d)** The umpire shall start the second game of a doubleheader, if at all possible, and play shall continue as long as ground conditions, local time restrictions, or weather permit. **(e)** When a regularly scheduled doubleheader is delayed in starting for any cause, any game that is started is the first game of the doubleheader. **(f)** When a rescheduled game is part of a doubleheader the rescheduled game shall be the second game, and the first game shall be the regularly scheduled game for that date.

4.14 The umpire-in-chief shall order the playing field lights turned on whenever in his opinion darkness makes further play in daylight hazardous.

4.15 A game may be forfeited to the opposing team when a team—**(a)** Fails to appear upon the field, or being upon the field, refuses to start play within five minutes after the umpire has called "Play" at the appointed hour for beginning the game, unless such delayed appearance is, in the umpire's judgment, unavoidable; **(b)** Employs tactics palpably designed to delay or shorten the game; **(c)** Refuses to continue play during a game unless the game has been suspended or terminated by the umpire; **(d)** Fails to resume play, after a suspension, within one minute after the umpire has called "Play;" **(e)** After warning by the umpire, willfully and persistently violates any rules of the game; **(f)** Fails to obey within a reasonable time the umpire's order for removal of a player from the game; **(g)** Fails to appear for the second game of a doubleheader within twenty minutes after the close of the first game unless the umpire-in-chief of the first game shall have extended the time of the intermission.

4.16 A game shall be forfeited to the visiting team if, after it has been suspended, the order of the umpire to groundskeepers respecting preparation of the field for resumption of play are not complied with.

4.17 A game shall be forfeited to the opposing team when a team is unable or refuses to place nine players on the field.

4.18 If the umpire declares a game forfeited he shall transmit a written report to the league president within twenty-four hours thereafter, but failure of such transmittal shall not affect the forfeiture.

4.19 PROTESTING GAMES. Each league shall adopt rules governing procedure for protesting a game, when a manager claims that an umpire's decision is in violation of these rules. No protest shall ever be permitted on judgment decisions by the umpire. In all protested games, the decision of the League President shall be final.

Even if it is held that the protested decision violated the rules, no replay of the game will be ordered unless in the opinion of the League President the violation adversely affected the protesting team's chances of winning the game.

Whenever a manager protests a game because of alleged misapplication of the rules the protest will not be recognized unless the umpires are notified at the time the play under protest occurs and before the next pitch is made or a runner is retired. A protest arising on a game-ending play may be filed until 12 noon the following day with the League Office.

5.00—PUTTING THE BALL IN PLAY. LIVE BALL

5.01 At the time set for beginning the game the umpire shall call "Play."

5.02 After the umpire calls "Play" the ball is alive and in play and remains alive and in play until for legal cause, or at the umpire's call of "Time" suspending play, the ball becomes dead. While the ball is dead no player may be put out, no bases may be run and no runs may be scored, except that runners may advance one or more bases as the result of acts which occurred while the ball was alive (such as, but not limited to a balk, an overthrow, interference, or a home run or other fair ball hit out of the playing field).

Should a ball come partially apart in a game, it is in play until the play is completed.

5.03 The pitcher shall deliver the pitch to the batter who may elect to strike the ball, or who may not offer at it, as he chooses.

5.04 The offensive team's objective is to have its batter become a runner, and its runners advance.

5.05 The defensive team's objective is to prevent offensive players from becoming runners, and to prevent their advance around the bases.

5.06 When a batter becomes a runner and touches all bases legally he shall score one run for his team.

A run legally scored cannot be nullified by subsequent action of the runner, such as but not limited to an effort to return to third base in the belief that he had left the base before a caught fly ball.

5.07 When three offensive players are legally put out, that team takes the field and the opposing team becomes the offensive team.

5.08 If a thrown ball accidently touches a base coach, or a pitched or thrown ball touches an umpire, the ball is alive and in play. However, if the coach interferes with a thrown ball, the runner is out.

5.09 The ball becomes dead and runners advance one base, or return to their bases, without liability to be put out, when—**(a)** A pitched ball touches a batter, or his clothing, while in his legal batting position; runners, if forced, advance; **(b)** The plate umpire interferes with the catcher's throw; runners may not advance.

NOTE: The interference shall be disregarded if the catcher's throw retires the runner.

(c) A balk is committed; runners advance; (See Penalty 8.05). **(d)** A ball is illegally batted; runners return; **(e)** A foul ball is not caught; runners return. The umpire shall not put the ball in play until all runners have retouched their bases; **(f)** A fair ball touches a runner or an umpire on fair territory before it touches an infielder including the pitcher, or touches an umpire before it has passed an infielder other than the pitcher;

If a fair ball touches an umpire working in the infield after it has bounded past, or over, the pitcher, it is a dead ball. If a batted ball is deflected by a fielder in fair territory and hits a runner or an umpire while still in flight and then caught by an infielder it shall not be a catch, but the ball shall remain in play.

If a fair ball goes through, or by, an infielder, and touches a runner immediately back of him, or touches a runner after being deflected by an infielder, the ball is in play and the umpire shall not declare the runner out. In making his decision the umpire must be convinced that the ball passed through, or by, the infielder and that no other infielder had the chance to make a play on the ball; runners advance, if forced:

(g) A pitched ball lodges in the umpire's or catcher's mask or paraphernalia, and remains out of play; runners advance one base;

If a foul tip hits the umpire and is caught by a fielder on the rebound, the ball is "dead" and the batsman cannot be called out. The same shall apply where such foul tip lodges in the umpire's mask or other paraphernalia.

If a third strike (not a foul tip) passes the catcher and hits an umpire, the ball is in play. If such ball rebounds and is caught by a fielder before it touches the ground, the batsman is not out on such a catch, but the ball remains in play and the batsman may be retired at first base, or touched with the ball for the out.

If a pitched ball lodges in the umpire's or catcher's mask or paraphernalia, and remains out of play, on the third strike or fourth ball, then the batter is entitled to first base and all runners advance one base. If the count on the batter is less than three balls, runners advance one base. **(h)** Any legal pitch touches a runner trying to score; runners advance.

5.10 The ball becomes dead when an umpire calls "Time." The umpire-in-chief shall call "Time"—**(a)** When in his judgment weather, darkness or similar conditions make immediate further play impossible; **(b)** When light failure makes it difficult or impossible for the umpires to follow the play;

NOTE: A league may adopt its own regulations governing games interrupted by light failure.

(c) When an accident incapacitates a player or an umpire; **(1)** If an accident to a runner is such as to prevent him from proceeding to a base to which he is entitled, as on a home run hit out of the playing field, or an award of one or more bases, a substitute runner shall be permitted to complete the play. **(d)** When a manager requests "Time" for a substitution, or for a conference with one of his players. **(e)** When the umpire wishes to examine the ball, to consult with either manager, or for any similar cause. **(f)** When a fielder, after catching a fly ball, falls into a bench or stand, or falls across ropes into a crowd when spectators are on the field. As pertains to runners, the provisions of 7.04 **(c)** shall prevail. If a fielder after making a catch steps into a bench, but does not fall, the ball is in play and runners may advance at their own peril. **(g)** When an umpire orders a player or any other person removed from the playing field. **(h)** Except in the cases stated in paragraphs **(b)** and **(c)** **(1)** of this rule, no umpire shall call "Time" while a play is in progress.

5.11 After the ball is dead, play shall be resumed when the pitcher takes his place on the pitcher's plate with a new ball or the same ball in his possession and the plate umpire calls "Play." The plate umpire shall call "Play" as soon as the pitcher takes his place on his plate with the ball in his possession.

6.00—THE BATTER

6.01 (a) Each player of the offensive team shall bat in the order that his name appears in his team's batting order. **(b)** The first batter in each inning after the first inning shall be the player whose name follows that of the last player who legally completed his time at bat in the preceding inning.

6.02 (a) The batter shall take his position in the batter's box promptly when it is his time at bat. **(b)** The batter shall not leave his position in the batter's box after the pitcher comes to Set Position, or starts his windup.

PENALTY: If the pitcher pitches, the umpire shall call "Ball" or "Strike," as the case may be.

The batter leaves the batter's box at the risk of having a strike delivered and called, unless he requests the umpire to call "Time." The batter is not at liberty to step in and out of the batter's box at will.

Once a batter has taken his position in the batter's box, he shall not be permitted to step out of the batter's box in order to use the resin or the pine tar rag, unless there is a delay in the game action or, in the judgment of the umpires, weather conditions warrant an exception.

Umpires will not call "Time" at the request of the batter or any member of his team once the pitcher has started his windup or has come to a set position even though the batter claims "dust in his eyes," "steamed glasses," "didn't get the sign" or for any other cause.

Umpires may grant a hitter's request for "Time" once he is in the batter's box, but the umpire should eliminate hitters walking out of the batter's box without reason. If umpires are not lenient, batters will understand that they are in the batter's box and they must remain there until the ball is pitched.

If pitcher delays once the batter is in his box and the umpire feels that the delay is not justified he may allow the batter to step out of the box momentarily.

If after the pitcher starts his windup or comes to a "set position" with a runner on, he does not go through with his pitch because the batter has stepped out of the box, it shall not be called a balk. Both the pitcher and batter have violated a rule and the umpire shall call time and both the batter and pitcher start over from "scratch."

(c) If the batter refuses to take his position in the batter's box during his time at bat, the umpire shall order the pitcher to pitch, and shall call "Strike" on each such pitch. The batter may take his proper position after any such pitch, and the regular ball and strike count shall continue, but if he does not take his proper position before three strikes are called, he shall be declared out.

6.03 The batter's legal position shall be with both feet within the batter's box.

APPROVED RULING: The lines defining the box are within the batter's box.

6.04 A batter has legally completed his time at bat when he is put out or becomes a runner.

6.05 A batter is out when—**(a)** His fair or foul fly ball (other than a foul tip) is legally caught by a fielder; **(b)** A third strike is legally caught by the catcher;

"Legally caught" means in the catcher's glove before the ball touches the ground. It is not legal if the ball lodges in his clothing or paraphernalia; or if it touches the umpire and is caught by the catcher on the rebound.

If a foul-tip first strikes the catcher's glove and then goes on through and is caught by both hands against his body or protector, before the ball touches the ground, it is a strike, and if third strike, batter is out. If smothered against his body or protector, it is a catch provided the ball struck the catcher's glove or hand first.

(c) A third strike is not caught by the catcher when first base is occupied before two are out; **(d)** He bunts foul on third strike; **(e)** An Infield Fly is declared; **(f)** He attempts to hit a third strike and the ball touches him; **(g)** His fair ball touches him before touching a fielder; **(h)** After hitting or bunting a fair ball, his bat hits the ball a second time in fair territory. The ball is dead and no runners may advance. If the batter-runner drops his bat and the ball rolls against the bat in fair territory and, in the umpire's judgment, there was no intention to interfere with the course of the ball, the ball is alive and in play;

If a bat breaks and part of it is in fair territory and is hit by a batted ball or part of it hits a runner or fielder, play shall continue and no interference called. If batted ball hits part of broken bat in foul territory, it is a foul ball.

If a whole bat is thrown into fair territory and interferes with a defensive player attempting to make a play, interference shall be called, whether intentional or not.

In cases where the batting helmet is accidently hit with a batted or thrown ball, the ball remains in play the same as if it has not hit the helmet.

If a batted ball strikes a batting helmet or any other object foreign to the natural ground while on foul territory, it is a foul ball and the ball is dead.

If, in the umpire's judgment, there is intent on the part of a baserunner to interfere with a batted or thrown ball by dropping the helmet or throwing it at the ball, then the runner would be out, the ball dead and runners would return to last base legally touched.

(i) After hitting or bunting a foul ball, he intentionally deflects the course of the ball in any manner while running to first base. The ball is dead and no runners may advance; **(j)** After a third strike or after he hits a fair ball, he or first base is tagged before he touches first base; **(k)** In running the last half of the distance from home base to first base, while the ball is being fielded to first base, he runs outside (to the right of) the three-foot line, or inside (to the left of) the foul line, and in the umpire's judgment in so doing interferes with the fielder taking the throw at first base; except that he may run outside (to the right of) the three-foot line or inside (to the left of) the foul line to avoid a fielder attempting to field a batted ball; **(l)** An infielder intentionally drops a fair fly ball or line drive, with first, first and second, first and third, or first, second and third base occupied before two are out. The ball is dead and runner or runners shall return to their original base or bases;

APPROVED RULING: In this situation, the batter is not out if the infielder permits the ball to drop untouched to the ground, except when the Infield Fly rule applies.

(m) A preceding runner shall, in the umpire's judgment, intentionally interfere with a fielder who is attempting to catch a thrown ball or to throw a ball in an attempt to complete any play:

The objective of this rule is to penalize the offensive team for deliberate, unwarranted, unsportsmanlike action by the runner in leaving the baseline for the obvious purpose of crashing the pivot man on a double play, rather than trying to reach the base. Obviously this is an umpire's judgment call.

(n) With two out, a runner on third base, and two strikes on the batter, the runner attempts to steal home base on a legal pitch and the ball touches the runner in the batter's strike zone. The umpire shall call "Strike Three," the batter is out and the run shall not count; before two are out, the umpire shall call "Strike Three," the ball is dead, and the run counts.

6.06 A batter is out for illegal action when—**(a)** He hits a ball with one or both feet on the ground entirely outside the batter's box.

If a batter hits a ball fair or foul while out of the batter's box, he shall be called out. Umpires should pay particular attention to the position of the batter's feet if he attempts to hit the ball while he is being intentionally passed. A batter cannot jump or step out of the batter's box and hit the ball.

(b) He steps from one batter's box to the other while the pitcher is in position ready to pitch; **(c)** He interferes with the catcher's fielding or throwing by stepping out of the batter's box or making any other movement that hinders the catcher's play at home base. EXCEPTION: Batter is not out if any runner attempting to advance is put out, or if runner trying to score is called out for batter's interference.

If the batter interferes with the catcher, the plate umpire shall call "interference." The batter is out and the ball dead. No player may advance on such interference (offensive interference) and all runners must return to the last base that was, in the judgment of the umpire, legally touched at the time of the interference.

If, however, the catcher makes a play and the runner attempting to advance is put out, it is to be assumed there was no actual interference and that runner is out—not the batter. Any other runners on the base at the time may advance as the ruling is that there is no actual interference if a runner is retired. In that case play proceeds just as if no violation had been called.

If a batter strikes at a ball and misses and swings so hard he carries the bat all the way around and, in the umpire's judgment, unintentionally hits the catcher or the ball in back of him on the backswing before the catcher has securely held the ball, it shall be called a strike only (not interference). The ball will be dead, however, and no runner shall advance on the play.

(d) He uses or attempts to use a bat that, in the umpire's judgment, has been altered or tampered with in such a way to improve the distance factor or cause an unusual reaction on the baseball. This includes bats that are filled, flat-surfaced, nailed, hollowed, grooved or covered with a substance such as paraffin, wax, etc.

No advancement on the bases will be allowed and any out or outs made during a play shall stand.

In addition to being called out, the player shall be ejected from the game and may be subject to additional penalties as determined by his League President.

6.07 BATTING OUT OF TURN. **(a)** A batter shall be called out, on appeal, when he fails to bat in his proper turn, and another batter completes a time at bat in his place. **(1)** The proper batter may take his place in the batter's box at any time before the improper batter becomes a runner or is put out, and any balls and strikes shall be counted in the proper batter's time at bat. **(b)** When an improper batter becomes a runner or is put out, and the defensive team appeals to the umpire before the first pitch to the next batter of either team, or before any play or attempted play, the umpire shall **(1)** declare the proper batter out; and **(2)** nullify any advance or score made because of a ball batted by the improper batter or because of the improper batter's advance to first base on a hit, an error, a base on balls, a hit batter or otherwise.

NOTE: If a runner advances, while the improper batter is at bat, on a stolen base, balk, wild pitch or passed ball, such advance is legal.

(c) When an improper batter becomes a runner or is put out, and a pitch is made to the next batter of either team before an appeal is made, the improper batter thereby becomes the proper batter, and the results of his time at bat become legal. **(d) (1)** When the proper batter is called out because he has failed to bat in turn, the next batter shall be the batter whose name follows that of the proper batter thus called out; **(2)** When an improper batter becomes a proper batter because no appeal is made before the next pitch, the next batter shall be the batter whose name follows that of such legalized improper batter. The instant an improper batter's actions are legalized, the batting order picks up with the name following that of the legalized improper batter.

The umpire shall not direct the attention of any person to the presence in the batter's box of an improper batter. This rule is designed to require constant vigilance by the players and managers of both teams.

There are two fundamentals to keep in mind: When a player bats out of turn, the proper batter is the player called out. If an improper batter bats and reaches base or is out and no appeal is made before a pitch to the next batter, or before any play or attempted play, that improper batter is considered to have batted in proper turn and establishes the order that is to follow.

APPROVED RULING

To illustrate various situations arising from batting out of turn, assume a first-inning batting order as follows:

Abel-Baker-Charles-Daniel-Edward-Frank-George-Hooker-Irwin.

PLAY **(1)**. Baker bats. With the count 2 balls and 1 strike, **(a)** the offensive team discovers the error or **(b)** the defensive team appeals. RULING: In either case, Abel replaces Baker, with the count on him 2 balls and 1 strike.

PLAY **(2)**. Baker bats and doubles. The defensive team appeals **(a)** immediately or **(b)** after a pitch to Charles. RULING: **(a)** Abel is called out and Baker is the proper batter; **(b)** Baker stays on second and Charles is the proper batter.

PLAY **(3)**. Abel walks. Baker walks. Charles forces Baker. Edward bats in Daniel's turn. While Edward is at bat, Abel scores and Charles goes to second on a wild pitch. Edward grounds out, sending Charles to third. The defensive team appeals **(a)** immediately or **(b)** after a pitch to Daniel. RULING: **(a)** Abel's run counts and Charles is entitled to second base since these advances were not made because of the improper batter batting a ball or advancing to first base. Charles must return to second base because his

advance to third resulted from the improper batter batting a ball. Daniel is called out, and Edward is the proper batter; **(b)** Abel's run counts and Charles stays on third. The proper batter is Frank.

PLAY **(4)**. With the bases full and two out. Hooker bats in Frank's turn, and triples, scoring three runs. The defensive team appeals **(a)** immediately, or **(b)** after a pitch to George. RULING: **(a)** Frank is called out and no runs score. George is the proper batter to lead off the second inning; **(b)** Hooker stays on third and three runs score. Irwin is the proper batter.

PLAY **(5)**. After Play **(4) (b)** above, George continues at bat. **(a)** Hooker is picked off third base for the third out, or **(b)** George flies out, and no appeal is made. Who is the proper leadoff batter in the second inning? RULING: **(a)** Irwin. He became the proper batter as soon as the first pitch to George legalized Hooker's triple; **(b)** Hooker. When no appeal was made, the first pitch to the leadoff batter of the opposing team legalized George's time at bat.

PLAY **(6)**. Daniel walks and Abel comes to bat. Daniel was an improper batter, and if an appeal is made before the first pitch to Abel, Abel is out, Daniel is removed from base, and Baker is the proper batter. There is no appeal, and a pitch is made to Abel. Daniel's walk is now legalized, and Edward thereby becomes the proper batter. Edward can replace Abel at any time before Abel is put out or becomes a runner. He does not do so. Abel flies out, and Baker comes to bat. Abel was an improper batter, and if an appeal is made before the first pitch to Baker, Edward is out, and the proper batter is Frank. There is no appeal, and a pitch is made to Baker. Abel's out is now legalized, and the proper batter is Baker. Baker walks. Charles is the proper batter. Charles flies out. Now Daniel is the proper batter, but he is on second base. Who is the proper batter? RULING: The proper batter is Edward. When the proper batter is on base, he is passed over, and the following batter becomes the proper batter.

6.08 The batter becomes a runner and is entitled to first base without liability to be put out (provided he advances to and touches first base) when—**(a)** Four "balls" have been called by the umpire;

A batter who is entitled to first base because of a base on balls must go to first base and touch the base before other base runners are forced to advance. This applies when bases are full and applies when a substitute runner is put into the game.

If, in advancing, the base runner thinks there is a play and he slides past the base before or after touching it he may be put out by the fielder tagging him. If he fails to touch the base to which he is entitled and attempts to advance beyond that base he may be put out by tagging him or the base he missed.

(b) He is touched by a pitched ball which he is not attempting to hit unless **(1)** The ball is in the strike zone when it touches the batter, or **(2)** The batter makes no attempt to avoid being touched by the ball;

If the ball is in the strike zone when it touches the batter, it shall be called a strike, whether or not the batter tries to avoid the ball. If the ball is outside the strike zone when it touches the batter, it shall be called a ball if he makes no attempt to avoid being touched.

APPROVED RULING: When the batter is touched by a pitched ball which does not entitle him to first base, the ball is dead and no runner may advance.

(c) The catcher or any fielder interferes with him. If a play follows the interference, the manager of the offense may advise the plate umpire that he elects to decline the interference penalty and accept the play. Such election shall be made immediately at the end of the play. However, if the batter reaches first base on a hit, an error, a base on balls, a hit batsman, or otherwise, and all other runners advance at least one base, the play proceeds without reference to the interference.

If catcher's interference is called with a play in progress the umpire will allow the play to continue because the manager may elect to take the play. If the batter-runner missed first base, or a runner misses his next base, he shall be considered as having reached the base, as stated in Note of Rule 7.04 **(d)**.

Examples of plays the manager might elect to take:

1. Runner on third, one out, batter hits fly ball to the outfield on which the runner scores but catcher's interference was called. The offensive manager may elect to take the run and have batter called out or have runner remain at third and batter awarded first base.

2. Runner on second base. Catcher interferes with batter as he bunts ball fairly sending runner to third base. The manager may rather have runner on third base with an out on the play than have runners on second and first.

In situations where the manager wants the "interference" penalty to apply, the following interpretation shall be made of 6.08 (c):

If the catcher (or any fielder) interferes with the batter, the batter is awarded first base. If, on such interference a runner is trying to score by a steal or squeeze from third base, the ball is dead and the runner on third scores and batter is awarded first base. If the catcher interferes with the batter with no runners trying to score from third on a squeeze or steal, then the ball is dead, batter is awarded first base and runners who are forced to advance, do advance. Runners not attempting to steal or not forced to advance remain on the base they occupied at the time of the interference.

If the catcher interferes with the batter before the pitcher delivers the ball, it shall not be considered interference on the batter under Rule 6.08 **(c)**. In such cases, the umpire shall call "Time" and the pitcher and batter start over from "scratch."

(d) A fair ball touches an umpire or a runner on fair territory before touching a fielder.

If a fair ball touches an umpire after having passed a fielder other than the pitcher, or having touched a fielder, including the pitcher, the ball is in play.

6.09 The batter becomes a runner when—**(a)** He hits a fair ball; **(b)** The third strike called by the umpire is not caught, providing **(1)** first base is unoccupied, or **(2)** first base is occupied with two out;

When a batter becomes a base runner on a third strike not caught by the catcher and starts for the dugout, or his position, and then realizes his situation and attempts then to reach first base, he is not out unless he or first base is tagged before he reaches first base. If, however, he actually reaches the dugout or dugout steps, he may not then attempt to go to first base and shall be out.

(c) A fair ball, after having passed a fielder other than the pitcher, or after having been touched by a fielder, including the pitcher, shall touch an umpire or runner on fair territory; **(d)** A fair ball passes over a fence or into the stands at a distance from home base of 250 feet or more. Such hit entitles the batter to a home run when he shall have touched all bases legally. A fair fly ball that passes out of the playing field at a point less than 250 feet from home base shall entitle the batter to advance to second base only; **(e)** A fair ball, after touching the ground, bounds into the stands, or passes through, over or under a fence, or through or under a scoreboard, or through or under shrubbery, or vines on the fence, in which case the batter and the runners shall be entitled to advance two bases; **(f)** Any fair ball which, either before or after touching the ground, passes through or under a fence, or through or under a scoreboard, or through any opening in the fence or scoreboard, or through or under shrubbery, or vines on the fence, or which sticks in a fence or scoreboard, in which case the batter and the runners shall be entitled to two bases; **(g)** Any bounding fair ball is deflected by the fielder into the stands, or over or under a fence on fair or foul territory, in which case the batter and all runners shall be entitled to advance two bases; **(h)** Any fair fly ball is deflected by the fielder into the stands, or over the fence into foul territory, in which case the batter shall be entitled to advance to second base; but if deflected into the stands or over the fence in fair territory, the batter shall be entitled to a home run. However, should such a fair fly be deflected at a point less than 250 feet from home plate, the batter shall be entitled to two bases only.

6.10 Any League may elect to use the Designated Hitter Rule. **(a)** In the event of inter-league competition between clubs of Leagues using the Designated Hitter Rule and clubs of Leagues not using the Designated Hitter Rule, the rule will be used as follows:

1. In World Series or exhibition games, the rule will be used or not used as is the practice of the home team.

2. In All-Star games, the rule will only be used if both teams and both Leagues so agree.

(b) The Rule provides as follows:

A hitter may be designated to bat for the starting pitcher and all subsequent pitchers in any game without otherwise affecting the status of the pitcher(s) in the game. A Designated Hitter for the pitcher must be selected prior to the game and must be included in the lineup cards presented to the Umpire in Chief.

The designated hitter named in the starting lineup must come to bat at least one time, unless the opposing club changes pitchers.

It is not mandatory that a club designate a hitter for the pitcher, but failure to do so prior to the game precludes the use of a Designated Hitter for that game.

Pinch hitters for a Designated Hitter may be used. Any substitute hitter for a Designated Hitter becomes the Designated Hitter. A replaced Designated Hitter shall not re-enter the game in any capacity.

The Designated Hitter may be used defensively, continuing to bat in the same position in the batting order, but the pitcher must then bat in the place of the substituted defensive player, unless more than one substitution is made, and the manager then must designate their spots in the batting order.

A runner may be substituted for the Designated Hitter and the runner assumes the role of Designated Hitter. A Designated Hitter may not pinch run.

A Designated Hitter is "locked" into the batting order. No multiple substitutions may be made that will alter the batting rotation of the Designated Hitter.

Once the game pitcher is switched from the mound to a defensive position this move shall terminate the Designated Hitter role for the remainder of the game.

Once a pinch hitter bats for any player in the batting order and then enters the game to pitch, this move shall terminate the Designated Hitter role for the remainder of the game.

Once the game pitcher bats for the Designated Hitter this move shall terminate the Designated Hitter role for the remainder of the game. (The game pitcher may only pinch-hit for the Designated Hitter).

Once a Designated Hitter assumes a defensive position this move shall terminate the Designated Hitter role for the remainder of the game. A substitute for the Designated Hitter need not be announced until it is the Designated Hitter's turn to bat.

7.00—THE RUNNER.

7.01 A runner acquires the right to an unoccupied base when he touches it before he is out. He is then entitled to it until he is put out, or forced to vacate it for another runner legally entitled to that base.

If a runner legally acquires title to a base, and the pitcher assumes his pitching position, the runner may not return to a previously occupied base.

7.02 In advancing, a runner shall touch first, second, third and home base in order. If forced to return, he shall retouch all bases in reverse order, unless the ball is dead under any provision of Rule 5.09. In such cases, the runner may go directly to his original base.

7.03 Two runners may not occupy a base, but if, while the ball is alive, two runners are touching a base, the following runner shall be out when tagged. The preceding runner is entitled to the base.

7.04 Each runner, other than the batter, may without liability to be put out, advance one base when—**(a)** There is a balk; **(b)** The batter's advance without liability to be put out forces the runner to vacate his base, or when the batter hits a fair ball that touches another runner or the umpire before such ball has been touched by, or has passed a fielder, if the runner is forced to advance;

A runner forced to advance without liability to be put out may advance past the base to which he is entitled only at his peril. If such a runner, forced to advance, is put out for the third out before a preceding runner, also forced to advance, touches home plate, the run shall score.

Play. Two out, bases full, batter walks but runner from second is overzealous and runs past third base toward home and is tagged out on a throw by the catcher. Even though two are out, the run would score on the theory that the run was forced home by the base on balls and that all the runners needed to do was proceed and touch the next base.

(c) A fielder, after catching a fly ball, falls into a bench or stand, or falls across ropes into a crowd when spectators are on the field;

A fielder or catcher may reach or step into, or go into the dugout with one or both feet to make a catch, and if he holds the ball, the catch shall be allowed. Ball is in play.

If the fielder or catcher, after having made a legal catch, should fall into a stand or among spectators or into the dugout after making a legal catch, or fall while in the dugout after making a legal catch, the ball is dead and runners advance one base without liability to be put out.

(d) While he is attempting to steal a base, the batter is interfered with by the catcher or any other fielder.

NOTE: When a runner is entitled to a base without liability to be put out, while the ball is in play, or under any rule in which the ball is in play after the runner reaches the base to which he is entitled, and the runner fails to touch the base to which he is entitled before attempting to advance to the next base, the runner shall forfeit his exemption from liability to be put out, and he may be put out by tagging the base or by tagging the runner before he returns to the missed base.

7.05 Each runner including the batter-runner may, without liability to be put out, advance—**(a)** To home base, scoring a run, if a fair ball goes out of the playing field in flight and he touches all bases legally; or if a fair ball which, in the umpire's judgment, would have gone out of the playing field in flight, is deflected by the act of a fielder in throwing his glove, cap, or any article of his apparel; **(b)** Three bases, if a fielder deliberately touches a fair ball with his cap, mask or any part of his uniform detached from its proper place on his person. The ball is in play and the batter may advance to home base at his peril; **(c)** Three bases, if a fielder deliberately throws his glove at and touches a fair ball. The ball is in play and the batter may advance to home base at his peril. **(d)** Two bases, if a fielder deliberately touches a thrown ball with his cap, mask or any part of his uniform detached from its proper place on his person. The ball is in play; **(e)** Two bases, if a fielder deliberately throws his glove at and touches a thrown ball. The ball is in play;

In applying (b-c-d-e) the umpire must rule that the thrown glove or detached cap or mask has touched the ball. There is no penalty if the ball is not touched.

Under (c-e) this penalty shall not be invoked against a fielder whose glove is carried off his hand by the force of a batted or thrown ball, or when his glove flies off his hand as he makes an obvious effort to make a legitimate catch.

(f) Two bases, if a fair ball bounces or is deflected into the stands outside the first or third base foul lines; or if it goes through or under a field fence, or through or under a scoreboard, or through or under shrubbery or vines on the fence; or if it sticks in such fence, scoreboard, shrubbery or vines; **(g)** Two bases when, with no spectators on the playing field, a thrown ball goes into the stands, or into a bench (whether or not the ball rebounds into the field), or over or under or through a field fence, or on a slanting part of the screen above the backstop, or remains in the meshes of a wire screen protecting spectators. The ball is dead. When such wild throw is the first play by an infielder, the umpire, in awarding such bases, shall be governed by the position of the runners at the time the ball was pitched; in all other cases the umpire shall be governed by the position of the runners at the time the wild throw was made;

APPROVED RULING: If all runners, including the batter-runner, have advanced at least one base when an infielder makes a wild throw on the first play after the pitch, the award shall be governed by the position of the runners when the wild throw was made.

In certain circumstances it is impossible to award a runner

two bases. Example: Runner on first. Batter hits fly to short right. Runner holds up between first and second and batter comes around first and pulls up behind him. Ball falls safely. Outfielder, in throwing to first, throws ball into stand.

APPROVED RULING: Since no runner, when the ball is dead, may advance beyond the base to which he is entitled, the runner originally on first base goes to third base and the batter is held at second base.

The term "when the wild throw was made" means when the throw actually left the player's hand and not when the thrown ball hit the ground, passes a receiving fielder or goes out of play into the stands.

The position of the batter-runner at the time the wild throw left the thrower's hand is the key in deciding the award of bases. If the batter-runner has not reached first base, the award is two bases at the time the pitch was made for all runners. The decision as to whether the batter-runner has reached first base before the throw is a judgment call.

If an unusual play arises where a first throw by an infielder goes into stands or dugout but the batter did not become a runner (such as catcher throwing ball into stands in attempt to get runner from third trying to score on passed ball or wild pitch) award of two bases shall be from the position of the runners at the time of the throw. (For the purpose of Rule 7.05 **(g)** a catcher is considered an infielder.)

PLAY. Runner on first base, batter hits a ball to the shortstop, who throws to second base too late to get runner at second, and second baseman throws toward first base after batter has crossed first base. Ruling—Runner at second scores. (On this play, only if batter-runner is past first base when throw is made is he awarded third base.)

(h) One base, if a ball, pitched to the batter, or thrown by the pitcher from his position on the pitcher's plate to a base to catch a runner, goes into a stand or a bench, or over or through a field fence or backstop. The ball is dead;

APPROVED RULING: When a wild pitch or passed ball goes through or by the catcher, or deflects off the catcher, and goes directly into the dugout, stands, above the break, or any area where the ball is dead, the awarding of bases shall be one base. One base shall also be awarded if the pitcher while in contact with the rubber, throws to a base, and the throw goes directly into the stands or into any area where the ball is dead.

If, however, the pitched or thrown ball goes through or by the catcher or through the fielder, and remains on the playing field, and is subsequently kicked or deflected into the dugout, stands or other area where the ball is dead, the awarding of bases shall be two bases from position of runners at the time of the pitch or throw.

(i) One base, if the batter becomes a runner on Ball Four or Strike Three, when the pitch passes the catcher and lodges in the umpire's mask or paraphernalia.

If the batter becomes a runner on a wild pitch which entitles the runners to advance one base, the batter-runner shall be entitled to first base only.

The fact a runner is awarded a base or bases without liability to be put out does not relieve him of the responsibility to touch the base he is awarded and all intervening bases. For example: batter hits a ground ball which an infielder throws into the stands but the

batter-runner missed first base. He may be called out on appeal for missing first base after the ball is put in play even though he was "awarded" second base.

If a runner is forced to return to a base after a catch, he must retouch his original base even though, because of some ground rule or other rule, he is awarded additional bases. He may retouch while the ball is dead and the award is then made from his original base.

7.06 When obstruction occurs, the umpire shall call or signal "Obstruction." **(a)** If a play is being made on the obstructed runner, or if the batter-runner is obstructed before he touches first base, the ball is dead and all runners shall advance, without liability to be put out, to the bases they would have reached, in the umpire's judgment, if there had been no obstruction. The obstructed runner shall be awarded at least one base beyond the base he had last legally touched before the obstruction. Any preceding runners, forced to advance by the award of bases as the penalty for obstruction, shall advance without liability to be put out.

When a play is being made on an obstructed runner, the umpire shall signal obstruction in the same manner that he calls "Time," with both hands overhead. The ball is immediately dead when this signal is given; however, should a thrown ball be in flight before the obstruction is called by the umpire, the runners are to be awarded such bases on wild throws as they would have been awarded had no obstruction occurred. On a play where a runner was trapped between second and third and obstructed by the third baseman going into third base while the throw is in flight from the shortstop, if such throw goes into the dugout the obstructed runner is to be awarded home base. Any other runners on base in this situation would also be awarded two bases from the base they last legally touched before obstruction was called.

(b) If no play is being made on the obstructed runner, the play shall proceed until no further action is possible. The umpire shall then call "Time" and impose such penalties, if any, as in his judgment will nullify the act of obstruction.

Under 7.06 (b) when the ball is not dead on obstruction and an obstructed runner advances beyond the base which, in the umpire's judgment, he would have been awarded because of being obstructed, he does so at his own peril and may be tagged out. This is a judgment call.

NOTE: The catcher, without the ball in his possession, has no right to block the pathway of the runner attempting to score. The base line belongs to the runner and the catcher should be there only when he is fielding a ball or when he already has the ball in his hand.

7.07 If, with a runner on third base and trying to score by means of a squeeze play or a steal, the catcher or any other fielder steps on, or in front of home base without possession of the ball, or touches the batter or his bat, the pitcher shall be charged with a balk, the batter shall be awarded first base on the interference and the ball is dead.

7.08 Any runner is out when—**(a) (1)** He runs more than three feet away from a direct line between bases to avoid being tagged unless his action is to avoid interference with a fielder fielding a batted ball; or **(2)** after touching first base, he leaves the baseline, obviously abandoning his effort to touch the next base;

Any runner after reaching first base who leaves the baseline heading for his dugout or his position believing that there is no further play, may be declared out if the umpire judges the act of the runner to be considered abandoning his efforts to run the bases. Even though an out is called, the ball remains in play in regard to any other runner.

This rule also covers the following and similar plays: Less than two out, score tied last of ninth inning, runner on first, batter hits a ball out of park for winning run, the runner on first passes second and thinking the home run automatically wins the game, cuts across diamond toward his bench as batter-runner circles bases. In this case, the base runner would be called out "for abandoning his effort to touch the next base" and batter-runner permitted to continue around bases to make his home run valid. If there are two out, home run would not count (see Rule 7.12). This is not an appeal play.

PLAY. Runner believing he is called out on a tag at first or third base starts for the dugout and progresses a reasonable distance still indicating by his actions that he is out, shall be declared out for abandoning the bases.

In the above two plays the runners are considered actually abandoning their base paths and are treated differently than the batter who struck out as described. APPROVED RULING OF 7.08 (a).

APPROVED RULING: When a batter becomes a runner on third strike not caught, and starts for his bench or position, he may advance to first base at any time before he enters the bench. To put him out, the defense must tag him or first base before he touches first base.

(b) He intentionally interferes with a thrown ball; or hinders a fielder attempting to make a play on a batted ball;

A runner who is adjudged to have hindered a fielder who is attempting to make a play on a batted ball is out whether it was intentional or not.

If, however, the runner has contact with a legally occupied base when he hinders the fielder, he shall not be called out unless, in the umpire's judgment, such hindrance, whether it occurs on fair or foul territory, is intentional. If the umpire declares the hindrance intentional, the following penalty shall apply: With less than two out, the umpire shall declare both the runner and batter out. With two out, the umpire shall declare the batter out.

If, in a run-down between third base and home plate, the succeeding runner has advanced and is standing on third base when the runner in a run-down is called out for offensive interference, the umpire shall send the runner standing on third base back to second base. This same principle applies if there is a run-down between second and third base and succeeding runner has reached second (the reasoning is that no runner shall advance on an interference play and a runner is considered to occupy a base until he legally has reached the next succeeding base).

(c) He is tagged, when the ball is alive, while off his base. EXCEPTION: A batter-runner cannot be tagged out after overrunning or oversliding first base if he returns immediately to the base;

APPROVED RULING: **(1)** If the impact of a runner breaks a base loose from its position, no play can be made on that runner at that base if he had reached the base safely.

APPROVED RULING: **(2)** If a base is dislodged from its position during a play, any following runner on the same play shall be considered as touching or occupying the base if, in the umpire's

judgment, he touches or occupies the point marked by the dislodged bag.

(d) He fails to retouch his base after a fair or foul ball is legally caught before he, or his base, is tagged by a fielder. He shall not be called out for failure to retouch his base after the first following pitch, or any play or attempted play. This is an appeal play;

Runners need not "tag up" on a foul tip. They may steal on a foul tip. If a so-called tip is not caught, it becomes an ordinary foul. Runners then return to their bases.

(e) He fails to reach the next base before a fielder tags him or the base, after he has been forced to advance by reason of the batter becoming a runner. However, if a following runner is put out on a force play, the force is removed and the runner must be tagged to be put out. The force is removed as soon as the runner touches the base to which he is forced to advance, and if he overslides or overruns the base, the runner must be tagged to be put out. However, if the forced runner, after touching the next base, retreats for any reason towards the base he had last occupied, the force play is reinstated, and he can again be put out if the defense tags the base to which he is forced;

PLAY. Runner on first and three balls on batter: Runner steals on the next pitch, which is fourth ball, but after having touched second he overslides or overruns that base. Catcher's throw catches him before he can return. Ruling is that runner is out. (Force out is removed.)

Oversliding and overrunning situations arise at bases other than first base. For instance, before two are out, and runners on first and second, or first, second and third, the ball is hit to an infielder who tries for the double play. The runner on first beats the throw to second base but overslides the base. The relay is made to first base and the batter-runner is out. The first baseman, seeing the runner at second base off the bag, makes the return throw to second and the runner is tagged off the base. Meanwhile runners have crossed the plate. The question is: Is this a force play? Was the force removed when the batter-runner was out at first base? Do the runs that crossed the plate during this play and before the third out was made when the runner was tagged at second, count? Answer: The runs score. It is not a force play. It is a tag play.

(f) He is touched by a fair ball in fair territory before the ball has touched or passed an infielder. The ball is dead and no runner may score, nor runners advance, except runners forced to advance. EXCEPTION: If a runner is touching his base when touched by an Infield Fly, he is not out, although the batter is out;

If two runners are touched by the same fair ball, only the first one is out because the ball is instantly dead.

If runner is touched by an Infield Fly when he is not touching his base, both runner and batter are out.

(g) He attempts to score on a play in which the batter interferes with the play at home base before two are out. With two out, the interference puts the batter out and no score counts; **(h)** He passes a preceding runner before such runner is out; **(i)** After he has acquired legal possession of a base, he runs the bases in reverse order for the purpose of confusing the defense or making a travesty of the game. The umpire shall immediately call "Time" and declare the runner out;

If a runner touches an unoccupied base and then thinks the ball was caught or is decoyed into returning to the base he last touched, he may be put out running back to that base, but if he reaches the previously occupied base safely he cannot be put out while in contact with that base.

(j) He fails to return at once to first base after overrunning or oversliding that base. If he attempts to run to second he is out when tagged. If, after overrunning or oversliding first base he starts toward the dugout, or toward his position, and fails to return to first base at once, he is out, on appeal, when he or the base is tagged;

Runner who touches first base in overrunning and is declared safe by the umpire has, within the intent of Rule 4.09 (a) "reached first base" and any run which scores on such a play counts, even though the runner subsequently becomes the third out for failure to return "at once," as covered in Rule 7.08 (j).

(k) In running or sliding for home base, he fails to touch home base and makes no attempt to return to the base, when a fielder holds the ball in his hand, while touching home base, and appeals to the umpire for the decision.

This rule applies only where runner is on his way to the bench and the catcher would be required to chase him. It does not apply to the ordinary play where the runner misses the plate and then immediately makes an effort to touch the plate before being tagged. In that case, runner must be tagged.

7.09 It is interference by a batter or a runner when—**(a)** After a third strike he hinders the catcher in his attempt to field the ball; **(b)** After hitting or bunting a fair ball, his bat hits the ball a second time in fair territory. The ball is dead and no runners may advance. If the batter-runner drops his bat and the ball rolls against the bat in fair territory and, in the umpire's judgment, there was no intention to interfere with the course of the ball, the ball is alive and in play; **(c)** He intentionally deflects the course of a foul ball in any manner; **(d)** Before two are out and a runner on third base, the batter hinders a fielder in making a play at home base; the runner is out; **(e)** Any member or members of the offensive team stand or gather around any base to which a runner is advancing, to confuse, hinder or add to the difficulty of the fielders. Such runner shall be declared out for the interference of his teammate or teammates; **(f)** Any batter or runner who has just been put out hinders or impedes any following play being made on a runner. Such runner shall be declared out for the interference of his teammate;

If the batter or a runner continues to advance after he has been put out, he shall not by that act alone be considered as confusing, hindering or impeding the fielders.

(g) If, in the judgment of the umpire, a base runner willfully and deliberately interferes with a batted ball or a fielder in the act of fielding a batted ball with the obvious intent to break up a double play, the ball is dead. The umpire shall call the runner out for interference and also call out the batter-runner because of the action of his teammate. In no event may bases be run or runs scored because of such action by a runner. **(h)** If, in the judgment of the umpire, a batter-runner willfully and deliberately interferes with a batted ball or a fielder in the act of fielding a batted ball, with the obvious intent to break up a double play, the ball is dead; the umpire shall call the batter-runner out for interference and shall also call out the runner who had advanced closest to the home plate regardless where the double play might have been possible. In no event shall bases be run because of such interference. **(i)** In the judgment of the umpire, the base coach at third base, or first base,

by touching or holding the runner, physically assists him in returning to or leaving third base or first base. **(j)** With a runner on third base, the base coach leaves his box and acts in any manner to draw a throw by a fielder; **(k)** In running the last half of the distance from home base to first base while the ball is being fielded to first base, he runs outside (to the right of) the three-foot line, or inside (to the left of) the foul line and, in the umpire's judgment, interferes with the fielder taking the throw at first base, or attempting to field a batted ball;

The lines marking the three foot lane are a part of that "lane" but the interpretation to be made is that a runner is required to have both feet within the three foot "lane" or on the lines marking the "lane."

(l) He fails to avoid a fielder who is attempting to field a batted ball, or intentionally interferes with a thrown ball, provided that if two or more fielders attempt to field a batted ball, and the runner comes in contact with one or more of them, the umpire shall determine which fielder is entitled to the benefit of this rule, and shall not declare the runner out for coming in contact with a fielder other than the one the umpire determines to be entitled to field such a ball;

When a catcher and batter-runner going to first base have contact when the catcher is fielding the ball, there is generally no violation and nothing should be called. "Obstruction" by a fielder attempting to field a ball should be called only in very flagrant and violent cases because the rules give him the right of way, but of course such "right of way" is not a license to, for example, intentionally trip a runner even though fielding the ball. If the catcher is fielding the ball and the first baseman or pitcher obstructs a runner going to first base "obstruction" shall be called and the base runner awarded first base.

(m) A fair ball touches him on fair territory before touching a fielder. If a fair ball goes through, or by, an infielder, and touches a runner immediately back of him, or touches the runner after having been deflected by a fielder, the umpire shall not declare the runner out for being touched by a batted ball. In making such decision the umpire must be convinced that the ball passed through, or by, the fielder, and that no other infielder had the chance to make a play on the ball. If, in the judgment of the umpire, the runner deliberately and intentionally kicks such a batted ball on which the infielder has missed a play, then the runner shall be called out for interference.

PENALTY FOR INTERFERENCE: The runner is out and the ball is dead.

7.10 Any runner shall be called out, on appeal, when—**(a)** After a fly ball is caught, he fails to retouch his original base before he or his original base is tagged;

"Retouch," in this rule, means to tag up and start from a contact with the base after the ball is caught. A runner is not permitted to take a flying start from a position in back of his base.

(b) With the ball in play, while advancing or returning to a base, he fails to touch each base in order before he, or a missed base, is tagged.

APPROVED RULING: **(1)** No runner may return to touch a missed base after a following runner has scored. **(2)** When the ball is dead, no runner may return to touch a missed base or one he has left after he has advanced to and touched a base beyond the missed base.

PLAY. **(a)** Batter hits ball out of park or ground rule double and misses first base (ball is dead)—he may return to first base to correct his mistake before he touches second but if he touches second he may not return to first and if defensive team appeals he is declared out at first.

PLAY. **(b)** Batter hits ball to shortstop who throws wild into stand (ball is dead)—batter-runner misses first base but is awarded second base on the overthrow. Even though the umpire has awarded the runner second base on the overthrow, the runner must touch first base before he proceeds to second base.

These are appeal plays. **(c)** He overruns or overslides first base and fails to return to the base immediately, and he or the base is tagged; **(d)** He fails to touch home base and makes no attempt to return to that base, and home base is tagged.

Any appeal under this rule must be made before the next pitch, or any play or attempted play. If the violation occurs during a play which ends a half-inning, the appeal must be made before the defensive team leaves the field.

An appeal is not to be interpreted as a play or an attempted play.

Successive appeals may not be made on a runner at the same base. If the defensive team on its first appeal errs, a request for a second appeal on the same runner at the same base shall not be allowed by the umpire. (Intended meaning of the word "err" is that the defensive team in making an appeal threw the ball out of play. For example, if the pitcher threw to first base to appeal and threw the ball into the stands, no second appeal would be allowed.)

Appeal plays may require an umpire to recognize an apparent "fourth out." If the third out is made during a play in which an appeal play is sustained on another runner, the appeal play decision takes precedence in determining the out. If there is more than one appeal during a play that ends a half-inning, the defense may elect to take the out that gives it the advantage. For the purpose of this rule, the defensive team has "left the field" when the pitcher and all infielders have left fair territory on their way to the bench or clubhouse.

If two runners arrive at home base about the same time and the first runner misses home plate but a second runner legally touches the plate, the first runner will be called out on appeal. If there are two out, and the first runner is tagged out on his attempt to come back and touch the base or is called out, on appeal, then he shall be considered as having been put out before the second runner scored and being the third out. Second runner's run shall not count, as provided in Rule 7.12.

If a pitcher balks when making an appeal, such act shall be a play. An appeal should be clearly intended as an appeal, either by a verbal request by the player or an act that unmistakably indicates an appeal to the umpire. A player, inadvertently stepping on the base with a ball in his hand, would not constitute an appeal. Time is not out when an appeal is being made.

7.11 The players, coaches or any member of an offensive team shall vacate any space (including both dugouts) needed by a fielder who is attempting to field a batted or thrown ball.

PENALTY: Interference shall be called and the batter or runner on whom the play is being made shall be declared out.

7.12 Unless two are out, the status of a following runner is not affected by a preceding runner's failure to touch or retouch a base. If, upon appeal, the preceding runner is the third out, no runners following him shall score. If such third out is the result of a force play, neither preceding nor following runners shall score.

8.01 Legal pitching delivery. There are two legal pitching positions, the Windup Position and the Set Position, and either position may be used at any time.

Pitchers shall take signs from the catcher while standing on the rubber.

Pitchers may disengage the rubber after taking their signs but may not step quickly onto the rubber and pitch. This may be judged a quick pitch by the umpire. When the pitcher disengages the rubber, he must drop his hands to his sides.

Pitchers will not be allowed to disengage the rubber after taking each sign. **(a)** The Windup Position. The pitcher shall stand facing the batter, his entire pivot foot on, or in front of and touching and not off the end of the pitcher's plate, and the other foot free. From this position any natural movement associated with his delivery of the ball to the batter commits him to the pitch without interruption or alteration. He shall not raise either foot from the ground, except that in his actual delivery of the ball to the batter, he may take one step backward, and one step forward with his free foot.

When a pitcher holds the ball with both hands in front of his body, with his entire pivot foot on, or in front of and touching but not off the end of the pitcher's plate, and his other foot free, he will be considered in the Windup Position.

The pitcher may have one foot, not the pivot foot, off the rubber and any distance he may desire back of a line which is an extension to the back edge of the pitcher's plate, but not at either side of the pitcher's plate.

With his "free" foot the pitcher may take one step backward and one step forward, but under no circumstances, to either side, that is to either the first base or third base side of the pitcher's rubber.

If a pitcher holds the ball with both hands in front of his body, with his entire pivot foot on or in front of and touching but not off the end of the pitcher's plate, and his other foot free, he will be considered in a windup position.

From this position he may: **(1)** deliver the ball to the batter, or **(2)** step and throw to a base in an attempt to pick-off a runner, or **(3)** disengage the rubber (if he does he must drop his hand to his sides).

In disengaging the rubber the pitcher must step off with his pivot foot and not his free foot first.

He may not go into a set or stretch position—if he does it is a balk.

(b) The Set Position. Set Position shall be indicated by the pitcher when he stands facing the batter with his entire pivot foot on, or in front of, and in contact with, and not off the end of the pitcher's plate, and his other foot in front of the pitcher's plate, holding the ball in both hands in front of his body and coming to a complete stop. From such Set Position he may deliver the ball to the batter, throw to a base or step backward off the pitcher's plate with his pivot foot. Before assuming Set Position, the pitcher may elect to make any natural preliminary motion such as that known as "the stretch." But if he so elects, he shall come to Set Position before delivering the ball to the batter. After assuming Set Position, any natural motion associated with his delivery of the ball to the batter commits him to the pitch without alteration or interruption.

Preparatory to coming to a set position, the pitcher shall have one hand on his side; from this position he shall go to his set position as defined in Rule 8.01 (b) without interruption and in one continuous motion.

The whole width of the foot in contact with the rubber must be on the rubber. A pitcher cannot pitch from off the end of the rubber with just the side of his foot touching the rubber.

The pitcher, following his stretch, must **(a)** hold the ball in both hands in front of his body and **(b)** come to a complete stop. This must be enforced. Umpires should watch this closely. Pitchers are constantly attempting to "beat the rule" in their efforts to hold runners on bases and in cases where the pitcher fails to make a complete "stop" called for in the rules, the umpire should immediately call a "Balk."

(c) At any time during the pitcher's preliminary movements and until his natural pitching motion commits him to the pitch, he may throw to any base provided he steps directly toward such base before making the throw.

The pitcher shall step "ahead of the throw." A snap throw followed by the step directly toward the base is a balk.

(d) If the pitcher makes an illegal pitch with the bases unoccupied, it shall be called a ball unless the batter reaches first base on a hit, an error, a base on balls, a hit batter or otherwise.

A ball which slips out of a pitcher's hand and crosses the foul line shall be called a ball; otherwise it will be called no pitch. This would be a balk with men on base.

(e) If the pitcher removes his pivot foot from contact with the pitcher's plate by stepping backward with that foot, he thereby becomes an infielder and if he makes a wild throw from that position, it shall be considered the same as a wild throw by any other infielder.

The pitcher, while off the rubber, may throw to any base. If he makes a wild throw, such throw is the throw of an infielder and what follows is governed by the rules covering a ball thrown by a fielder.

8.02 The pitcher shall not—**(a) (1)** Bring his pitching hand in contact with his mouth or lips while in the 18 foot circle surrounding the pitching rubber. EXCEPTION: Provided it is agreed to by both managers, the umpire prior to the start of a game played in cold weather, may permit the pitcher to blow on his hand.

PENALTY: For violation of this part of this rule the umpires shall immediately call a ball. However, if the pitch is made and a batter reaches first base on a hit, an error, a hit batsman or otherwise, and no other runner is put out before advancing at least one base, the play shall proceed without reference to the violation. Repeated offenders shall be subject to a fine by the league president.

(2) Apply a foreign substance of any kind to the ball; **(3)** expectorate on the ball, either hand or his glove; **(4)** rub the ball on his glove, person or clothing; **(5)** deface the ball in any manner; **(6)** deliver what is called the "shine" ball, "spit" ball, "mud" ball or "emery" ball. The pitcher, of course, is allowed to rub the ball between his bare hands.

PENALTY: For violation of any part of this rule 8.02 **(a)** (2 to 6) the umpire shall: **(a)** Call the pitch a ball, warn the pitcher and have announced on the public address system the reason for the action. **(b)** In the case of a second offense by the same pitcher in the same game, the pitcher shall be disqualified from the game. **(c)** If a

play follows the violation called by the umpire, the manager of the offense may advise the plate umpire that he elects to accept the play. Such election shall be made immediately at the end of the play. However, if the batter reaches first base on a hit, an error, a base on balls, a hit batsman, or otherwise, and no other runner is put out before advancing at least one base, the play shall proceed without reference to the violation. **(d)** Even though the offense elects to take the play, the violation shall be recognized and the penalties in **(a)** and **(b)** will still be in effect. **(e)** The umpire shall be sole judge on whether any portion of this rule has been violated.

All umpires shall carry with them one official rosin bag. The umpire-in-chief is responsible for placing the rosin bag on the ground back of the pitcher's plate. If at any time the ball hits the rosin bag it is in play. In the case of rain or wet field, the umpire may instruct the pitcher to carry the rosin bag in his hip pocket. A pitcher may use the rosin bag for the purpose of applying rosin to his bare hand or hands. Neither the pitcher nor any other player shall dust the ball with the rosin bag; neither shall the pitcher nor any other player be permitted to apply rosin from the bag to his glove or dust any part of his uniform with the rosin bag.

(b) Have on his person, or in his possession, any foreign substance. For such infraction of this section **(b)** the penalty shall be immediate ejection from the game. **(c)** Intentionally delay the game by throwing the ball to players other then the catcher, when the batter is in position, except in an attempt to retire a runner.

PENALTY: If, after warning by the umpire, such delaying action is repeated, the pitcher shall be removed from the game.

(d) Intentionally Pitch at the Batter.

If, in the umpire's judgment, such a violation occurs, the umpire may elect either to:

1. Expel the pitcher, or the manager and the pitcher, from the game, or

2. may warn the pitcher and the manager of both teams that another such pitch will result in the immediate expulsion of that pitcher (or a replacement) and the manager.

If, in the umpire's judgment, circumstances warrant, both teams may be officially "warned" prior to the game or at any time during the game. (League Presidents may take additional action under authority provided in Rule 9.05)

To pitch at a batter's head is unsportsmanlike and highly dangerous. It should be—and is—condemned by everybody. Umpires should act without hesitation in enforcement of this rule.

8.03 When a pitcher takes his position at the beginning of each inning, or when he relieves another pitcher, he shall be permitted to pitch not to exceed eight preparatory pitches to his catcher during which play shall be suspended. A league by its own action may limit the number of preparatory pitches to less than eight preparatory pitches. Such preparatory pitches shall not consume more than one minute of time. If a sudden emergency causes a pitcher to be summoned into the game without any opportunity to warm up, the umpire-in-chief shall allow him as many pitches as the umpire deems necessary.

8.04 When the bases are unoccupied, the pitcher shall deliver the ball to the batter within 20 seconds after he receives the ball. Each time the pitcher delays the game by violating this rule, the umpire shall call "Ball."

The intent of this rule is to avoid unnecessary delays. The umpire shall insist that the catcher return the ball promptly to the pitcher, and that the pitcher take his position on the rubber promptly. Obvious delay by the pitcher should instantly be penalized by the umpire.

8.05 If there is a runner, or runners, it is a balk when—**(a)** The pitcher, while touching his plate, makes any motion naturally associated with his pitch and fails to make such delivery;

If a lefthanded or righthanded pitcher swings his free foot past the back edge of the pitcher's rubber, he is required to pitch to the batter except to throw to second base on a pick-off-play.

(b) The pitcher, while touching his plate, feints a throw to first base and fails to complete the throw; **(c)** The pitcher, while touching his plate, fails to step directly toward a base before throwing to that base;

Requires the pitcher, while touching his plate, to step directly toward a base before throwing to that base. If a pitcher turns or spins off of his free foot without actually stepping or if he turns his body and throws before stepping, it is a balk.

A pitcher is to step directly toward a base before throwing to that base but does not require him to throw (except to first base only) because he steps. It is possible, with runners on first and third, for the pitcher to step toward third and not throw, merely to bluff the runner back to third; then seeing the runner on first start for second, turn and step toward and throw to first base. This is legal. However, if, with runners on first and third, the pitcher, while in contact with the rubber, steps toward third and then immediately and in practically the same motion "wheels" and throws to first base, it is obviously an attempt to deceive the runner at first base, and in such a move it is practically impossible to step directly toward first base before the throw to first base, and such a move shall be called a balk. Of course, if the pitcher steps off the rubber and then makes such a move, it is not a balk.

(d) The pitcher, while touching his plate, throws, or feints a throw to an unoccupied base, except for the purpose of making a play; **(e)** The pitcher makes an illegal pitch;

A quick pitch is an illegal pitch. Umpires will judge a quick pitch as one delivered before the batter is reasonably set in the batter's box. With runners on base the penalty is a balk; with no runners on base, it is a ball. The quick pitch is dangerous and should not be permitted.

(f) The pitcher delivers the ball to the batter while he is not facing the batter; **(g)** The pitcher makes any motion naturally associated with his pitch while he is not touching the pitcher's plate; **(h)** The pitcher unnecessarily delays the game; **(i)** The pitcher, without having the ball, stands on or astride the pitcher's plate or while off the plate, he feints a pitch; **(j)** The pitcher, after coming to a legal pitching position, removes one hand from the ball other than in an actual pitch, or in throwing to a base; **(k)** The pitcher, while touching his plate, accidentally or intentionally drops the ball; **(l)** The pitcher, while giving an intentional base on balls, pitches when the catcher is not in the catcher's box; **(m)** The pitcher delivers the pitch from Set Position without coming to a stop.

PENALTY: The ball is dead, and each runner shall advance one base without liability to be put out, unless the batter reaches first on a hit, an error, a base on balls, a hit batter, or otherwise,

and all other runners advance at least one base, in which case the play proceeds without reference to the balk.

APPROVED RULING: In cases where a pitcher balks and throws wild, either to a base or to home plate, a runner or runners may advance beyond the base to which he is entitled at his own risk.

APPROVED RULING: A runner who misses the first base to which he is advancing and who is called out on appeal shall be considered as having advanced one base for the purpose of this rule.

Umpires should bear in mind that the purpose of the balk rule is to prevent the pitcher from deliberately deceiving the base runner. If there is doubt in the umpire's mind, the "intent" of the pitcher should govern. However, certain specifics should be borne in mind: **(a)** Straddling the pitcher's rubber without the ball is to be interpreted as intent to deceive and ruled a balk. **(b)** With a runner on first base the pitcher may make a complete turn, without hesitating toward first, and throw to second. This is not to be interpreted as throwing to an unoccupied base.

8.06 A professional league shall adopt the following rule pertaining to the visit of the manager or coach to the pitcher: **(a)** This rule limits the number of trips a manager or coach may make to any one pitcher in any one inning; **(b)** A second trip to the same pitcher in the same inning will cause this pitcher's automatic removal; **(c)** The manager or coach is prohibited from making a second visit to the mound while the same batter is at bat, but **(d)** if a pinch-hitter is substituted for this batter, the manager or coach may make a second visit to the mound, but must remove the pitcher.

A manager or coach is considered to have concluded his visit to the mound when he leaves the 18-foot circle surrounding the pitcher's rubber.

If the manager or coach goes to the catcher or infielder and that player then goes to the mound or the pitcher comes to him at his position before there is an intervening play (a pitch or other play) that will be the same as the manager or coach going to the mound.

Any attempt to evade or circumvent this rule by the manager or coach going to the catcher or an infielder and then that player going to the mound to confer with the pitcher shall constitute a trip to the mound.

If the coach goes to the mound and removes a pitcher and then the manager goes to the mound to talk with the new pitcher, that will constitute one trip to that new pitcher that inning.

In a case where a manager has made his first trip to the mound and then returns the second time to the mound in the same inning with the same pitcher in the game and the same batter at bat, after being warned by the umpire that he cannot return to the mound, the manager shall be removed from the game and the pitcher required to pitch to the batter until he is retired or gets on base. After the batter is retired, or becomes a base runner, then this pitcher must be removed from the game. The manager should be notified that his pitcher will be removed from the game after he pitches to one hitter, so he can have a substitute pitcher warmed up.

The substitute pitcher will be allowed eight preparatory pitches or more if in the umpire's judgment circumstances justify.

9.01 (a) The league president shall appoint one or more umpires to officiate at each league championship game. The umpires shall be responsible for the conduct of the game in accordance with these official rules and for maintaining discipline and order on the playing field during the game. **(b)** Each umpire is the representative of the league and of professional baseball, and is authorized and required to enforce all of these rules. Each umpire has authority to order a player, coach, manager or club officer or employee to do or refrain from doing anything which affects the administering of these rules, and to enforce the prescribed penalties. **(c)** Each umpire has authority to rule on any point not specifically covered in these rules. **(d)** Each umpire has authority to disqualify any player, coach, manager or substitute for objecting to decisions or for unsportsmanlike conduct or language, and to eject such disqualified person from the playing field. If an umpire disqualifies a player while a play is in progress, the disqualification shall not take effect until no further action is possible in that play. **(e)** Each umpire has authority at his discretion to eject from the playing field **(1)** any person whose duties permit his presence on the field, such as ground crew members, ushers, photographers, newsmen, broadcasting crew members, etc., and **(2)** any spectator or other person not authorized to be on the playing field.

9.02 (a) Any umpire's decision which involves judgment, such as, but not limited to, whether a batted ball is fair or foul, whether a pitch is a strike or a ball, or whether a runner is safe or out, is final. No player, manager, coach or substitute shall object to any such judgment decisions. **(a)** Players leaving their position in the field or on base, or managers or coaches leaving the bench or coaches box, to argue on BALLS AND STRIKES will not be permitted. They should be warned if they start for the plate to protest the call. If they continue, they will be ejected from the game. **(b)** If there is reasonable doubt that any umpire's decision may be in conflict with the rules, the manager may appeal the decision and ask that a correct ruling be made. Such appeal shall be made only to the umpire who made the protested decision. **(c)** If a decision is appealed, the umpire making the decision may ask another umpire for information before making a final decision. No umpire shall criticize, seek to reverse or interfere with another umpire's decision unless asked to do so by the umpire making it. **(c)** The manager or the catcher may request the plate umpire to ask his partner for help on a half swing when the plate umpire calls the pitch a ball, but not when the pitch is called a strike. The manager may not complain that the umpire made an improper call, but only that he did not ask his partner for help. Field umpires must be alerted to the request from the plate umpire and quickly respond. Managers may not protest the call of a ball or strike on the pretense they are asking for information about a half swing.

Appeals on a half swing may be made only on the call of ball and when asked to appeal, the home plate umpire must refer to a base umpire for his judgment on the half swing. Should the base umpire call the pitch a strike, the strike call shall prevail.

Baserunners must be alert to the possibility that the base umpire on appeal from the plate umpire may reverse the call of a ball to the call of a strike, in which event the runner is in jeopardy of being out by the catcher's throw. Also, a catcher must be alert in a base stealing situation if a ball call is reversed to a strike by the base umpire upon appeal from the plate umpire.

The ball is in play on appeal on a half swing.

On a half swing, if the manager comes out to argue with first or third base umpire and if after being warned he persists in arguing, he can be ejected as he is now arguing over a called ball or strike.

(d) No umpire may be replaced during a game unless he is injured or becomes ill.

9.03 (a) If there is only one umpire, he shall have complete jurisdiction in administering the rules. He may take any position on the playing field which will enable him to discharge his duties (usually behind the catcher, but sometimes behind the pitcher if there are runners). **(b)** If there are two or more umpires, one shall be designated umpire-in-chief and the others field umpires.

9.04 (a) The umpire-in-chief shall stand behind the catcher. (He usually is called the plate umpire.) His duties shall be to: **(1)** Take full charge of, and be responsible for, the proper conduct of the game; **(2)** Call and count balls and strike; **(3)** Call and declare fair balls and fouls except those commonly called by field umpires; **(4)** Make all decisions on the batter; **(5)** Make all decisions except those commonly reserved for the field umpires; **(6)** Decide when a game shall be forfeited; **(7)** If a time limit has been set, announce the fact and the time set before the game starts; **(8)** Inform the official scorer of the official batting order, and any changes in the lineups and batting order, on request; **(9)** Announce any special ground rules, at his discretion. **(b)** A field umpire may take any position on the playing field he thinks best suited to make impending decisions on the bases. His duties shall be to: **(1)** Make all decisions on the bases except those specifically reserved to the umpire-in-chief; **(2)** Take concurrent jurisdiction with the umpire-in-chief in calling "Time," balks, illegal pitches, or defacement or discoloration of the ball by any player. **(3)** Aid the umpire-in-chief in every manner in enforcing the rules, and excepting the power to forfeit the game, shall have equal authority with the umpire-in-chief in administering and enforcing the rules and maintaining discipline. **(c)** If different decisions should be made on one play by different umpires, the umpire-in-chief shall call all the umpires into consultation, with no manager or player present. After consultation, the umpire-in-chief (unless another umpire may have been designated by the league president) shall determine which decision shall prevail, based on which umpire was in best position and which decision was most likely correct. Play shall proceed as if only the final decision had been made.

9.05 (a) The umpire shall report to the league president within twelve hours after the end of a game all violations of rules and other incidents worthy of comment, including the disqualification of any trainer, manager, coach or player, and the reasons therefor. **(b)** When any trainer, manager, coach or player is disqualified for a flagrant offense such as the use of obscene or indecent language, or an assault upon an umpire, trainer, manager, coach or player, the umpire shall forward full particulars to the league president within four hours after the end of the game. **(c)** After receiving the umpire's report that a trainer, manager, coach or player has been disqualified, the league president shall impose such penalty as he deems justified, and shall notify the person penalized and the manager of the club of which the penalized person is a member. If the penalty includes a fine, the penalized person shall pay the amount of the fine to the league within five days after receiving notice of the fine. Failure to pay such fine within five days shall result in the offender being debarred from participation in any game and from sitting on the players' bench during any game, until the fine is paid.

GENERAL INSTRUCTIONS TO UMPIRE

Umpires, on the field, should not indulge in conversation with players. Keep out of the coaching box and do not talk to the coach on duty.

Keep your uniform in good condition. Be active and alert on the field.

Be courteous, always, to club officials; avoid visiting in club offices and thoughtless familiarity with officers or employees of contesting clubs. When you enter a ball park your sole duty is to umpire a ball game as the representative of baseball.

Do not allow criticism to keep you from studying out bad situations that may lead to protested games. Carry your rule book. It is better to consult the rules and hold up the game ten minutes to decide a knotty problem than to have a game thrown out on protest and replayed.

Keep the game moving. A ball game is often helped by energetic and earnest work of the umpires.

You are the only official representative of baseball on the ball field. It is often a trying position which requires the exercise of much patience and good judgment, but do not forget that the first essential in working out of a bad situation is to keep your own temper and self-control.

You no doubt are going to make mistakes, but never attempt to "even up" after having made one. Make all decisions as you see them and forget which is the home or visiting club.

Keep your eye everlastingly on the ball while it is in play. It is more vital to know just where a fly ball fell, or a thrown ball finished up, than whether or not a runner missed a base. Do not call the plays too quickly, or turn away too fast when a fielder is throwing to complete a double play. Watch out for dropped balls after you have called a man out.

Do not come running with your arm up or down, denoting "out" or "safe." Wait until the play is completed before making any arm motion.

Each umpire team should work out a simple set of signals, so the proper umpire can always right a manifestly wrong decision when convinced he has made an error. If sure you got the play correctly, do not be stampeded by players' appeals to "ask the other man." If not sure, ask one of your associates. Do not carry this to extremes, be alert and get your own plays. But remember! The first requisite is to get decisions correctly. If in doubt don't hesitate to consult your associate. Umpire dignity is important but never as important as "being right."

A most important rule for umpires is always "BE IN POSITION TO SEE EVERY PLAY." Even though your decision may be 100% right, players still question it if they feel you were not in a spot to see the play clearly and definitely.

Finally, be courteous, impartial and firm, and so compel respect from all.

Index

10.00—THE OFFICIAL SCORER.

10.01 (a) The league president shall appoint an official scorer for each league championship game. The official scorer shall observe the game from a position in the press box. The scorer shall have sole authority to make all decisions involving judgment, such as whether a batter's advance to first base is the result of a hit or an error. He shall communicate such decisions to the press box and broadcasting booths by hand signals or over the press box loud-speaker system, and shall advise the public address announcer of such decisions if requested.

The Official Scorer must make all decisions concerning judgment calls within twenty-four (24) hours after a game has been officially concluded. No judgment decision shall be changed thereafter except, upon immediate application to the League President, the scorer may request a change, citing the reasons for such. In all cases, the official scorer is not permitted to make a scoring decision which is in conflict with the scoring rules.

After each game, including forfeited and called games, the scorer shall prepare a report, on a form prescribed by the league president, listing the date of the game, where it was played, the names of the competing clubs and the umpires, the full score of the game, and all records of individual players compiled according to the system specified in these Official Scoring Rules. He shall forward this report to the league office within thirty-six hours after the game ends. He shall forward the report of any suspended game within thirty-six hours after the game has been completed, or after it becomes an official game because it cannot be completed, as provided by the Official Playing Rules.

(b) (1) To achieve uniformity in keeping the records of championship games, the scorer shall conform strictly to the Official Scoring Rules. The scorer shall have authority to rule on any point not specifically covered in these rules. (2) If the teams change sides before three men are put out, the scorer shall immediately inform the umpire of the mistake. (3) If the game is protested or suspended, the scorer shall make a note of the exact situation at the time of the protest or suspension, including the score, the number of outs, the position of any runners, and the ball and strike count on the batter.

NOTE: It is important that a suspended game resume with exactly the same situation as existed at the time of suspension. If a protested game is ordered replayed from the point of protest, it must be resumed with exactly the situation that existed just before the protested play.

(4) The scorer shall not make any decision conflicting with the Official Playing Rules, or with an umpire's decision. (5) The scorer shall not call the attention of the umpire or of any member of either team to the fact that a player is batting out of turn. (c) (1) The scorer is an official representative of the league, and is entitled to the respect and dignity of his office, and shall be accorded full protection by the league president. The scorer shall report to the president any indignity expressed by any manager, player, club employee or club officer in the course of, or as the result of, the discharge of his duties.

10.02 The official score report prescribed by the league president shall make provisions for entering the information listed below, in a form convenient for the compilation of permanent statistical records: **(a)** The following records for each batter and runner: **(1)** Number of times he batted, except that no time at bat shall be charged against a player when (i) He hits a sacrifice bunt or sacrifice fly (ii) He is awarded first base on four called balls (iii) He is hit by a pitched ball (iv) He is awarded first base because of interference or obstruction. **(2)** Number of runs scored **(3)** Number of safe hits **(4)** Number of runs batted in **(5)** Two-base hits **(6)** Three-base hits **(7)** Home runs **(8)** Total bases on safe hits **(9)** Stolen bases **(10)** Sacrifice bunts **(11)** Sacrifice flies **(12)** Total number of bases on balls **(13)** Separate listing of any intentional bases on balls **(14)** Number of times hit by a pitched ball **(15)** Number of times awarded first base for interference or obstruction. **(16)** Strikeouts **(b)** The following records for each fielder: **(1)** Number of putouts **(2)** Number of assists **(3)** Number of errors **(4)** Number of double plays participated in **(5)** Number of triple plays participated in **(c)** The following records for each pitcher: **(1)** Number of innings pitched.

NOTE: In computing innings pitched, count each putout as one-third of an inning. If a starting pitcher is replaced with one out in the sixth inning, credit that pitcher with 5-1/3 innings. If a starting pitcher is replaced with none out in the sixth inning, credit that pitcher with 5 innings, and make the notation that he faced———batters in the sixth. If a relief pitcher retires two batters and is replaced, credit that pitcher with 2/3 inning pitched.

(2) Total number of batters faced **(3)** Number of batters officially at bat against pitcher computed according to 10.02 (a) (1). **(4)** Number of hits allowed **(5)** Number of runs allowed **(6)** Number of earned runs allowed **(7)** Number of home runs allowed **(8)** Number of sacrifice hits allowed **(9)** Number of sacrifice flies allowed **(10)** Total number of bases on balls allowed **(11)** Separate listing of any intentional bases on balls allowed **(12)** Number of batters hit by pitched balls **(13)** Number of strikeouts **(14)** Number of wild pitches **(15)** Number of balks **(d)** The following additional data: **(1)** Name of the winning pitcher **(2)** Name of the

losing pitcher **(3)** Names of the starting pitcher and the finishing pitcher for each team. **(4)** Name of pitcher credited with save. **(e)** Number of passed balls allowed by each catcher. **(f)** Name of players participating in double plays and triple plays.

EXAMPLE: Double Plays—Jones, Roberts and Smith **(2)**. Triple Play—Jones and Smith.

(g) Number of runners left on base by each team. This total shall include all runners who get on base by any means and who do not score and are not put out. Include in this total a batter-runner whose batted ball results in another runner being retired for the third out. **(h)** Names of batters who hit home runs with bases full. **(i)** Names of batters who ground into force double plays and reverse force double plays. **(j)** Names of runners caught stealing. **(k)** Number of outs when winning run scored, if game is won in last half-inning. **(l)** The score by innings for each team. **(m)** Names of umpires, listed in this order **(1)** plate umpire, **(2)** first base umpire, **(3)** second base umpire, **(4)** third base umpire. **(n)** Time required to play the game, with delays for weather or light failure deducted.

10.03 **(a)** In compiling the official score report, the official scorer shall list each player's name and his fielding position or positions in the order in which the player batted, or would have batted if the game ends before he gets to bat.

NOTE: When a player does not exchange positions with another fielder but is merely placed in a different spot for a particular batter, do not list this as a new position.

EXAMPLES: **(1)** Second baseman goes to the outfield to form a four-man outfield. **(2)** Third baseman moves to a position between shortstop and second baseman.

(b) Any player who enters the game as a substitute batter or substitute runner, whether or not he continues in the game thereafter, shall be identified in the batting order by a special symbol which shall refer to a separate record of substitute batters and runners. Lower case letters are recommended as symbols for substitute batters, and numerals as symbols for substitute runners. The record of substitute batters shall describe what the substitute batter did.

EXAMPLES—"a-Singled for———in third inning; b-Flied out———in sixth inning; c-Forced———for———in seventh inning; d-Grounded out for———in ninth inning; 1-Ran for———in ninth inning.

The record of substitute batters and runners shall include the name of any such substitute whose name is announced, but who is removed for a second substitute before he actually gets into the game. Such substitution shall be recorded as "e-Announced as substitute for———in seventh inning." Any such second substitute shall be recorded as batting or running for the first announced substitute.

HOW TO PROVE A BOX SCORE **(c)** A box score is in balance (or proved) when the total of the team's times at bat, bases on balls received, hit batters, sacrifice bunts, sacrifice flies and batters awarded first base because of interference or obstruction equals the total of that team's runs, players left on base and the opposing team's putouts.

WHEN PLAYER BATS OUT OF TURN **(d)** When a player bats out of turn, and is put out, and the proper batter is called out before the ball is pitched to the next batter, charge the proper batter with a time at bat and score the putout and any assists the same as if the correct batting order had been followed. If an improper batter becomes a runner and the proper batter is called out for having missed his turn at bat, charge the proper batter with a time at bat, credit the putout to the catcher, and ignore everything entering into the improper batter's safe arrival on base. If more than one batter bats out of turn in succession score all plays just as they occur, skipping the turn at bat of the player or players who first missed batting in the proper order.

CALLED AND FORFEITED GAMES (e) (1) If a regulation game is called, include the record of all individual and team actions up to the moment the game ends, as defined in Rules 4.10 and 4.11. If it is a tie game, do not enter a winning or losing pitcher. (2) If a regulation game is forfeited, include the record of all individual and team actions up to the time of forfeit. If the winning team by forfeit is ahead at the time of forfeit, enter as winning and losing pitchers the players who would have qualified if the game had been called at the time of forfeit. If the winning team by forfeit is behind or if the score is tied at the time of forfeit, do not enter a winning or losing pitcher. If a game is forfeited before it becomes a regulation game, include no records. Report only the fact of the forfeit.

RUNS BATTED IN

10.04 (a) Credit the batter with a run batted in for every run which reaches home base because of the batter's safe hit, sacrifice bunt, sacrifice fly, infield out or fielder's choice; or which is forced over the plate by reason of the batter becoming a runner with the bases full (on a base on balls, or an award of first base for being touched by a pitched ball, or for interference or obstruction). (1) Credit a run batted in for the run scored by the batter who hits a home run. Credit a run batted in for each runner who is on base when the home run is hit and who scores ahead of the batter who hits the home run. (2) Credit a run batted in for the run scored when, before two are out, an error is made on a play on which a runner from third base ordinarily would score. (b) Do not credit a run batted in when the batter grounds into a force double play or a reverse force double play. (c) Do not credit a run batted in when a fielder is charged with an error because he muffs a throw at first base which would have completed a force double play. (d) Scorer's judgment must determine whether a run batted in shall be credited for a run which scores when a fielder holds the ball, or throws to a wrong base. Ordinarily, if the runner keeps going, credit a run batted in; if the runner stops and takes off again when he notices the misplay, credit the run as scored on a fielder's choice.

BASE HITS

10.05 A base hit shall be scored in the following cases: (a) When a batter reaches first base (or any succeeding base) safely on a fair ball which settles on the ground or touches a fence before being touched by a fielder, or which clears a fence; (b) When a batter reaches first base safely on a fair ball hit with such force, or so slowly, that any fielder attempting to make a play with it has no opportunity to do so;

NOTE: A hit shall be scored if the fielder attempting to handle the ball cannot make a play, even if such fielder deflects the ball from or cuts off another fielder who could have put out a runner.

(c) When a batter reaches first base safely on a fair ball which takes an unnatural bounce so that a fielder cannot handle it with ordinary effort, or which touches the pitcher's plate or any base, (including home plate), before being touched by a fielder and bounces so that a fielder cannot handle it with ordinary effort; (d) When a batter reaches first base safely on a fair ball which has not been touched by a fielder and which is in fair territory when it reaches the outfield unless in the scorer's judgment it could have been handled with ordinary effort; (e) When a fair ball which has not been touched by a fielder touches a runner or an umpire. EXCEPTION: Do not score a hit when a runner is called out for having been touched by an Infield Fly; (f) When a fielder unsuccessfully attempts to put out a preceding runner, and in the scorer's judgment the batter-runner would not have been put out at first base by ordinary effort.

NOTE: In applying the above rules, always give the batter the benefit of the doubt. A safe course to follow is to score a hit when exceptionally good fielding of a ball fails to result in a putout.

10.06 A base hit shall not be scored in the following cases: (a) When a runner is forced out by a batted ball, or would have been forced out except for a fielding error; (b) When the batter apparently hits safely and a runner who is forced to advance by reason of the batter becoming a runner fails to touch the first base to which he is advancing and is called out on appeal. Charge the batter with a time at bat but no hit; (c) When the pitcher, the catcher or any infielder handles a batted ball and puts out a preceding runner who is attempting to advance one base or to return to his original base, or would have put out such runner with ordinary effort except for a fielding error. Charge the batter with a time at bat but no hit; (d) When a fielder fails in an attempt to put out a preceding runner, and in the scorer's judgment the batter-runner could have been put out at first base.

NOTE: This shall not apply if the fielder merely looks toward or feints toward another base before attempting to make the putout at first base;

(e) When a runner is called out for interference with a fielder attempting to field a batted ball, unless in the scorer's judgment the batter-runner would have been safe had the interference not occurred.

DETERMINING VALUE OF BASE HITS

10.07 Whether a safe hit shall be scored as one-base hit, two-base hit, three-base hit or home run when no error or putout results shall be determined as follows: (a) Subject to the provisions of 10.07 (b) and (c), it is a one-base hit if the batter stops at first base; it is a two-base hit if the batter stops at second base; it is a three-base hit if the batter stops at third base; it is a home run if the batter touches all bases and scores. (b) When, with one or more runners on base, the batter advances more than one base on a safe hit and the defensive team makes an attempt to put out a preceding runner, the scorer shall determine whether the batter made a legitimate two-base hit or three-base hit, or whether he advanced beyond first base on the fielder's choice.

NOTE: Do not credit the batter with a three-base hit when a preceding runner is put out at the plate, or would have been out but for an error. Do not credit the batter with a two-base hit when a preceding runner trying to advance from first base is put out at third base, or would have been out but for an error. However, with the exception of the above, do not determine the value of base-hits by the number of bases advanced by a preceding runner. A batter may deserve a two-base hit even though a preceding runner advances one or no bases; he may deserve only a one-base hit even though he reaches second base and a preceding runner advances two bases.

EXAMPLES: **(1)** Runner on first, batter hits to right fielder, who throws to third base in unsuccessful attempt to put out runner. Batter takes second base. Credit batter with one-base hit. **(2)** Runner on second. Batter hits fair fly ball. Runner holds up to determine if ball is caught, and advances only to third base, while batter takes second. Credit batter with two-base hit. **(3)** Runner on third. Batter hits high fair fly. Runner takes lead, then runs back to tag up, thinking ball will be caught. Ball falls safe, but runner cannot score, although batter has reached second. Credit batter with two-base hit.

(c) When the batter attempts to make a two-base hit or a three-base hit by sliding, he must hold the last base to which he advances. If he overslides and is tagged out before getting back to the base safely, he shall be credited with only as many bases as he attained safely. If he overslides second base and is tagged out, he shall be credited with a one-base hit; if he overslides third base and is tagged out, he shall be credited with a two-base hit.

NOTE: If the batter overruns second or third base and is tagged out trying to return, he shall be credited with the last base he touched. If he runs past second base after reaching that base on his feet, attempts to return and is tagged out, he shall be credited with a two-base hit. If he runs past third base after reaching that base on his feet, attempts to return and is tagged out, he shall be credited with a three-base hit.

(d) When the batter, after making a safe hit, is called out for having failed to touch a base, the last base he reached safely shall determine if he shall be credited with a one-base hit, a two-base hit or a three-base hit. If he is called out after missing home base, he shall be credited with a three-base hit. If he is called out for missing third base, he shall be credited with a two-base hit. If he is called out for missing second base, he shall be credited with a one-base hit. If he is called out for missing first base, he shall be charged with a time at bat, but no hit. **(e)** When the batter-runner is awarded two bases, three bases or a home run under the provisions of Playing Rules 7.05 or 7.06 **(a)**, he shall be credited with a two-base hit, a three-base hit or a home run, as the case may be.

GAME-ENDING HITS

(f) Subject to the provisions of 10.07 **(g)**, when the batter ends a game with a safe hit which drives in as many runs as are necessary to put his team in the lead, he shall be credited with only as many bases on his hit as are advanced by the runner who scores the winning run, and then only if the batter runs out his hit for as many bases as are advanced by the runner who scores the winning run.

NOTE: Apply this rule even when the batter is theoretically entitled to more bases because of being awarded an "automatic" extra-base hit under various provisions of Playing Rules 6.09 and 7.05.

(g) When the batter ends a game with a home run hit out of the playing field, he and any runners on base are entitled to score.

STOLEN BASES

10.08 A stolen base shall be credited to a runner whenever he advances one base unaided by a hit, a putout, an error, a force-out, a fielder's choice, a passed ball, a wild pitch or a balk, subject to the following: **(a)** When a runner starts for the next base before the pitcher delivers the ball and the pitch results in what ordinarily is scored a wild pitch or passed ball, credit the runner with a stolen base and do not charge the misplay. EXCEPTION: If, as a result of the misplay, the stealing runner advances an extra base, or another runner also advances, score the wild pitch or passed ball as well as the stolen base. **(b)** When a runner is attempting to steal, and the catcher, after receiving the pitch, makes a wild throw trying to prevent the stolen base, credit a stolen base. Do not charge an error unless the wild throw permits the stealing runner to advance one or more extra bases, or permits another runner to advance, in which case credit the stolen base and charge one error to the catcher. **(c)** When a runner, attempting to steal, or after being picked off base, evades being put out in a run-down play and advances to the next base without the aid of an error, credit the runner with a stolen base. If another runner also advances on the play, credit both runners with stolen bases. If a runner advances while another runner, attempting to steal, evades being put out in a run-down play and returns safely, without the aid of an error, to the base he originally occupied, credit a stolen base to the runner who advances. **(d)** When a double or triple steal is attempted and one runner is thrown out before reaching and holding the base he is attempting to steal, no other runner shall be credited with a stolen base. **(e)** When a runner is tagged out after oversliding a base, while attempting either to return to that base or to advance to the next base, he shall not be credited with a stolen base. **(f)** When in the scorer's judgment a runner attempting to steal is safe because of a muffed throw, do not credit a stolen base. Credit an assist to the fielder who made the throw; charge an error to the fielder who muffed the throw, and charge the runner with "caught stealing." **(g)** No stolen base shall be scored when a runner advances solely because of the defensive team's indifference to his advance. Score as a fielder's choice.

CAUGHT STEALING

(h) A runner shall be charged as "Caught Stealing" if he is put out, or would have been put out by errorless play when he **(1)** Tries to steal. **(2)** Is picked off a base and tries to advance (any move toward the next base shall be considered an attempt to advance). **(3)** Overslides while stealing.

NOTE: In those instances where a pitched ball eludes the catcher and the runner is put out trying to advance, no caught stealing shall be charged. No caught stealing should be charged when a runner is awarded a base due to obstruction.

SACRIFICES

10.09 (a) Score a sacrifice bunt when, before two are out, the batter advances one or more runners with a bunt and is put out at first base, or would have been put out except for a fielding error. **(b)** Score a sacrifice bunt when, before two are out, the fielders handle a bunted ball without error in an unsuccessful attempt to put out a preceding runner advancing one base. EXCEPTION: When an attempt to turn a bunt into a putout of a preceding runner fails, and in the scorer's judgment perfect play would not have put out the batter at first base, the batter shall be credited with a one-base hit and not a sacrifice. **(c)** Do not score a sacrifice bunt when any runner is put out attempting to advance one base on a bunt. Charge the batter with a time at bat. **(d)** Do not score a sacrifice bunt when, in the judgment of the scorer, the batter is bunting primarily for a base hit and not for the purpose of advancing a runner or runners. Charge the batter with a time at bat

NOTE: In applying the above rule, always give the batter the benefit of the doubt.

(e) Score a sacrifice fly when, before two are out, the batter hits a fly ball or a line drive handled by an outfielder or an infielder running in the outfield which **(1)** is caught, and a runner scores after the catch, or **(2)** is dropped, and a runner scores, if in the scorer's judgment the runner could have scored after the catch had the fly been caught.

NOTE: Score a sacrifice fly in accordance with 10.09 **(e) (2)** even though another runner is forced out by reason of the batter becoming a runner.

PUTOUTS

10.10 A putout shall be credited to each fielder who **(1)** catches a fly ball or a line drive, whether fair or foul; **(2)** catches a thrown ball which puts out a batter or runner, or **(3)** tags a runner when the runner is off the base to which he legally is entitled. **(a)** Automatic putouts shall be credited to the catcher as follows: **(1)** When the batter is called out for an illegally batted ball; **(2)** When the batter is called out for bunting foul for his third strike; (Note exception in 10.17 (a) (4). **(3)** When the batter is called out for being touched by his own batted ball; **(4)** When the batter is called out for interfering with the catcher. **(5)** When the batter is called out for failing to bat in his proper turn; (See 10.03 (d)). **(6)** When the batter is called out for refusing to touch first base after receiving a base on balls; **(7)** When a runner is called out for refusing to advance from third base to home with the winning run. **(b)** Other automatic putouts shall be credited as follows (Credit no assists on these plays except as specified): **(1)** When the batter is called out on an Infield Fly which is not caught, credit the putout to the fielder who the scorer believes could have made the catch; **(2)** When a runner is called out for being touched by a fair ball (including an Infield Fly), credit the putout to the fielder nearest the ball; **(3)** When a runner is called out for running out of line to avoid being tagged, credit the putout to the fielder whom the runner avoided; **(4)** When a runner is called out for passing another runner, credit the putout to the fielder nearest the point of passing; **(5)** When a runner is called out for running the bases in reverse order, credit the putout to the fielder covering the base he left in starting his reverse run; **(6)** When a runner is called out for having interfered with a fielder, credit the putout to the fielder with whom the runner interfered, unless the fielder was in the act of throwing the ball when the interference occurred, in which case credit the putout to the fielder for whom the throw was intended, and credit an assist to the fielder whose throw was interfered with; **(7)** When the batter-runner is called out because of interference by a preceding runner, as provided in Playing Rule 6.05 **(m)**, credit the putout to the first baseman. If the fielder interfered with was in the act of throwing the ball, credit him with an assist, but credit only one assist on any one play under the provisions of 10.10 **(b) (6)** and **(7)**.

ASSISTS

10.11 An assist shall be credited to each fielder who throws or deflects a batted or thrown ball in such a way that a putout results, or would have resulted except for a subsequent error by any fielder. Only one assist and no more shall be credited to each fielder who throws or deflects the ball in a run-down play which results in a putout, or would have resulted in a putout, except for a subsequent error.

NOTE: Mere ineffective contact with the ball shall not be considered an assist. "Deflect" shall mean to slow down or change the direction of the ball and thereby effectively assist in putting out a batter or runner.

(a) Credit an assist to each fielder who throws or deflects the ball during a play which results in a runner being called out for interference, or for running out of line. **(b)** Do not credit an assist to the pitcher on a strikeout. EXCEPTION: Credit an assist if the pitcher fields an uncaught third strike and makes a throw which results in a putout. **(c)** Do not credit an assist to the pitcher when, as the result of a legal pitch received by the catcher, a runner is put out, as when the catcher picks a runner off base, throws out a runner trying to steal, or tags a runner trying to score. **(d)** Do not credit an assist to a fielder whose wild throw permits a runner to advance, even though the runner subsequently is put out as a result of continuous play. A play which follows a misplay (whether or not it is an error) is a new play, and the fielder making any misplay shall not be credited with an assist unless he takes part in the new play.

DOUBLE PLAYS—TRIPLE PLAYS

10.12 Credit participation in the double play or triple play to each fielder who earns a putout or an assist when two or three players are put out between the time a pitch is delivered and the time the ball next becomes dead or is next in possession of the pitcher in pitching position, unless an error or misplay intervenes between putouts.

NOTE: Credit the double play or triple play also if an appeal play after the ball is in possession of the pitcher results in an additional putout.

ERRORS

10.13 An error shall be charged for each misplay (fumble, muff or wild throw) which prolongs the time at bat of a batter or which prolongs the life of a runner, or which permits a runner to advance one or more bases.

NOTE **(1)** Slow handling of the ball which does not involve mechanical misplay shall not be construed as an error.

NOTE **(2)** It is not necessary that the fielder touch the ball to be charged with an error. If a ground ball goes through a fielder's legs or a pop fly falls untouched and in the scorer's judgment the fielder could have handled the ball with ordinary effort, an error shall be charged.

NOTE **(3)** Mental mistakes or misjudgments are not to be scored as errors unless specifically covered in the rules.

(a) An error shall be charged against any fielder when he muffs a foul fly, to prolong the time at bat of a batter whether the batter subsequently reaches first base or is put out. **(b)** An error shall be charged against any fielder when he catches a thrown ball or a ground ball in time to put out the batter-runner and fails to tag first base or the batter-runner. **(c)** An error shall be charged against any fielder when he catches a thrown ball or a ground ball in time to put out any runner on a force play and fails to tag the base or the runner. **(d) (1)** An error shall be charged against any fielder whose wild throw permits a runner to reach a base safely, when in the scorer's judgment a good throw would have put out the runner. EXCEPTION: No error shall be charged under this section if the wild throw is made attempting to prevent a stolen base. **(2)** An error shall be charged against any fielder whose wild throw in attempting to prevent a runner's advance permits that runner or any other runner to advance one or more bases beyond the base he would have reached had the throw not been wild. **(3)** An error shall be charged against any fielder whose throw takes an unnatural bounce, or touches a base or the pitcher's plate, or touches a runner, a fielder or an umpire, thereby permitting any runner to advance.

NOTE: Apply this rule even when it appears to be an injustice to a fielder whose throw was accurate. Every base advanced by a runner must be accounted for.

(4) Charge only one error on any wild throw, regardless of the number of bases advanced by one or more runners. **(e)** An error shall be charged against any fielder whose failure to stop, or try to stop, an accurately thrown ball permits a runner to advance, providing there was occasion for the throw. If such throw be made to second base, the scorer shall determine whether it was the duty of the second baseman or the shortstop to stop the ball, and an error shall be charged to the negligent player.

NOTE: If in the scorer's judgment there was no occasion for the throw, an error shall be charged to the fielder who threw the ball.

(f) When an umpire awards the batter or any runner or runners one or more bases because of interference or obstruction, charge the fielder who committed the interference or obstruction with one error, no matter how many bases the batter, or runner or runners, may be advanced.

NOTE: Do not charge an error if obstruction does not change the play in the opinion of the scorer.

10.14 No error shall be charged in the following cases: **(a)** No error shall be charged against the catcher when after receiving the pitch, he makes a wild throw attempting to prevent a stolen base, unless the wild throw permits the stealing runner to advance one or more extra bases, or permits any other runner to advance one or more bases. **(b)** No error shall be charged against any fielder who makes a wild throw if in the scorer's judgment the runner would not have been put out with ordinary effort by a good throw, unless such wild throw permits any runner to advance beyond the base he would have reached had the throw not been wild. **(c)** No error shall be charged against any fielder when he makes a wild throw in attempting to complete a double play or triple play, unless such wild throw enables any runner to advance beyond the base he would have reached had the throw not been wild.

NOTE: When a fielder muffs a thrown ball which, if held, would have completed a double play or triple play, charge an error to the fielder who drops the ball and credit an assist to the fielder who made the throw.

(d) No error shall be charged against any fielder when, after fumbling a ground ball or dropping a fly ball, a line drive or a thrown ball, he recovers the ball in time to force out a runner at any base. **(e)** No error shall be charged against any fielder who permits a foul fly to fall safe with a runner on third base before two are out, if in the scorer's judgment the fielder deliberately refuses the catch in order that the runner on third shall not score after the catch. **(f)** Because the pitcher and catcher handle the ball much more than other fielders, certain misplays on pitched balls are defined in Rule 10.15 as wild pitches and passed balls. No error shall be charged when a wild pitch or passed ball is scored. **(1)** No error shall be charged when the batter is awarded first base on four called balls or because he was touched by a pitched ball, or when he reaches first base as the result of a wild pitch or passed ball. **(i)** When the third strike is a wild pitch, permitting the batter to reach first base, score a strikeout and a wild pitch. (ii) When the third strike is a passed ball, permitting the batter to reach first base, score a strikeout and a passed ball. **(2)** No error shall be charged when a runner or runners advance as the result of a passed ball, a wild pitch or a balk. **(i)** When the fourth called ball is a wild pitch or a passed ball, and as a result **(a)** the batter-runner advances to a base beyond first base; **(b)** any runner forced to advance by the base on balls advances more than one base, or **(c)** any runner, not forced to advance, advances one or more bases, score the base on balls, and also the wild pitch or passed ball, as the case may be; (ii) When the catcher recovers the ball after a wild pitch or passed ball on the third strike, and throws out the batter-runner at first base, or tags out the batter-runner, but another runner or runners advance, score the strikeout, the putout and assists, if any, and credit the advance of the other runner or runners as having been made on the play.

WILD PITCHES—PASSED BALLS

10.15 (a) A wild pitch shall be charged when a legally delivered ball is so high, or so wide, or so low that the catcher does not stop and control the ball by ordinary effort, thereby permitting a runner or runners to advance. **(1)** A wild pitch shall be charged when a legally delivered ball touches the ground before reaching home plate and is not handled by the catcher, permitting a runner or runners to advance. **(b)** A catcher shall be charged with a passed ball when he fails to hold or to control a legally pitched ball which should have been held or controlled with ordinary effort, thereby permitting a runner or runners to advance.

BASES ON BALLS

10.16 (a) A base on balls shall be scored whenever a batter is awarded first base because of four balls having been pitched outside the strike zone, but when the fourth such ball touches the batter it shall be scored as a "hit batter." (See 10.18 **(h)** for procedure when more than one pitcher is involved in giving a base on balls: Also see 10.17 **(b)** relative to substitute batter who receives base on balls.) **(b)** Intentional base on balls shall be scored when the pitcher makes no attempt to throw the last pitch to the batter into the strike zone but purposely throws the ball wide to the catcher outside the catcher's box. **(1)** If a batter awarded a base on balls is called out for refusing to advance to first base, do not credit the base on balls. Charge a time at bat.

STRIKEOUTS

10.17 (a) A strikeout shall be scored whenever: **(1)** A batter is put out by a third strike caught by the catcher; **(2)** A batter is put out by a third strike not caught when there is a runner on first before two are out; (3) A batter becomes a runner because a third strike is not caught; (4) A batter bunts foul on third strike. EXCEPTION: If such bunt on third strike results in a foul fly caught by any fielder, do not score a strikeout. Credit the fielder who catches such foul fly with a putout. (b) When the batter leaves the game with two strikes against him, and the substitute batter completes a strikeout, charge the strikeout and the time at bat to the first batter. If the substitute batter completes the turn at bat in any other manner, including a base on balls, score the action as having been that of the substitute batter.

EARNED RUNS

10.18 An earned run is a run for which the pitcher is held accountable. In determining earned runs, the inning should be reconstructed without the errors (which include catcher's interference) and passed balls, and the benefit of the doubt should always be given to the pitcher in determining which bases would have been reached by errorless play. For the purpose of determining earned runs, an intentional base on balls, regardless of the circumstances, shall be construed in exactly the same manner as any other base on balls. (a) An earned run shall be charged every time a runner reaches home base by the aid of safe hits, sacrifice bunts, a sacrifice fly, stolen bases, putouts, fielder's choices, bases on balls, hit batters, balks or wild pitches (including a wild pitch on third strike which permits a batter to reach first base) before fielding chances have been offered to put out the offensive team. For the purpose of this rule, a defensive interference penalty shall be construed as a fielding chance. (1) A wild pitch is solely the pitcher's fault, and contributes to an earned run just as a base on balls or a balk. (b) No run shall be earned when scored by a runner who reaches first base (1) on a hit or otherwise after his time at bat is prolonged by a muffed foul fly; (2) because of interference or obstruction or (3) because of any fielding error. (c) No run shall be earned when scored by a runner whose life is prolonged by an error, if such runner would have been put out by errorless play. (d) No run shall be earned when the runner's advance is aided by an error, a passed ball, or defensive interference or obstruction, if the scorer judges that the run would not have scored without the aid of such misplay. (e) An error by a pitcher is treated exactly the same as an error by any other fielder in computing earned runs. (f) Whenever a fielding error occurs, the pitcher shall be given the benefit of the doubt in determining to which bases any runners would have advanced had the fielding of the defensive team been errorless. (g) When pitchers are changed during an inning, the relief pitcher shall not be charged with any run (earned or unearned) scored by a runner who was on base at the time he entered the game, nor for runs scored by any runner who reaches base on a fielder's choice which puts out a runner left on base by the preceding pitcher.

NOTE: It is the intent of this rule to charge each pitcher with the number of runners he put on base, rather than with the individual runners. When a pitcher puts runners on base, and is relieved, he shall be charged with all runs subsequently scored up to and including the number of runners he left on base when he left the game, unless such runners are put out without action by the batter, i.e., caught stealing, picked off base, or called out for inter-

ference when a batter-runner does not reach first base on the play. EXCEPTION: see example 7.

EXAMPLES: (1) P1 walks A and is relieved by P2. B grounds out, sending A to second. C flies out. D singles, scoring A. Charge run to P1. (2) P1 walks A and is relieved by P2. B forces A at second. C grounds out, sending B to second. D singles, scoring B. Charge run to P1. (3) P1 walks A and is relieved by P2. B singles, sending A to third. C grounds to short, and A is out at home, B going to second. D flies out. E singles, scoring B. Charge run to P1. (4) P1 walks A and is relieved by P2. B walks. C flies out. A is picked off second. D doubles, scoring B from first. Charge run to P2. (5) P1 walks A and is relieved by P2. P2 walks B and is relieved by P3. C forces A at third. D forces B at third. E hits home run, scoring three runs. Charge one run to P1; one run to P2, one run to P3. (6) P1 walks A, and is relieved by P2, P2 walks B. C singles, filling the bases. D forces A at home. E singles, scoring B and C. Charge one run to P1 and one run to P2. (7) P1 walks A, and is relieved by P2. P2 allows B to single, but A is out trying for third. B takes second on the throw. C singles, scoring B. Charge run to P2.

(h) A relief pitcher shall not be held accountable when the first batter to whom he pitches reaches first base on four called balls if such batter has a decided advantage in the ball and strike count when pitchers are changed. (1) If, when pitchers are changed, the count is

2 balls, no strike,
2 balls, 1 strike,
3 balls, no strike,
3 balls, 1 strike,
3 balls, 2 strikes,

and the batter gets a base on balls, charge that batter and the base on balls to the preceding pitcher, not to the relief pitcher. (2) Any other action by such batter, such as reaching base on a hit, an error, a fielder's choice, a force-out, or being touched by a pitched ball, shall cause such a batter to be charged to the relief pitcher.

NOTE: The provisions of 10.18 (h) (2) shall not be construed as affecting or conflicting with the provisions of 10.18 (g).

(3) If, when pitchers are changed, the count is

2 balls, 2 strikes,
1 ball, 2 strikes,
1 ball, 1 strike,
1 ball, no strike,
no ball, 2 strikes,
no ball, 1 strike,

charge that batter and his actions to the relief pitcher. (i) When pitchers are changed during an inning, the relief pitcher shall not have the benefit of previous chances for outs not accepted in determining earned runs.

NOTE: It is the intent of this rule to charge relief pitchers with earned runs for which they are solely responsible. In some instances, runs charged as earned against the relief pitcher can be charged as unearned against the team.

EXAMPLES: (1) With two out, P1 walks A. B reaches base on an error. P2 relieves P1. C hits home run, scoring three runs. Charge two unearned runs to P1, one earned run to P2. (2) With two out, P1 walks A and B and is relieved by P2. C reaches base on an error. D hits home run, scoring four runs. Charge two unearned runs to P1, two unearned runs to P2. (3) With none out,

P1 walks A. B reaches base on an error. P2 relieves P1. C hits home run, scoring three runs. D and E strike out. F reaches base on an error. G hits home run, scoring two runs. Charge two runs, one earned, to P1. Charge three runs, one earned, to P2.

WINNING AND LOSING PITCHER

10.19 (a) Credit the starting pitcher with a game won only if he has pitched at least five complete innings and his team not only is in the lead when he is replaced but remains in the lead the remainder of the game. **(b)** The "must pitch five complete innings" rule in respect to the starting pitcher shall be in effect for all games of six or more innings. In a five-inning game, credit the starting pitcher with a game won only if he has pitched at least four complete innings and his team not only is in the lead when he is replaced but remains in the lead the remainder of the game. **(c)** When the starting pitcher cannot be credited with the victory because of the provisions of 10.19 **(a)** or **(b)** and more than one relief pitcher is used, the victory shall be awarded on the following basis: **(1)** When, during the tenure of the starting pitcher, the winning team assumes the lead and maintains it to the finish of the game, credit the victory to the relief pitcher judged by the scorer to have been the most effective; **(2)** Whenever the score is tied the game becomes a new contest insofar as the winning and losing pitcher is concerned; **(3)** Once the opposing team assumes the lead all pitchers who have pitched up to that point are excluded from being credited with the victory except that if the pitcher against whose pitching the opposing team gained the lead continues to pitch until his team regains the lead, which it holds to the finish of the game, that pitcher shall be the winning pitcher; **(4)** The winning relief pitcher shall be the one who is the pitcher of record when his team assumes the lead and maintains it to the finish of the game. EXCEPTION: Do not credit a victory to a relief pitcher who is ineffective in a brief appearance, when a succeeding relief pitcher pitches effectively in helping his team maintain the lead. In such cases, credit the succeeding relief pitcher with the victory. **(d)** When a pitcher is removed for a substitute batter or substitute runner, all runs scored by his team during the inning in which he is removed shall be credited to his benefit in determining the pitcher of record when his team assumes the lead. **(e)** Regardless of how many innings the first pitcher has pitched, he shall be charged with the loss of the game if he is replaced when his team is behind in the score, or falls behind because of runs charged to him after he is replaced, and his team thereafter fails either to tie the score or gain the lead. **(f)** No pitcher shall be credited with pitching a shutout unless he pitches the complete game, or unless he enters the game with none out before the opposing team has scored in the first inning, puts out the side without a run scoring and pitches all the rest of the game. When two or more pitchers combine to pitch a shutout a notation to that effect should be included in the league's official pitching records. **(g)** In some non-championship games (such as the Major League All-Star Game) it is provided in advance that each pitcher shall work a stated number of innings, usually two or three. In such games, it is customary to credit the victory to the pitcher of record, whether starter or reliever, when the winning team takes a lead which it maintains to the end of the game, unless such pitcher is knocked out after the winning team has a commanding lead, and the scorer believes a subsequent pitcher is entitled to credit for the victory.

SAVES FOR RELIEF PITCHERS

10.20 Credit a pitcher with a save when he meets all three of the following conditions: **(1)** He is the finishing pitcher in a game won by his club; and **(2)** He is not the winning pitcher; and **(3)** He qualifies under one of the following conditions: **(a)** He enters the game with a lead of no more than three runs and pitches for at least one inning; or **(b)** He enters the game, regardless of the count, with the potential tying run either on base, or at bat, or on deck (that is, the potential tying run is either already on base or is one of the first two batsmen he faces); or **(c)** He pitches effectively for at least three innings.

No more than one save may be credited in each game.

STATISTICS

10.21 The league president shall appoint an official statistician. The statistician shall maintain an accumulative record of all the batting, fielding, running and pitching records specified in 10.02 for every player who appears in a league championship game.

The statistician shall prepare a tabulated report at the end of the season, including all individual and team records for every championship game, and shall submit this report to the league president. This report shall identify each player by his first name and surname, and shall indicate as to each batter whether he bats righthanded, lefthanded or both ways; as to each fielder and pitcher, whether he throws righthanded or lefthanded.

When a player listed in the starting lineup for the visiting club is substituted for before he plays defensively, he shall not receive credit in the defensive statistics (fielding), unless he actually plays that position during a game. All such players, however, shall be credited with one game played (in "batting statistics") as long as they are announced into the game or listed on the official lineup card.

Any games played to break a divisional tie shall be included in the statistics for that championship season.

DETERMINING PERCENTAGE RECORDS

10.22 To compute **(a)** Percentage of games won and lost, divide the number of games won by the total games won and lost; **(b)** Batting average, divide the total number of safe hits (not the total bases on hits) by the total times at bat, as defined in 10.02 **(a)**; **(c)** Slugging percentage, divide the total bases of all safe hits by the total times at bat, as defined in 10.02 **(a)**; **(d)** Fielding average, divide the total putouts and assists by the total of putouts, assists and errors; **(e)** Pitcher's earned-run average, multiply the total earned runs charged against his pitching by 9, and divide the result by the total number of innings he pitched.

NOTE: Earned-run averages shall be calculated on the basis of total innings pitched including fractional innings. EXAMPLE: 9-1/3 innings pitched and 3 earned runs is an earned-run average of 2.89 (3 ER times 9 divided by 9-1/3 equals 2.89).

(f) On-base percentage, divide the total of hits, all bases on balls, and hit by pitch by the total of at bats, all bases on balls, hit by pitch and sacrifice flies.

NOTE: For the purpose of computing on-base percentage, ignore being awarded first base on interference or obstruction.

MINIMUM STANDARDS FOR
INDIVIDUAL CHAMPIONSHIPS

10.23 To assure uniformity in establishing the batting, pitching and fielding championships of professional leagues, such champions shall meet the following minimum performance standards: **(a)** The individual batting champion or slugging champion shall be the player with the highest batting average or slugging percentage, provided he is credited with as many or more total appearances at the plate in League Championship games as the number of games scheduled for each club in his league that season, multiplied by 3.1 in the case of a major league player. EXCEPTION: However, if there is any player with fewer than the required number of plate appearances whose average would be the highest, if he were charged with the required number of plate appearances or official at bats, then that player shall be awarded the batting championship or slugging championship.

EXAMPLE: If a major league schedules 162 games for each club, 502 plate appearances qualify (162 times 3.1 equals 502). If a National Association league schedules 140 games for each club, 378 plate appearances qualify (140 times 2.7 equals 378).

Total appearances at the plate shall include official times at bat, plus bases on balls, times hit by pitcher, sacrifice hits, sacrifice flies and times awarded first base because of interference or obstruction.

(b) The individual pitching champion shall be the pitcher with the lowest earned-run average, provided that he has pitched at least as many innings as the number of games scheduled for each club in his league that season. EXCEPTION: However, pitchers in National Association leagues shall qualify for the pitching championship by having the lowest earned-run average and having pitched at least as many innings as 80% of the number of games scheduled for each club in his league that season. **(c)** The individual fielding champions shall be the fielders with the highest fielding average at each position, provided: **(1)** A catcher must have participated as a catcher in at least one-half the number of games scheduled for each club in his league that season; **(2)** An infielder or outfielder must have participated at his position in at least two-thirds of the number of games scheduled for each club in his league that season; **(3)** A pitcher must have pitched at least as many innings as the number of games scheduled for each club in his league that season. EXCEPTION: If another pitcher has a fielding average as high or higher, and has handled more total chances in a lesser number of innings, he shall be the fielding champion.

GUIDELINES FOR
CUMULATIVE PERFORMANCE RECORDS

10.24 CONSECUTIVE HITTING STREAKS. **(a)** A consecutive hitting streak shall not be terminated if the plate appearance results in a base on balls, hit batsman, defensive interference or a sacrifice bunt. A sacrifice fly shall terminate the streak. **(b)** CONSECUTIVE-GAME HITTING STREAKS. A consecutive-game hitting streak shall not be terminated if all the player's plate appearances (one or more) result in a base on balls, hit batsman, defensive interference or a sacrifice bunt. The streak shall terminate if the player has a sacrifice fly and no hit. The player's individual consecutive-game hitting streak shall be determined by the consecutive games in which the player appears and is not determined by his club's games. **(c)** CONSECUTIVE PLAYING STREAK. A consecutive-game playing streak shall be extended if the player plays one half-inning on defense, or if he completes a time at bat by reaching base or being put out. A pinch-running appearance only shall not extend the streak. If a player is ejected from a game by an umpire before he can comply with the requirements of this rule, his streak shall continue. **(d)** SUSPENDED GAMES. For the purpose of this rule, all performances in the completion of a suspended game shall be considered as occurring on the original date of the game.

INDEX

Infield Fly—2.00, 6.05 (e) and (l) Note, 7.08 (f).

Intentionally Dropped Ball—6.05 (l).

Interference—Defensive 2.00, 6.08 (c); 7.04 (d), 7.07; Offensive 2.00, 5.09 (f), (g), 6.05 (h) (i) (m) and (n), 6.06 (c), 6.08 (d), 7.08 (b) (f) and (g), 7.09, 7.11; Spectator 2.00, 3.16; Umpires 2.00, 5.09 (b), (f); 6.08 (d).

Light Failure—4.12 (a-b), 5.10 (b).

Missed Base—7.02, 7.04—Note, 7.08 (k), 7.10 (b), 7.12, 8.05 Penalty—Approved Ruling.

Obstruction—7.06.

Official Scorer—Rule 10.00.

Overrunning First Base—7.08 (c) and (j), 7.10 (c).

Penalties—2.00 (See LEAGUE PRESIDENT.)

Pitcher—Legal Position 8.01 (a-b); Becomes Infielder 8.01 (e); Preparatory Pitches 8.03; Take Signs While on Rubber 8.01; Throwing at Batter 8.02 (d); Throwing to a Base 7.05 (h), 8.01 (c); Visits by Manager or Coach 8.06.

Players' Positions—4.03.

Playing Field—1.04. (Includes Diagrams of Mound and Diamond Layout and Playing Lines.)

Police Protection—3.18.

Postponement Responsibility—3.10.

Protested Games—4.19.

Regulation Game—4.10, 4.11. (7-inning Games 4.10 (a)—Note).

Resuming Play After Dead Ball—5.11.

Restrictions on Players—

No Fraternizing 3.09; Barred from Stands 3.09; Confined to Bench 3.17.

Runner—Entitled to Base 7.01, 7.03; Touch Requirements 7.02, 7.08 (d), 7.10; Runners Advance 7.04, 7.05, 7.06; Reverse Run Prohibited 7.08 (i); Runner Out 7.08, 7.09 (e-m), 7.10, 7.11; Running Out of Line 6.05 (k), 7.08 (a).

Score of Game—4.11.

Scoring Rules—Rule 10.00

Scoring Runs—4.09, 6.05 (n), 7.07, 7.12.

Spectators—Barred from Field 3.15; Touching Batted or Thrown Ball 3.16.

Strike—2.00 (See STRIKE AND STRIKE ZONE), 6.08 (b).

Substitutions—3.03, 3.04, 3.05, 3.06, 3.07, 3.08, 4.04.

Suspended Games—4.12.

Time Limits—9.04 (a) (7).

Umpire—Rule 9.00.

Inspects Equipment and Playing Lines 3.01; Judge of Playing Conditions 3.10 (c-d), 5.10 (a); Controls Ground Crew 3.11; Controls Lights 4.14; Calls "Time" 5.10; Controls Newsmen and Photographers 9.01 (e); Time Limits 9.04 (a) (7); Umpire's Interference 5.09 (b) and (f), 6.08 (d); Touched by Pitch or Thrown Ball 5.08, 5.09 (h), 7.05 (i).

Unsportsmanlike Conduct—4.06 (b).

Wild Throws—5.08, 7.05 (g-h-i).

INDEX

THE RULES OF BASEBALL

sacrifices, 203, 252–253
St. Louis Browns, 26, 75, 123, 187, 195
St. Louis Cardinals, 10, 43, 66, 79, 111, 116, 165
St. Louis Maroons, 40, 46
St. Louis Terriers, 74
Sanders, Deion, 121
San Diego Padres, 94, 141
Sanford, Fred, 126
San Francisco Giants, 91, 106, 140
Schacht, Al, 21
Schaefer, Germany, 134–135
Schafer, Harry, 45
Schappert, John, 103
Scheffing, Bob (manager), 52
Schmidt, Mike, 115
Schoendienst, Red, 108
Schultz, Barney, 114
Schwarts, Harry (umpire), 146
scorers, official, 191–194, 249–250
    and game-winning RBI, 197
    ruling hits as errors, 199–200
    rulings on putouts and assists, 204–205
    rulings on stolen bases, 200–202
Seaver, Tom, 72
Selee, Frank, 32
Serena, Bill, 146
Sewell, Rip, 150
Seymour, Cy, 7
Shanks, Howard, 145
Sharman, Bill, 67
Sharrott, Jack, 49
Shea Stadium (New York), 181
Shellenback, Frank, 45
Sherdel Willie, 165
Sheridan, John (scorer-umpire), 103, 199–200
Shibe Park (Philadelphia), 136
Shocker, Urban, 44
"Shoe Polish" incident, 108–109
shoes, regulations concerning, 19–20
Shore, Ernie, 210
Short, Bob (owner), 60

Shorten, Chick, 187
Shotton, Burt (manager), 65
Siemer, Oscar, 120
Simmons, Curt, 96
Sisler, Dick, 112
sliding into first base, 135
Smith, Al, 129
Smith, Bob, 86
Smith, Earl, 84
Smith, Germany, 174
"soaking," 36
Sommers, Benjamin (umpire), 170
Sothoron, Allan, 44
South Side Park (Chicago), 63
Spahn, Warren, 107
Spalding, Al (owner), 22, 192
Spalding (ball), 9
Spalding's Official Baseball Guide, 92
Special Baseball Records Committee, 69, 193
spectator interference, 59–61
Sporting News, The, 211, 213
Sportsman's Park (St. Louis), 76, 96, 123, 165, 199
sportswriters, 191
squeeze play, 230
stadiums, 28
Stanky, Eddie (player-manager), 76, 99, 137
Start, Joe, 111
Staub, Rusty, 117
Steinbrenner, George, 11
Stello, Dick (umpire), 98
Stengel, Casey (manager), 138
Stenzel, Jake, 215
Stewart, Bill (umpire), 100
Stewart, Dave, 151
Stirnweiss, Snuffy, 71
stolen bases, 164, 166, 200–202, 252
Stovey, Harry, 124, 212
Stoyle, Don, 144
Stricker, Cub, 165
Strief, George, 124
strike, 33–35, 230
    one-bounce-out rule, 92–94

THE   RULES   OF   BASEBALL

Washington Unions, 76
weather conditions, 54, 86
Weaver, Buck, 199
Weaver, Earl (manager), 96
Weeghman, Charles (owner), 39
Weeghman Park. *See* Wrigley Field
Weidman, Stump, 102
Welch, Curt, 41
Welch, Micky, 207
Wendelstadt, Harry (umpire), 106
Wertz, Johnny, 118
Western Association, 97
Western Carolina League, 113
Western International League, 53, 90
Western League, 114
Wheat, Zach, 111
White, Bill, 174
White, Devon, 121
White, Will, 103, 152
Wilhelm, Hoyt, 20, 219
Will, George, viii
Williams, Charlie (umpire), 87
Williams, Cy, 195
Williams, Elisa Green (scorer), 192
Williams, Ted, 50, 194, 216
Williamson, Ned, 3
"Williams Shift," the, 195
Wilson, Swamp Baby, 97
Wiltse, Hooks, 104
Winfield, Dave, 117
Wise, Sam, 110
Wisneski, Bill, 53
Wolf, Jimmy, 184–185
Worcester Ruby Legs, 29

World Series
 1884; 1890, 56
 1903, 63
 1911, 136
 1925, 84
 1928, 165
 1939, 82
 1951, 137
 1957, 107
 1969, 95
 1973, 182
 1975, 97
 1976, 116
 1978, 139
 1985, 188
 1992, 121
Wright, George, 9
Wright, Taffy, 214
Wrigley Field (Chicago), 39, 79
Wynegar, Butch, 175

Yankee Stadium (New York), 11, 67, 139
Yastrzemski, Carl, 8
You've Got to Have B*lls to Make It in This League (Postema), 101
Young, Anthony, 56
Young, Cy, 152
Yount, Larry, 52

Zabala, Adrian, 167, 178
Zimmer, Chief, 102
Zimmerman, Heinie, 214
Ziruolo, Herman (umpire), 53
Zisk, Richie, 181